Stylish F#

Crafting Elegant Functional Code
for .NET and .NET Core

Kit Eason

Stylish F#: Crafting Elegant Functional Code for .NET and .NET Core

Kit Eason
Farnham, Surrey, UK

ISBN-13 (pbk): 978-1-4842-3999-5   ISBN-13 (electronic): 978-1-4842-4000-7
https://doi.org/10.1007/978-1-4842-4000-7

Library of Congress Control Number: 2018963299

Managing Director, Apress Media LLC: Welmoed Spahr
Acquisitions Editor: Joan Murray
Development Editor: Laura Berendson
Coordinating Editor: Jill Balzano

Cover image designed by Kit Eason. Contains OS data © Crown copyright and database right 2018

Distributed to the book trade worldwide by Springer Science+Business Media New York, 233 Spring Street, 6th Floor, New York, NY 10013. Phone 1-800-SPRINGER, fax (201) 348-4505, e-mail orders-ny@springer-sbm.com, or visit www.springeronline.com. Apress Media, LLC is a California LLC and the sole member (owner) is Springer Science + Business Media Finance Inc (SSBM Finance Inc). SSBM Finance Inc is a **Delaware** corporation.

For information on translations, please e-mail rights@apress.com, or visit http://www.apress.com/rights-permissions.

Apress titles may be purchased in bulk for academic, corporate, or promotional use. eBook versions and licenses are also available for most titles. For more information, reference our Print and eBook Bulk Sales web page at http://www.apress.com/bulk-sales.

Any source code or other supplementary material referenced by the author in this book is available to readers on GitHub via the book's product page, located at www.apress.com/9781484239995. For more detailed information, please visit http://www.apress.com/source-code.

Printed on acid-free paper

To Val, Matt, Meg, Kate, Noah, and Darwin:
my own persistent collection.

Table of Contents

About the Author

Kit Eason is a software developer and educator with more than 20 years of experience. He has been programming in F# since 2011 and is employed at Perpetuum Ltd., working on an extensive network of energy-harvesting vibration sensors fitted to railway rolling stock. Kit is an avid F# user who is passionate about teaching others. He has contributed to several publications, as well as to the books *Beginning F# 4.0* (Apress 2016) and *F# Deep Dives* (Manning 2014). He often teaches and presents on F#, and his popular videos appear on Lynda.com and YouTube.

About the Technical Reviewer

Quinton Coetzee was born and raised in a small town not too far from Johannesburg, South Africa, which means he can just about remember how to speak Afrikaans. He played paintball at a relatively high level (for a South African team), traveling to the USA and Europe to compete, before moving to the UK in 2011 to pursue career opportunities in London. Since then, he has worked on real-time trading systems and various applications in one way or another related to trading, primarily in F#. As a productivity tool, F# is really hard to beat and would be his first choice in most production environments. That said, he enjoys playing with other functional languages like Clojure and Scala in his spare time.

Acknowledgments

I am grateful for the generous help I received in putting *Stylish F#* together. Thanks to Quinton Coetzee for his exceedingly diligent and constructive technical reviews. To Val Eason for reading every chapter before submission, detecting many typos and poor turns of phrase. To Jon Harrop for providing detailed technical feedback on Chapter 12, and to several other F# community members who reviewed a code sample for Chapter 8. To Jason Heeris for kindly giving permission to reproduce the cartoon in Chapter 1. To Don Syme and the F# community for the never-ending stream of compiler and tooling improvements that propel F# forward. And to Matt Jones and the amazing team at Perpetuum for providing the best working environment I've ever experienced. Thanks also to the tireless crew at Apress: Joan Murray, Jill Balzano, and Laura Berendson.

Any errors, omissions, or plain wrong-headedness are, of course, still my own responsibility.

Introduction

There are three distinct philosophies that you can apply to computer programming. You can think of programming as a *science*, where the measure of progress is how well you discover and reflect fundamental mathematical concepts in your code. You can think of it as a *discipline*, where you seek to establish and follow rules about how code should be written and organized. Or, best of all, you can think of it as a *craft*, where, yes, you apply some of the science and some of the discipline; but you leaven those with a generous helping of human creativity. To do this successfully, you need a fair bit of experience, because crafting something is an inherently intuitive process. This book aims to get you to a level where you can craft code confidently. It does this by distilling and passing on my own experience of writing F# systems in numerous different industries over the past eight years.

Before you start this book, you'll need at least some knowledge of F# syntax and concepts. Maybe you've read some of the wide range of beginner material that's available, and probably you'll have written at least a few simple F# programs yourself. You may well have deeper experience of other languages and environments, such as C# and .NET. That said, I have framed the book so that C# knowledge is not a hard prerequisite: I learned F# before I learned C#, and if I can do it, so can you! Also you definitely don't need any background in Computer Science or functional programming. I don't have even a trace of formal education in either of these areas.

So what's between the covers? In Chapter 1, I'll establish some *principles* that will help us decide whether we are coding well, and say a little bit about why coding stylishly is important. In Chapter 2, we'll pick up the basic tools of our craft and learn to chisel out elegant and reliable *functions*. In Chapter 3, we'll tackle the thorny issue of *missing data*, learning some effective techniques for writing dependable code when certain values might not be available. In Chapter 4, we'll pick up some more powerful crafting tools: the so-called *collection functions*, and explore how you can use them to achieve a surprising amount with very little code. In Chapter 5, we'll delve into the strange world of *immutability*: how you can write programs that achieve a result without explicitly changing anything. In Chapter 6, we'll look at *pattern matching*, a concept you may have looked at a little when you learned F# syntax, but which is surprisingly pervasive and powerful in quality F# code. In Chapter 7, we'll explore *record types*, F#'s go-to structure for storing groups of labeled values. In Chapter 8, we'll cover some ground that might already be familiar to C# developers: *object oriented classes*. In Chapter 9, we'll return to the topic of F# *functions*, and explore what it means for a function to also be a first-class value. In Chapter 10, we'll tame the apparent complexity of *asynchronous and parallel programming*: it needn't be as hard as you think! In Chapter 11, we'll look at *Railway Oriented Programming*, an interesting metaphor you can use to help you think about processing pipelines. In Chapter 12, we'll investigate *performance*: can you really write code that is both elegant and fast? In Chapter 13, we'll establish some useful techniques for *laying out* your code and *naming* items to maximize readability. In Chapter 14, I'll briefly reiterate what we've learned.

As this book is primarily about the language, you'll find relatively few references to other libraries. Of course, to build substantial systems, you'll almost always want to pull in Nuget packages for requirements such as unit testing, serialization, web serving, and so forth. But these libraries constitute a large and fast-changing landscape, so I've chosen to pare things down to the F# essentials for this book. This also means that almost all the examples can be typed in and simply run as F# scripts, and they are provided in script form in the downloadable code samples. In the small number of cases where you need to write a compilable program, I take you through the process alongside the example.

Likewise, you won't find many references to specific integrated development environments (IDEs) such as Visual Studio, Visual Studio Code, Xamarin Studio, or JetBrains Rider. Any of these can be used to edit and run the examples in this book, and all are available as free editions if you don't already have something installed. If your IDE doesn't know about F# "out of the box," simply search online for "F# <your IDE> getting started" to find setup instructions. The samples should work without change on any platform where F# is installed, except you may need to change some paths where the sample code accesses local files.

I very much hope you enjoy sharing my F# experience as much as I enjoyed acquiring it. Don't forget to have fun!

CHAPTER 1

The Sense of Style

Mystification is simple; clarity is the hardest thing of all.

—Julian Barnes, English Novelist

Why a Style Guide?

In this chapter I will talk a little about why we as F# developers need a style guide, and what such a guide should look like. I'll also outline a few principles that, independent of language, great developers follow. These principles will be our guiding light in the many decisions we'll examine in future chapters.

One of the most common issues for developers beginning their journey into F# is that the language is neither old enough nor corporate enough to have acquired universally accepted and comprehensive idioms. There simply isn't the same depth of "best practice" and "design patterns" as there is in older languages such as C# and Java. Newcomers are often brought to a standstill by the openness of the choices before them, and by a lack of mental tools for making those choices.

Traditionally, teams and language communities have dealt with this kind of problem by adopting "coding standards," together with tools to support and enforce them, such as "StyleCop" and "Resharper." But I must admit to having a horror of anything so prescriptive. For me they smack too much of the "human wave" approach to software development, in which a large number of programmers are directed toward a coding task, and "standards" are used to try and bludgeon them into some approximation of a unified team. It can work, but it's expensive and depressing. This is not the F# way!

1

Understanding Beats Obedience

So how *are* we to assist the budding F# developer, in such a way that their creativity and originality are respected and utilized, while still giving them a sense of how to make choices that will be understood and supported by their peers? The answer, I believe, is to offer not *coding standards*, but a *style guide*. I mean "guide" in the truest sense of the word: something that suggests rather than mandates, and something that gives the reader the tools to understand when and why certain choices might be for the best, and when perhaps the developer should strike out on their own and do something completely original.

In coming to this conclusion, I've been inspired by Steven Pinker's superb guide to writing in English, *The Sense of Style* (Penguin Books, 2014). The book is a triumph of guidance over prescription, and my hope is to set the same tone here. Pinker makes the point that stylish writing isn't merely an aesthetic exercise: it is also a means to an end, that end being the spread of ideas. Exactly the same is true of stylish coding, in F# or any other computer language. The aim is not to impress your peers, to adhere slavishly to this or that "best practice," or to wring every possible drop of processing power out of the computer. No, the aim is to *communicate*. The only fundamental metric is how effectively we communicate using our language of choice. Therefore, the measure of the usefulness of a style guide is how much it improves the reader's ability to communicate with peers, and with the computer, via the code they write.

Good Guidance from Bad Code

Let's begin by defining what kinds of communication problems we are trying to avoid. We can get to the bottom of this by looking at the common characteristics of codebases which everyone would agree are bad. Avoid those characteristics and we can hope that our code can indeed communicate well!

Regardless of the era or technology involved, hard-to-work-with codebases tend to have the following characteristics in common.

Characteristic 1: It's hard to work out what's going on when looking closely at any particular piece of code.

To understand any one part of the program, the reader must think simultaneously about what is going on in various other widely scattered pieces of code and configuration. This cartoon (Figure 1-1) sums up the situation brilliantly.

THIS IS WHY YOU SHOULDN'T INTERRUPT A PROGRAMMER

© Jason Heeris 2013   Printed with permission of Jason Heeris   heeris.id.au

Figure 1-1. *This is why you shouldn't interrupt a programmer*

Interrupting busy programmers is bad, but the whistling coffee carrier isn't the only villain in this cartoon. The other is the code, which requires the developer to keep so much context in their personal working memory. When we write such code, we fail to communicate with people (including our future selves) who will have to maintain and extend it.

3

Note   I'll describe the kind of code that isn't readable with minimum context as having poor *semantic focus*. In other words, relevant meaning isn't concentrated in a particular place but is spread about the codebase.

Listing 1-1 shows an example of code that has poor *semantic focus* (along with a number of other problems!).

Listing 1-1. Code with bad semantic focus

```
let addInterest (interestType:int, amt:float, rate:float, y:int) =
    let rate = checkRate rate
    let mutable amt = amt
    checkAmount(&amt)
    let mutable intType = interestType
    if intType <= 0 then intType <- 1
    if intType = 1 then
        let yAmt = amt * rate / 100.
        amt + yAmt * (float y)
    else
        amt * System.Math.Pow(1. + (rate/100.), float y)
```

It is literally impossible to predict the behavior of this code without looking at other code elsewhere. What are checkRate and checkAmount doing? Is it OK that the value interestType can be any value from 2 upward with the same result? What happens when any of the parameters is negative? Or are some or all of the invalid range cases prevented elsewhere, or within checkRate and checkAmount? Could those protections ever get changed by accident?

And you can bet that when you see code like this, then the other code you then have to look at, such as the bodies of checkRate and checkAmount, are going to have similar issues. The number of "what if?" questions increases – literally exponentially – as one explores the call chain.

By the way, when I was writing this example, part of me was thinking "no professional would ever do this," and a larger part of me was remembering all the times when I had seen code exactly like it.

Characteristic 2: It's hard to be sure that any change will have the effects one wants, and only those effects.

In hard-to-maintain code, it's also difficult to answer questions such as:

- Can I refactor with confidence, or does the mess I'm looking at conceal some special cases that won't be caught properly by apparently cleaner code?

- Can I extend the code to handle circumstances it wasn't originally designed for, and be confident that both the old circumstances and the new circumstances are all correctly handled?

- Could the code here be undermined in the future by some change elsewhere?

Again, this is fundamentally a failure of communication with a human audience.

Note   I'll describe code that is difficult to change safely as having poor *revisability*, because the consequences of any local revision are not readily predictable.

I'll give some specific examples in Chapter 5, "Immutability and Mutation," but I'll bet that if you've been in the industry more than five minutes, you can provide plenty of your own!

Characteristic 3: It's hard to be certain of the author's intent.

A bad codebase raises similar unsettling questions in the area of authorial intent:

- What did the author mean by a particular section of code? Does the code actually do what they apparently think it should do? Is that even the right thing in the context of the system as a whole?

- If there appear to be gaps in the logic in the code, did the author realize they were there? Who is wrong, the author or the reader?

- If there are logic gaps, are the circumstances where they could manifest themselves prevented from occurring, or are the resulting errors handled elsewhere? Or have they never happened due to good luck? Or do they sometimes happen, but no one noticed or complained?

As if reading code wasn't hard enough, the maintainer is now placed in a position of having to read the mind of the original author, or worse still, the minds of every author who has touched the code. Not the recipe for a good day at work, and another failure to communicate.

Note   I'll describe the kind of code where the author's intentions are unclear as having poor *motivational transparency*. We can't readily tell what the author was thinking, and whether they were right when they were thinking it.

Here's a great example of some code (in C# as it happens) where it's hard to divine the author's intention. This is code that is published by a major cloud service provider, apparently with a perfectly straight face, as an example of how to iterate over stored objects. Perhaps a little cruelly, I've removed some helpful code comments (Listing 1-2).

Listing 1-2. Code with bad motivational transparency

```
ListVersionsRequest request = new ListVersionsRequest()
{
    BucketName = bucketName,
    MaxKeys = 2
};
do
{
    ListVersionsResponse response = client.ListVersions(request);
    foreach (ObjectVersion entry in response.Versions)
    {
        Console.WriteLine("key = {0} size = {1}",
            entry.Key, entry.Size);
    }

    if (response.IsTruncated)
    {
        request.KeyMarker = response.NextKeyMarker;
        request.VersionIdMarker = response.NextVersionIdMarker;
    }
```

```
    else
    {
        request = null;
    }
} while (request != null);
```

My problem with this code is that `request` is used both as an object embodying a client request; and as a sort of break marker, used to transport to the end of the loop the fact that `response.IsTruncated` has become `true`. Thus, it forces you to carry two distinct meanings of the label `"request"` in your head.

This immediately makes the reader start wondering, "Is there some reason why the author did this, something which I'm not understanding when I'm reading the code? For example, will any resources allocated when `request` was instantiated be released promptly when the assignment to `null` occurs. Was this therefore an attempt at prompt disposal?" (Would you know, without googling it, if resources are disposed promptly on assignment to `null`? I *have* googled it and I still don't know.) This is on top of the mental overhead caused by the way the code has to transport state (`KeyMarker` and `VersionIdMarker`) from the response to the request. Admittedly this isn't the sample author's fault as it is part of the API design, but with some careful coding it might have been possible to mitigate the issue.

All in all, reading this code starts a great many mental threads in the user's head, for no good reason. We can do better.

Characteristic 4: It's hard to tell without experimentation whether the code will be efficient.

Any algorithm can be expressed in myriad ways, but only a very few of these will make decent use of the available hardware and runtime resources. If you're looking at code with a tangle of flags, special cases, and ill-thought-out data structures, it is going to be very difficult to keep efficiency and performance in mind. You'll end up getting to the end of a hard day fiddling with such code, and thinking: "Oh well, at least it works!" As data volumes and user expectations grow exponentially, this will come back to bite you – hard!

Note   I'll describe code that isn't obviously efficient as having poor *mechanical sympathy*.

Again, it's a failure of communication. The code should be written in a way that satisfies both the human and electronic audiences, so the human maintainer can understand it, and the computer can execute it efficiently. I'll give some bad and good examples in Chapter 12, "Performance."

Generally, the term "mechanical sympathy" means the ability to get the best out of a machine by having some insight into how the machine operates. In a world of perfect abstractions (such as perfect automatic gearboxes or perfect computer languages), we wouldn't need mechanical sympathy. But we do not yet live in such a world. Incidentally the term is sometimes attributed to racing driver Jackie Stewart, but although he used it, a quick glance at Google Ngrams suggests it predates him as a well-used phrase.

What About Testability?

If you are worrying that I have missed out another characteristic of bad code, poor testability, don't worry. Testability is always at the forefront of my mind, but it's my belief that it would be hard to write code that had good *semantic focus*, good *revisability*, good *motivational transparency*, and good *mechanical sympathy*, without it automatically turning out to have good *testability*. Test Driven Design aficionados would put the cart and the horse the other way around, which is fine by me, but it's not the way I want to tackle things in this book.

Complexity Explosions

Everyone would agree that maintaining bad, poorly communicating code is an unpleasant experience for the individual. But why does this matter in a broader sense for software engineering? Why should we spend extra time polishing code when we could be rushing on to the next requirement?

The reason is that these sources of uncertainty exert an inexorable pressure toward a *complexity explosion*. A complexity explosion occurs when developers, under all sorts of time and commercial pressures, give up trying to fully reason about existing code and start to commit sins such as:

- Duplicating code, because that feels safer then generalizing existing code to handle both old and new cases.

- Programming by coincidence, in which one keeps changing code until it "seems to work," because the code is just too hard to reason about comprehensively.

- Avoiding refactoring, because it seems too risky or time consuming in the short term to be worth doing.

The reason why I refer to such situations as *explosions* is because these bad practices lead to further uncertainty, which leads to more widespread bad practice, and so forth. Complexity explosions are the reason why, when joining a team working on an established codebase, the new developer is so often tempted to say, "Shouldn't we just rewrite the whole thing?" Complexity explosions are expensive and hard to recover from! To prevent them, it's important to write code that doesn't put others (or your future self) into a position where the sins look more tempting than the path of righteousness.

Everything about this book is designed to help you minimize the risk of complexity explosions. If any of the techniques I suggest seem a little hard at first, consider the cost and pain of the alternative!

Summary

I hope I've convinced you that writing good code is a worthwhile investment of time; and that I've helped you spot some of the characteristics of bad code, so that you can see the practical advantages of every recommendation in this book.

The great news is that the F# language makes it easier than ever to avoid writing bad code, by making it easy to write programs that are *semantically focused*, *revisable*, *motivationally transparent*, and *mechanically sympathetic*. In the following chapters, you'll learn to write such great code and to enjoy doing it. For once in life, the path to righteousness is downhill!

CHAPTER 2

Designing Functions Using Types

When you remove layers, simplicity and speed happen.

—Ginni Rometty, CEO, IBM

Object Oriented (OO) programming is currently the dominant design approach in almost all software development. In OO, the natural unit of work is, unsurprisingly, the "object" or "class," and design effort is focused on defining classes that have the right shapes, behaviors, and relationships for the tasks at hand. In F#, by contrast, the natural units of work are *types*, which describe the shape of data; and *functions*, units of code that take some (typed) input and produce some (typed) output in a predictable fashion. It makes sense, therefore, to start our journey into stylish F# coding by looking at how best to design and code relatively simple types and functions. It's a surprisingly rich and rewarding topic.

Miles and Yards (No, Really!)

For the examples in this chapter, I'm going to choose a deliberately messy business domain. No cherry-picked, simplified examples here! Let me induct you into the weird and wonderful world of pre-metrication units and the British railroad (in British parlance "railway") system. British railways are still measured, for some purposes at least, in miles and yards. A yard is just under one meter, and will be familiar to American and most British readers. A mile is 1,760 yards, and again will be familiar to many readers (Table 2-1).

© Kit Eason 2018
K. Eason, *Stylish F#*, https://doi.org/10.1007/978-1-4842-4000-7_2

Table 2-1. *Some Rail Units of Distance*

Name	Equal to
yard	0.9144 meters
mile	1760 yards

That's simple enough, but it might surprise you to learn how miles and yards are recorded in some British railway systems. They use a single floating-point value, where the whole miles are in the whole part of the number, and the yards are in the fractional part, using .0 for zero yards and .1759 for 1,759 yards. For example, a mile and a half would be 1.0880, because half a mile is 880 yards. A fractional part greater than .1759 would be invalid, because at 1,760 yards we are at the next mile.

Now you know why I chose British railway mileages as a nice gnarly domain for our coding examples.[1] Clearly some rather specific coding is needed to allow railway systems to do apparently straightforward things like reading, calculating with, storing and printing such *miles.yards* distances. This gives us a great opportunity to exercise our type- and function-design skills.

Converting Miles and Yards to Decimal Miles

Let's start with the conversion from a miles-and-yards value, as perhaps read from a railway GIS (Geographic Information System), to a more conventional floating-point representation of miles and fractional miles, which would be useful for calculation. This conversion is needed, because, for example, you can't just add two miles-and-yards values, as the fractional part would not add properly. (Think about adding 1.0880 [one-and-a-half miles] to another 1.0880. Would you get three miles?) Because of the ever-present risk of confusion, I'll use very specific terminology for the two representations (Table 2-2).

Table 2-2. *Miles Terminolgy*

Term	Example Value	Real-World Meaning
miles.yards	1.0880	One and a half miles
decimal miles	1.5	One and a half miles

---

[1]Just be grateful that, for now at least, I'm ignoring another common railway unit, the "chain," which is equal to, wait for it, 22 yards or 1/80th of a mile.

How to Design a Function

Here is my thought process for coding any function. I'll list the steps first, then work through the example.

- Sketch the signature of the function – naïvely, what types of inputs does it take, and what type does it return? What should the function itself be called? Does the planned signature fit well into code that would need to call it?

- Code the body of the function, perhaps making some deliberately naïve assumptions if this helps get quickly to a "first cut."

- Ask, does the sketched signature cover the use cases, and eliminate as many potential errors as possible? If not, refine the signature, then the body to match.

- In coding the body, did you learn anything about the domain? Did you think of some new error cases that could have been eliminated at the signature level? Is the function name still a good reflection of what it does? Refine the name, signature, and body accordingly.

- Rinse and repeat as necessary.

In outlining these steps, I've dodged the whole issue of tests. How and when unit tests are written is an important topic, but I'm not getting into that here.

Now let us apply these steps to the *miles.yards* to *decimal miles* problem.

Sketch the Signature of the Function

You can sketch out the signature of a function straight into code, by typing the let-binding of the function, using specified rather than inferred types, and making the body of the function simply raise an exception. Listing 2-1 shows my initial thought on the *miles.yards* to *decimal miles* converter.

Listing 2-1. Sketching out a function signature

```
open System

let convertMilesYards (milesPointYards : float) : float =
    raise <| NotImplementedException()
```

Here we are saying, "We'll have a function called `convertMilesYards` that takes a floating-point input and returns a floating-point result." The function will compile, meaning that you could even experiment with calling it in other code if you wanted. But there is no danger of forgetting to code the logic of the body, because it will immediately fail if actually called.

Naïvely Code the Body of the Function

Now we can replace the exception in the body of the function with some real code. In the *miles.yards* example, this means separating the "whole miles" element (for instance, the "1" part of 1.0880) from the fractional part (the 0.0880), and dividing the fractional part by 0.1760 (remembering that there are 1,760 yards in a mile). Listing 2-2 shows how this looks in code.

Listing 2-2. Naïvely coded function body

```
let convertMilesYards (milesPointYards : float) : float =
    let wholeMiles = milesPointYards |> floor
    let fraction = milesPointYards - float(wholeMiles)
    wholeMiles + (fraction / 0.1760)

// val decimalMiles : float = 1.5
let decimalMiles = 1.0880 |> convertMilesYards
```

As you can see from the example at the end of Listing 2-2, this actually works fine. If you wanted, you could stop at this point, add some unit tests if you hadn't written these already, and move on to another task. In fact, for many purposes, particularly scripts and prototypes, the code as it is would be perfectly acceptable. As you go through the next few sections of this chapter, please bear in mind that the changes we make there are refinements rather than absolute necessities. You should make a mental cost-benefit analysis at every stage, depending on how polished and "bullet proof" you need the code to be.

Review the Signature for Type Safety

The next step in the refinement process is to reexamine the signature, to check whether there are any errors we could eliminate using the signature alone. It's all very well to detect errors using if/then style logic in the body of a function, but how much better it would be to make these errors impossible to even code. Prominent OCaml[2] developer Yaron Minsky calls this "making illegal state unrepresentable." It's an important technique for making code *motivationally transparent* and *revisable* – but it can be a little hard to achieve in code where numeric values are central.

In our example, think about what would happen if we called our naïve function with an argument of 1.1760. If you try this, you'll see that you get a result of 2.0, which is understandable because (fraction / 0.1760) is 1.0 and, in case you'd forgotten, 1.0 + 1.0 is 2.0. But we already said that fractional parts over 0.1759 are invalid, because from 0.1760 onward, we are into the next mile. If this happened in practice, it would probably indicate that we were calling the conversion function using some other floating-point value that wasn't intended to represent *miles.yards* distances, perhaps because we accessed the wrong field in that hypothetical railway GIS. Our current code leaves the door open to this kind of thing happening silently, and when a bug like that gets embedded deep in a system, it can be very hard to find.

A traditional way of handling this would be to check the fractional part in the body of the conversion function, and to raise an exception when it was out of range. Listing 2-3 shows that being done.

Listing 2-3. Bounds checking within the conversion function

```
open System

let convertMilesYards (milesPointYards : float) : float =
    let wholeMiles = milesPointYards |> floor
    let fraction = milesPointYards - float(wholeMiles)
    if fraction > 0.1759 then
        raise <| ArgumentOutOfRangeException("milesPointYards",
                    "Fractional part must be <= 0.1759")
    wholeMiles + (fraction / 0.1760)

// System.ArgumentOutOfRangeException: Fractional part must be <= 0.1759
// Parameter name: milesPointYards
let decimalMiles = 1.1760 |> convertMilesYards
```

---

[2]OCaml is a language closely related to F#.

But this isn't making illegal state *unrepresentable*; it's detecting an invalid state *after it has happened*. It's not obvious how to fix this, because the `milesPointYards` input is inherently a floating-point value, and (in contrast to, say Discriminated Unions), we don't have a direct way to restrict the range of values that can be expressed. Nonetheless, we can bring the error some way forward in the chain.

We start the process by noting that *miles.yards* could be viewed as a pair of integers, one for the miles and one for the yards. (In railways *miles.yards* distances, we disregard fractional yards.) This leads naturally to representing *miles.yards* as a *Single-Case Discriminated Union* (Listing 2-4.)

Listing 2-4. Miles and yards as a Single-Case Discriminated Union

```
type MilesYards = MilesYards of wholeMiles : int * yards : int
```

Just in case you aren't familiar with Discriminated Unions, we are declaring a type called `MilesYards`, with two integer fields called `wholeMiles` and `yards`. From a construction point of view, it's broadly the same as the C# in Listing 2-5. Consumption-wise though, it's very different, as we'll discover in a moment.

Listing 2-5. An immutable class in C#

```
public class MilesYards
{
    private readonly int wholeMiles;
    private readonly int yards;

    public MilesYards(int wholeMiles, int yards)
    {
        this.wholeMiles = wholeMiles;
        this.yards = yards;
    }

    public int WholeMiles { get { return this.wholeMiles; } }
    public int Yards { get { return this.yards; } }
}
```

I should also mention that in Discriminated Union declarations, the field names (in this case `wholeMiles` and `yards`) are optional, so you will often encounter declarations without them, as in Listing 2-6. I prefer to use field names, even though it's a little wordier, because this improves *motivational transparency*.

16

Listing 2-6. A Single-Case Discriminated Union without field names

```
type MilesYards = MilesYards of int * int
```

Going back to our function design task: we've satisfied the need for a type that models the fact that *miles.yards* is really two integers. How do we integrate that with the computation we set out to do? The trick is to isolate the *construction* of a `MilesYards` instance from any *computation*. This is an extreme version of "separation of concerns": here the concern of constructing a valid instance of *miles.yards* is a separate one from the concern of using it in a computation. Listing 2-7 shows the construction phase.

Listing 2-7. Constructing and validating a MilesYards instance

```
open System

type MilesYards = MilesYards of wholeMiles : int * yards : int

let create (milesPointYards : float) : MilesYards =
    let wholeMiles = milesPointYards |> floor |> int
    let fraction = milesPointYards - float(wholeMiles)
    if fraction > 0.1759 then
        raise <| ArgumentOutOfRangeException("milesPointYards",
                    "Fractional part must be <= 0.1759")
    let yards = fraction * 10_000. |> round |> int
    MilesYards(wholeMiles, yards)
```

Note the carefully constructed signature of the `create` function: it takes a floating-point value (from some external, less strictly-typed source like a GIS) and returns our nice strict `MilesYards` type. For the body, we've brought across some of the code from the previous iteration of our function, including the range validation of the fractional part. Finally, we've constructed a `MilesYards` instance using whole miles and yards.

All this may seem a trifle pernickety, but it has a number of benefits.

- The mapping from floating point to `MilesYards` is separately testable from the conversion to decimal yards.

- We could use the independent `MilesYards` type in other useful ways, such as overriding its `ToString()` method to provide a standard string representation.

- The signature and implementation are *motivationally transparent*. Even if a reader wasn't familiar with the strange *miles.yards* convention in British railways, they'd see instantly what we were trying to do, and they'd be very clear that we were doing it deliberately.

- Likewise, it's *semantically focused*: the reader only has to worry about one thing at a time, in this case the construction of a miles and yards figure consisting of two integers.

- The code is also *revisable*. For example, if a new requirement appeared to create distance values from miles and *chains* (a chain in railways is 22 yards, and yes, this unit is widely used), it would be obvious what to do.

Now it only remains to implement the computation. Listing 2-8 shows a first cut of code to do that.

Listing 2-8. Computing decimal miles from a MilesYards instance

```
let milesYardsToDecimalMiles (milesYards : MilesYards) : float =
    match milesYards with
    | MilesYards(wholeMiles, yards) ->
        (float wholeMiles) + ((float yards) / 1760.)
```

Again, the signature is super explicit: `MilesYards -> float`. In the body we use pattern matching to recover the `wholeMiles` and `yards` payload values from the `MilesYards` instance. Then we use the recovered values in a simple computation to produce decimal miles. Incidentally, if you aren't familiar with Discriminated Unions, the `match` expression is how we get at the fields of the DU. This is one way in which a DU differs from an immutable class such as the C# example in Listing 2-5.

Review and Refine

At this point, we have a somewhat safer and more explicit implementation. But it's not time to rest yet: we should still ruthlessly review the signature, naming, and implementation to ensure they are the best they can be.

The first thing that might jump out at you is the naming of the `create` function. "Create" is rather a vague word. What if we wanted to create an instance from some other type, such as a string? We could perhaps rename `create` to `fromMilesPointYards` - but that still leaves open the issue of what we are creating. And if we incorporated the result type in the name as well, it would be too long.[3] How about moving the whole thing to a module (Listing 2-9)?

Listing 2-9. Using a module to represent a business class

```
module MilesYards =

    type MilesYards = MilesYards of wholeMiles : int * yards : int

    let fromMilesPointYards (milesPointYards : float) : MilesYards =
        // ... Same body as 'create' before ...

    let toDecimalMiles (milesYards : MilesYards) : float =
        // ... Same body as 'milesYardsToDecimalMiles' before ...
```

This style of creation, using a `from...` function within a module, is nice because it leaves open the possibility that we might add additional ways of creating a `MilesYards` instance. For example, we might later add a `fromString` function. From the point of view of the caller, they would be doing a `MilesYards.fromMilesPointYards` or a `MilesYards.fromString`, which is just about as motivationally transparent as you could wish. We were also able to simplify the name of the conversion function from `milesYardsToDecimalMiles` to `toDecimalMiles`.

One thing you might not like about Listing 2-9 is that we have a *type* called `MilesYards` with a *DU case* called `MilesYards`, all inside a *module* called `MilesYards`. Before F# 4.1, having a type inside a module of the same name was actually illegal (unless you used a special attribute). It's now legal, but it can be confusing to users and even other compilers. On the other hand, it's quite difficult to think of different names for the module and the main module type, as they are "about" the same thing. To get around this, some people use a convention of giving the name "T" to the main business type in the module (Listing 2-10). (I'm told the convention originated in the ML language, and it's also been seen in the wild in ReasonML and Elixir.)

---

[3]The longest item name I ever created was `EventModuleBlockBedroomAllocationDelegates`. I'm not proud.

Listing 2-10. Avoiding repetitive naming using the T convention

```
module MilesYards =

    type T = MilesYards of wholeMiles : int * yards : int

    let fromMilesPointYards (milesPointYards : float) : T =
        // ... Same body as before ...

    let toDecimalMiles (milesYards : T) : float =
        // ... Same body as before ...
```

Frankly, I have experimented with both the "T" convention and the double-naming convention, and was undecided about which is best. So I ran a Twitter poll (Figure 2-1), and the definite majority was against the "T" convention.

Kit Eason
@kitlovesfsharp

Do you like the #fsharp convention of type T = ... within a module. (I.e. using the module name to name the domain object and literally 'T' as the name of the 'main' type within it.) Not trying to make a point - I genuinely want to know. ;-)

10% I do this and love it

12% I do this grudgingly

54% I don't like this

24% I don't understand

83 votes • Final results

Figure 2-1. *A Twitter poll on the popularity on the T convention for domain types*

In cases like this, it's probably best to go with what the community is doing. If you do use T, make sure you explain it to anyone who has to maintain the code, especially if they aren't familiar with this convention. Another alternative, which you might have to resort to if calling your code from another language that is confused by the double naming, is to add the word `Module` to the module name, for example, `module MilesYardsModule`. In the rest of this chapter, I stick with the `MilesYards.MilesYards` style of naming.

Another objection to our current code is that we haven't quite achieved "making illegal state unrepresentable." Someone could simply construct their own invalid `MilesYards.MilesYards` instance like this:

```
let naughty = MilesYards.MilesYards(1, 1760)
```

Thus, they'd bypass our carefully crafted `fromMilesPointYards` function. That's OK: it turns out you can prevent this by adding the keyword `private` after the = sign in the type definition:

```
type MilesYards = private MilesYards of wholeMiles : int * yards : int
```

Listing 2-11 shows this in context.

Listing 2-11. Hiding the DU constructor

```
module MilesYards =

    type MilesYards =
        private MilesYards of wholeMiles : int * yards : int
```

Now the only way to create a `MilesYards` instance is to go via the `fromMilesPointYards` function or via any other creation functions we might add in the future.

Note   Sometimes making a DU case constructor private in this way can cause problems. For example, test code or serialization/deserialization sometimes needs to see the constructor. Also, you won't be able to pattern match to recover the underlying values. If using private constructors causes more problems than it solves, just make the case public again (i.e., remove the keyword `private`), and don't worry too much about it.

A Final Polish

Time for a last look at the code to see if there is anything we can improve or simplify. Listing 2-12 shows where we are so far.

Listing 2-12. A pretty good implementation of miles.yards conversion

```
module MilesYards =

    open System

    type MilesYards =
        private MilesYards of wholeMiles : int * yards : int

    let fromMilesPointYards (milesPointYards : float) : MilesYards =
        let wholeMiles = milesPointYards |> floor |> int
        let fraction = milesPointYards - float(wholeMiles)
        if fraction > 0.1759 then
            raise <| ArgumentOutOfRangeException("milesPointYards",
                            "Fractional part must be <= 0.1759")
        let yards = fraction * 10_000. |> round |> int
        MilesYards(wholeMiles, yards)

    let toDecimalMiles (milesYards : MilesYards) : float =
        match milesYards with
        | MilesYards(wholeMiles, yards) ->
            (float wholeMiles) + ((float yards) / 1760.)
```

I now only have a couple of objections to this code, and they are both in the area of conciseness. The first is that we can avoid the match expression in the body of toDecimalMiles. Perhaps surprisingly, the way to do that is to move the pattern matching into the parameter declaration! Listing 2-13 shows before-and-after versions of the function.

Listing 2-13. Pattern matching in parameter declarations

```
/// Before:
let toDecimalMiles (milesPointYards : MilesYards) : float =
    match milesYards with
```

```
    | MilesYards(wholeMiles, yards) ->
        (float wholeMiles) + ((float yards) / 1760.)

/// After:
let toDecimalMiles (MilesYards(wholeMiles, yards)) : float =
    (float wholeMiles) + ((float yards) / 1760.)
```

This trick, which only works safely with single-case Discriminated Unions, causes the pattern match to occur at the caller/callee function boundary, rather than within the body of callee. From the caller's point of view, the type they have to provide (a MilesYards DU instance) is unchanged; but within the callee we have direct access to the fields of the DU, in this case the wholeMiles and yards values. I'm laboring this point slightly, because the first time you see this approach in the wild, it's incredibly confusing.

Another thing we can tighten up a little is the repeated casting to float, such as in this line:

```
(float wholeMiles) + ((float yards) / 1760.)
```

This casting is necessary because F# is stricter when mixing integers and floating-point types than, for example, C#. You have to explicitly cast in one direction or the other, which is intended to help you focus on your code's intentions, and thus to avoid subtle floating-point bugs. However, all those brackets and float keywords do make the code a little wordy. We can get around this by creating a little operator to do the work. Listing 2-14 shows how this looks. (Obviously you can put the operator in a different scope if you want to use it more widely.)

Listing 2-14. Using an operator to simplify mixing floating point and integer values

```
module MilesYards =

    let private (~~) = float

    ...

    let toDecimalMiles (MilesYards(wholeMiles, yards)) : float =
        ~~wholeMiles + (~~yards / 1760.)
```

The reason I chose ~~ as the name of this operator is that the wavy characters are reminiscent of an analog signal.

I personally find this a very useful trick when writing computational code. That said, many F# developers are reluctant to create their own operators, as it can obfuscate code as much as it simplifies. I'll leave the choice to you.

Recommendations

Here are the key points I want you to take away from this chapter.

- To write a function, first define the required signature, then write the body. Refine the signature and body until as many errors as possible are eliminated declaratively at the signature (type) level; and remaining errors are handled imperatively in the function body.

- To model a business type, consider using a Single-Case Discriminated Union, perhaps with a private case constructor, embedded in a module. Only allow instances to be created via functions in the same module, and validate inputs in those functions. Provide other functions to act on the type (for example, to convert to other types) in that same module.

- Be aware of the existence of the "T" convention for naming business types, but be cautious about using it in new code.

- Consider using operators – sparingly - to simplify code. In particular, consider declaring conversion operators such as ~~ to simplify code that mixes floating point and integer values.

Summary

In this chapter you learned how to design and write a function. You started by thinking about types: what type or types the function should take as parameters, and what type it should return. Then you coded the body of the function, before circling back to the type signature to try and eliminate possible errors. You learned how to embed a type representing some business item in a module, together with supporting functions to instantiate the type, and to transform the type to another type. You learned the importance of single-case Discriminated Unions, and about the usefulness of hiding the constructor to maximize type safety. Finally, you learned a couple of tricks to simplify your code: doing pattern matching in the declaration of a function parameter, and using operators to simplify common operations such as casting to float.

In the next chapter, we'll look at *missing data*: how best to express the concept that a data item is missing or irrelevant in a particular context.

Exercises

Here are some exercises to help you hone the skills you've gained so far. Exercise solutions are at the end of the chapter.

EXERCISE 2-1 – HANDLING NEGATIVE DISTANCES

There's a hole in the validation presented above: we haven't said anything about what happens when the input distance is negative. If we decided that negative distances simply aren't valid (because *miles.yards* values always represent a physical position on a railway network), what would you need to change in the code to prevent negative values entering the domain?

Hint: You could do this around the same point in the code where we already check the range of the yards value.

EXERCISE 2-2 – HANDLING DISTANCES INVOLVING CHAINS

For some purposes, British railway distances aren't expressed in miles and yards, but in miles and *chains*, where a chain is defined as 22 yards (see Figure 2-2).

Figure 2-2. *A sign identifying a British railway bridge. The figures at the very bottom represent a distance from some datum, in miles and chains.*

Write a new module that can create a distance in whole miles and chains, and convert such a miles-and-chains distance to decimal miles. The only way to create the new `MilesChains` distance should be by supplying a whole miles and a chains input (i.e., two positive integers), so unlike `MilesYards` you won't need a `fromMilesPointYards` function.

Hint: There are 80 chains in a mile.

Exercise Solutions

EXERCISE 2-1 – HANDLING NEGATIVE DISTANCES

To complete this exercise, you just need to add a couple of lines to validate `milesPointYards` using an `if` expression, then raise an `ArgumentOutOfRangeException`.

```
open System

module MilesYards =

    type MilesYards = private MilesYards of wholeMiles : int * yards : int
```

```
let fromMilesPointYards (milesPointYards : float) : MilesYards =

    if milesPointYards < 0.0 then
        raise <| ArgumentOutOfRangeException("milesPointYards",
        "Must be > 0.0")

    // As existing code...

    MilesYards(wholeMiles, yards)

let toDecimalMiles (milesYards : MilesYards) : float =
    // As existing code...
```

EXERCISE 2-2 – HANDLING DISTANCES INVOLVING CHAINS

To complete this exercise, you need to create a Single-Case Discriminated Union much like the `MilesYards` DU, but with `wholeMiles` and `chains` as its fields. Add a `fromMilesChains` function that range-validates the `wholeMiles` and `chains` arguments, then uses them to make a `MilesChains` instance.

To convert to decimal miles, create a `toDecimalMiles` function that pattern matches to retrieve the `wholeMiles` and `chains` values, then uses the 80-chains-per-mile conversion factor to calculate decimal miles.

```
open System

module MilesChains =

    type MilesChains =
        private MilesChains of wholeMiles : int * chains : int

    let fromMilesChains(wholeMiles : int, chains : int) =
        if wholeMiles < 0 then
            raise <| ArgumentOutOfRangeException("wholeMiles",
                        "Must be >= 0")
```

```
    if chains < 0 || chains >= 80 then
        raise <| ArgumentOutOfRangeException("chains",
                    "Must be >= 0 and < 80")
    MilesChains(wholeMiles, chains)

let toDecimalMiles (MilesChains(wholeMiles, chains)) : float =
    (float wholeMiles) + ((float chains) / 80.)
```

CHAPTER 3

Missing Data

Not even a thought has arisen; is there still a sin or not?

—Zen Koan, 10th Century CE

This is a chapter about nothing! Specifically, it's about how we handle the absence of data in our programs. It's a more important topic than you might think at first: bugs caused by incorrect handling of missing data, typically manifested as "null reference errors," are distressingly common in Object Oriented programs. And this still happens, despite code to avoid such errors forming a significant proportion of the line count of many C# codebases.

In this chapter I'll try to convince you how serious a problem this is, and show you the many features and idioms that F# offers to mitigate and even eliminate this class of error.

A Brief History of Null

When computer scientist Tony Hoare invented the concept of null in 1965, his purpose was to represent a thing or property that is *potentially* present, but might not be present in a particular situation. Take the ALGOL W program in Listing 3-1, where null values are used extensively. (ALGOL W was implemented by Tony Hoare.)

Listing 3-1. Some ALGOL W code that uses null

```
RECORD PERSON (
    STRING(20) NAME;
    INTEGER AGE;
    LOGICAL MALE;
    REFERENCE(PERSON) FATHER, MOTHER, YOUNGESTOFFSPRING, ELDERSIBLING
);
```

© Kit Eason 2018
K. Eason, *Stylish F#*, https://doi.org/10.1007/978-1-4842-4000-7_3

```
REFERENCE(PERSON) PROCEDURE YOUNGESTUNCLE (REFERENCE(PERSON) R);
    BEGIN
        REFERENCE(PERSON) P, M;
        P := YOUNGESTOFFSPRING(FATHER(FATHER(R)));
        WHILE (P ¬= NULL) AND (¬ MALE(P)) OR (P = FATHER(R)) DO
            P := ELDERSIBLING(P);
        M := YOUNGESTOFFSPRING(MOTHER(MOTHER(R)));
        WHILE (M ¬= NULL) AND (¬ MALE(M)) DO
            M := ELDERSIBLING(M);
        IF P = NULL THEN
            M
        ELSE IF M = NULL THEN
            P
        ELSE
            IF AGE(P) < AGE(M) THEN P ELSE M
    END
```

Here the ability to have a null or an actual value is used to model – for example - the fact that a person might or might not have an elder sibling. Null and non-null instance values are used as flags to go down various branches of code. The modeling is definitely a bit fuzzy: for instance, FATHER and MOTHER are also nullable, even though everyone has a mother and father. Perhaps this models the fact that we might not know who they are. This kind of ambiguity was excusable in the 1960s, but coding patterns in the style of Listing 3-1 are still surprisingly common, even though there are now well-known techniques for modeling such relationships much more explicitly.

Of course, things have improved somewhat since 1965: in C#, for example, we now have the null coalescing operator ??, which allows us to retrieve either the non-null value of some source item, or some other value, typically a default. As of C# 6.0, we also have the null-conditional operators ?. and ?[] that allow us to reach into an object or array for a property or indexed item and safely return null if either the object with the property, or the property itself, is null.

Despite these improvements, we all regularly see problems caused by null-based modeling. Spotting a ticketing machine or timetable display that has crashed with a null reference error can brighten any programmer's commute. Figure 3-1 shows a less high-profile but equally typical example: Team Explorer in Visual Studio 2017 exposing a null reference exception during a git syncing operation.

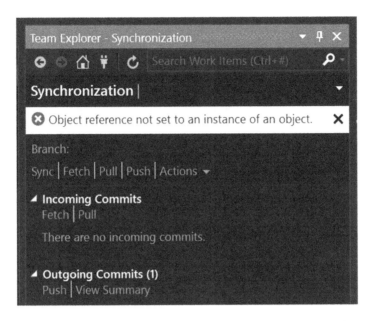

Figure 3-1. *Visual Studio 2017 Team Explorer Exposing a Null Reference Exception*

What has happened in these cases (typically) is that code has tried to access some property or method of an object, which is itself null, such as the arrival time of the first train when there is no known first train.

It's common to blame the programmer in these situations, attributing such errors either to incompetence or to outdated practices and technologies. But it isn't as simple as that. I took a look at the GitHub issue list of a very modern, reputable, high-profile C# codebase. (I won't be so rude as to name it.) When I checked (in April 2018) for mentions of null references in that GitHub issue list, I got hundreds of hits, many of which were still open (Table 3-1). (There will of course be some double counting in these figures.)

Table 3-1. *Null Reference Mentions in a Major C# Codebase Issue List*

Search Term	Open	Closed
NullReferenceException	78	338
null reference	77	275
null-ref	66	387
nullref	2	22

Clearly it isn't just "bad programmers" making these mistakes: null reference errors are accidents waiting to happen. Rather than blaming the operator, we should follow the basic principles of ergonomics, and design such errors out of the technology.

At the time of writing, the primary approach in C# is to "code around" the problem of null, which works (if you remember to do it) but does have a cost. I analyzed several open source C# codebases and found that the proportion of lines involved in managing nulls (null checks, uses of null-coalescing and null-conditional operators) amounted to between 3% and 5% of the significant lines of code. Not crippling by any means, but certainly a significant distraction. Anything we can do to make this process easier has a worthwhile payoff.

The conclusion must be that paying attention to missing data, and spending some time learning the techniques handle to it correctly, or avoid it completely, are among the most useful things you can do as you learn idiomatic F# coding.

By the way, in case you were wondering: no, we aren't going to port the youngest-uncle algorithm from ALGOL W to F# in this book! Aside from the use of nulls, the modeling here is so strange that it's not straightforward to build a concise implementation that is comparable with the original.

Option Types versus Null

F#'s answer to the problem of potentially absent values is the *option type*. If you've coded in F# at all, you are probably familiar with option types, but please bear with me for a few moments while I establish very clearly what option types are, and what they are not.

Fundamentally, the option type is just another *Discriminated Union* (DU), a type that can take several *case* values, each of which may have a different type of *payload*. Just in case you aren't fully conversant with DU's, Listing 3-2 shows a general example: a type that can represent the dimensions of a square, a rectangle, or a circle. The Shape DU is made generic (the "T" part) so that we could express the dimensions in any type we wanted – single precision, double precision, integer pixels, or whatever.

Listing 3-2. Example of a Discriminated Union

```
type Shape<'T> =
| Square of height:'T
| Rectangle of height:'T * width:'T
| Circle of radius:'T
```

Conceptually, the F# option type is just the same: you can think of it as being a generic DU as shown in Listing 3-3. (Actually, within the compiler, it's not quite as simple as that. For one thing, the option type has its own keyword: `option`.)

Listing 3-3. The Option type viewed as a Discriminated Union

```
type Option<'T> =
| Some of 'T
| None
```

One obvious difference between `Shape` and `Option` is that one of the cases of `Option` takes no payload at all - which makes sense because we can't know the value of something that, by definition, doesn't exist. DU cases without payloads are perfectly fine.

Listings 3-4 and 3-5 show us creating, and pattern matching on the `Shape` DU and the `Option` DU in exactly the same way, to illustrate that there is nothing really magical about the `Option` DU.

Listing 3-4. Creating and Using the Shape DU

```
type Shape<'T> =
| Square of height:'T
| Rectangle of height:'T * width:'T
| Circle of radius:'T

let describe (shape : Shape<float>) =
    match shape with
    | Square h -> sprintf "Square of height %f" h
    | Rectangle(h, w) -> sprintf "Rectangle %f x %f" h w
    | Circle r -> sprintf "Circle of radius %f" r

let goldenRect = Rectangle(1.0, 1.61803)

// Rectangle 1.000000 x 1.618030
printfn "%s" (describe goldenRect)
```

Listing 3-5. Creating and Using the Option DU

```
let myMiddleName = Some "Brian"
let herMiddleName = None

let displayMiddleName (name : Option<string>) =
    match name with
```

```
        | Some s -> s
        | None -> ""
    // >>>Brian<<<
    printfn ">>>%s<<<" (displayMiddleName myMiddleName)
    // >>><<<
    printfn ">>>%s<<<" (displayMiddleName herMiddleName)
```

The Shape type and the (built-in) Option type are treated in comparable ways in Listings 3-4 and 3-5 – the only real difference is that we could have declared the displayMiddleName function's argument using string option instead of Option<string>, thus:

```
    let displayMiddleName (name : string option) = ...
```

I could have done this because the compiler offers a special keyword for option types. I only used the Option<string> version in Listing 3-5 to highlight the fact that option types are DUs. In practice you should use the option keyword.

Consuming Option Types

How does all this help us step away from the risky world of nullable types, where we are always one null-check away from a NullReferenceException? The difference from using nulls is that – provided we don't deliberately bypass F# idioms – we are forced by the compiler to consider both the Some and None cases whenever we consume an option type. Consider Listing 3-6, where we have a billing details record that might, or might not, have a separate delivery address. (Again, this isn't great modeling – see the next few sections for some improvements.)

Listing 3-6. Modeling an optional delivery address using an Option type

```
    type BillingDetails = {
        name : string
        billing :  string
        delivery : string option }
```

```
let myOrder = {
    name = "Kit Eason"
    billing = "112 Fibonacci Street\nErehwon\n35813"
    delivery = None }

let hisOrder = {
    name = "John Doe"
    billing = "314 Pi Avenue\nErewhon\n15926"
    delivery = Some "16 Planck Parkway\nErewhon\n62291" }

// Error: the expression was expected to have type 'string'
// but here has type 'string option'
printfn "%s" myOrder.delivery
printfn "%s" hisOrder.delivery
```

Note how at the end of Listing 3-6, we try to treat the orders' delivery addresses as strings, not as string *options*, which are a different type. This causes a compiler error for both the myOrder and hisOrder cases, not just a runtime error in the myOrder case. This is the option type magic protecting us, by forcing us to consider the has-data and no-data possibilities at the point of consumption.

This begs the question: How *are* we supposed to access the underlying value or payload? There are several ways to do this, some more straightforward than others, so in the next few sections we'll go through these and examine their benefits and costs.

Pattern Matching on Option Types

Since an option type is a Discriminated Union, the obvious way to get at its payload (when there is one) is using pattern matching using a *match expression* (Listing 3-7).

Listing 3-7. Accessing an option type's payload using Pattern Matching

```
// BillingDetails type and examples as Listing 3-6.

let addressForPackage (details : BillingDetails) =
    let address =
        match details.delivery with
        | Some s -> s
        | None -> details.billing
    sprintf "%s\n%s" details.name address
```

```
// Kit Eason
// 112 Fibonacci Street
// Erehwon
// 35813
printfn "%s" (addressForPackage myOrder)

// John Doe
// 16 Planck Parkway
// Erewhon
// 62291
printfn "%s" (addressForPackage hisOrder)
```

Consuming option types using explicit pattern matching in this way has clear trade-offs. The big advantage is that it's simple: everyone familiar with the basics of F# syntax will be familiar with it, and the reader doesn't require knowledge of other libraries (or even Computer Science theory!) to understand what is going on. The disadvantage is that it's a little verbose and pipeline unfriendly.

I'll present alternatives in future sections, but before I do, let me say this: if you, and anyone maintaining your code, aren't *completely* comfortable with the basics of option types – comfortable to the extent that everyone is ready and keen to move onto more fluent methods of consumption – I'd advise that you stick with good old-fashioned pattern matching, at least for a while. As with many other areas of F# coding, trying to get too clever too quickly can lead to some pretty obscure code, and a definite blurring of the principles of *motivational transparency* and *semantic focus*.

The Option Module

Once you are ready to go beyond pattern matching, you can start using some of the functions available in the `Option` module. I personally found the `Option` module functions a little hard to get my head around at first. I suspect this is because English language descriptions of these functions don't make much sense without examples – so take this section slowly!

The Option.defaultValue Function

Let me start off with the equivalent code, in the `Option` module world, to that presented in Listing 3-7 – that is, getting either a string representing a delivery address, or a default value (Listing 3-8).

Listing 3-8. Defaulting an Option Type Instance using Option.defaultValue

```
type BillingDetails = {
    name : string
    billing :  string
    delivery : string option }

let addressForPackage (details : BillingDetails) =
    let address =
        Option.defaultValue details.billing details.delivery

    sprintf "%s\n%s" details.name address
```

The usage of `addressForPackage` is exactly the same as in Listing 3-7 so I haven't repeated the usage here.

`Option.defaultValue` is pretty straightforward: you give it an option type as its second argument (in this case `details.delivery`), and it'll either return the underlying value of that instance if there is one, or instead the value you give it in the first parameter (in this case `details.billing`). One thing that might confuse you is the ordering of the parameters – the default value first and the option value second. The reason for this is to make the function "pipeline friendly." The value of this becomes clear if we apply `Option.defaultValue` as part of a pipeline, as in Listing 3-9.

Listing 3-9. Using Option.defaultValue in a pipeline

```
let addressForPackage (details : BillingDetails) =
    let address =
        details.delivery
        |> Option.defaultValue details.billing

    sprintf "%s\n%s" details.name address
```

The Option.iter Function

The Option module also offers a function to do something imperative with an option type, for example, printing out its payload or writing it to a file. It's called Option. iter, by analogy with functions like Array.iter that "do something imperative" with each element of a collection. If the value is Some, it performs the specified imperative action once using the payload; otherwise is does nothing at all. The function printDeliveryAddress in Listing 3-10 prints "Delivery address: <address>" if there is such an address; otherwise it takes no action.

Listing 3-10. Using Option.iter to take an imperative action if a value is populated

```
let printDeliveryAddress (details : BillingDetails) =
    details.delivery
    |> Option.iter
        (fun address -> printfn "%s\n%s" details.name address)

// No output at all
myOrder |> printDeliveryAddress

// Delivery address:
// John Doe
// 16 Planck Parkway
// Erewhon
// 62291
hisOrder |> printDeliveryAddress
```

Other Option module functions that are analogous to their collection-based cousins are Option.count, which produces 1 if the value is Some, otherwise 0; and Option. toArray and Option.toList, which produce a collection of length 1 containing the underlying value, otherwise an empty collection.

Option.map and Option.bind

The two Option module functions that I personally struggled most with were Option.map and Option.bind, so we'll spend a little more time on them. The documented behavior of these functions is a good example of descriptions of function behavior in English not being terribly useful (Table 3-2). (It may be that the descriptions are more helpful if – unlike me – you have a Computer Science or formal functional programming background!)

Table 3-2. *Documented Behavior of the Option.map and Option.bind Functions*

Function	Description
Option.map	Transforms an option value by using a specified mapping function.
Option.bind	Invokes a function on an optional value that itself yields an option.

The Option.map Function

Option.map is a way to apply a function to the underlying value of an option type if it exists, and to return the result as a Some case; and if the input value is None, to return None without using the function at all. An example probably says it better: Listing 3-11 is a variation on printDeliveryAddress.

Listing 3-11. Using Option.map to optionally apply a function, returning an option type

```
let printDeliveryAddress (details : BillingDetails) =
    details.delivery
    |> Option.map
        (fun address -> address.ToUpper())
    |> Option.iter
        (fun address ->
            printfn "Delivery address:\n%s\n%s"
                (details.name.ToUpper()) address)

// No output at all
myOrder |> printDeliveryAddress

// Delivery address:
// JOHN DOE
// 16 PLANCK PARKWAY
// EREWHON
// 62291
hisOrder |> printDeliveryAddress
```

Here the requirement is to print a delivery address in capitals if it exists, otherwise to do nothing. We combine Option.map, to do the uppercasing when necessary, with Option.iter, to do the printing.

Another way of thinking of Option.map is in diagram form (Figure 3-2).

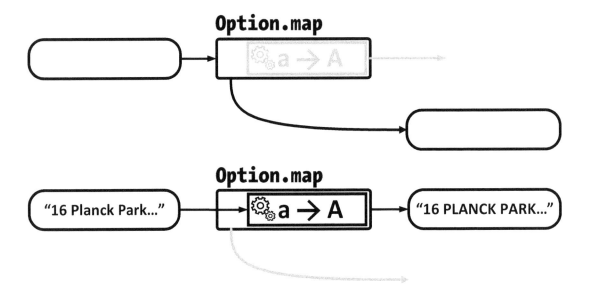

Figure 3-2. *Option.map as a diagram*

In the None case (top of the diagram), the None effectively passes through untouched and never goes near the uppercasing operation. In the Some case (bottom of diagram), the payload is uppercased and comes out as a Some value. At this point we begin to see the beginnings of the "Railway Oriented Programming" paradigm, which we'll discuss in detail in Chapter 11.

The Option.bind Function

Option.bind is so similar to Option.map that I found it very hard to get my head around the difference. (Indeed, I still often catch myself trying each of them until the compiler errors go away!) I think the best way to start is to compare the signatures of Option.map and Option.bind (Table 3-3).

Table 3-3. *Type Signatures for Option.map and Option.bind*

Function	Signature
Option.map	('T -> 'U) -> 'T option -> 'U option
Option.bind	('T -> 'U **option**) -> 'T option -> 'U option

Look at them carefully: the only difference is that the "binder" function needs to return an option type ("U" option) rather than an unwrapped type ("U"). The usefulness of this is that if you have a series of operations, each of which might succeed (returning Some value) or fail (returning None), you can pipe them together without any additional ceremony. Execution of your pipeline effectively "bails out" after the first step that returns None, because subsequent steps just pass the None through to the end without attempting to do any processing.

Think about a situation where we need to take the delivery address from the previous example, pull out the last line of the address, check that it is a postal code by trying to convert it into an integer, then look up a delivery hub (a package-sorting center) based on the postal code. The point is that several of these operations might "fail," in the sense of returning None.

- The delivery address might not be specified (i.e., have a value of None).

- The delivery address might exist but be an empty string, hence having no last line from which to get the postal code.

- The last line might not be convertible to a postal code.

(I've made some simplifying assumptions here: I'm ignoring the billing address, I'm ignoring any validation that might in practice mean the delivery address isn't an empty string; I'm assuming that a postal code must simply be an integer; and I'm assuming that the hub lookup always succeeds.) What does the code look like to achieve all this? (Listing 3-12).

Listing 3-12. Using Option.bind to create a pipeline of might-fail operations

```
open System

type BillingDetails = {
    name : string
    billing :  string
    delivery : string option }
```

```
let tryLastLine (address : string) =
    let parts =
        address.Split([|'\n'|],
                      StringSplitOptions.RemoveEmptyEntries)
    // Could also just do parts |> Array.tryLast
    match parts with
    | [||] ->
        None
    | parts ->
        parts |> Array.last |> Some

let tryPostalCode (codeString : string) =
    match Int32.TryParse(codeString) with
    | true, i -> i |> Some
    | false, _ -> None

let postalCodeHub (code : int) =
    if code = 62291 then
        "Hub 1"
    else
        "Hub 2"

let tryHub (details : BillingDetails) =
    details.delivery
    |> Option.bind tryLastLine
    |> Option.bind tryPostalCode
    |> Option.map postalCodeHub

let myOrder = {
    name = "Kit Eason"
    billing = "112 Fibonacci Street\nErewhon\n35813"
    delivery = None }

let hisOrder = {
    name = "John Doe"
    billing = "314 Pi Avenue\nErewhon\n15926"
    delivery = Some "16 Planck Parkway\nErewhon\n62291" }
```

```
// None
myOrder |> tryHub

// Some "Hub 1"
hisOrder |> tryHub
```

In Listing 3-12 we have a `trylastLine` function that splits the address by line breaks, and returns the last line *if there is one*, otherwise `None`. Similarly, `tryPostalCode` attempts to convert a string to an integer, and returns `Some  value` only if that succeeds. The `postalCodeHub` function does a super-naïve lookup (in reality, it would be some kind of database lookup) and always returns a value. We bring all these together in `tryHub`, which uses two `Option.bind` calls and an `Option.map` call to apply each of these operations in turn to get us from an optional delivery address to an optional delivery hub.

This is a really common pattern in idiomatic F# code: a series of `Option.bind` and `Option.map` calls to get from one state to another, using several steps, each of which can fail. Common though it is, it is quite a high level of abstraction, and it's one of those things where you have to understand *everything* before you understand *anything*. So, if you aren't comfortable using it for now – don't. A bit of nested pattern matching isn't the worst thing in the world! I'll return to this topic in Chapter 11 when we talk about "Railway Oriented Programming," at which point perhaps it'll make a little more sense.

Option Type No-Nos

Using option types can be frustrating at first. There's often a strong temptation to bypass the pattern-matching or `bind`/`map` approach, and instead tear open the package by examining the `IsSome` and `Value` properties that the option type offers (Listing 3-13).

Listing 3-13. Antipattern: accessing Option type payloads using hasValue and Value

```
// Accessing payload via .IsSome and .Value
// Don't do this!
let printDeliveryAddress (details : BillingDetails) =
    if details.delivery.IsSome then
        printfn "Delivery address:\n%s\n%s"
            (details.name.ToUpper())
            (details.delivery.Value.ToUpper())
```

Don't do this! You'd be undermining the whole infrastructure we have built up for handling potentially-missing values in a composable way.

Some people would also consider explicit pattern matching using a match expression (in the manner of Listing 3-7) an antipattern too, and would have you always use the equivalent functions from the `Option` module. But as I've said, I think that's a "counsel of perfection": that is, advice that's great in principle but isn't always easy to follow. You'll get to fluency with `Option.map`, `Option.bind`, or so forth in due course. In the meantime, a bit of pattern matching isn't going to hurt anyone, and the lower level of abstraction may make your code more comprehensible to non-advanced collaborators.

Designing Out Missing Data

So far, we've been accepting the admittedly not-great modeling embodied in our original `BillingDetails` type. (As a reminder this is repeated in Listing 3-14.)

Listing 3-14. The BillingDetails type

```
type BillingDetails = {
    name : string
    billing :  string
    delivery : string option }
```

The reason I say this is not great is that it isn't clear under what circumstances the delivery address might not be there. (You might have to look elsewhere in the code to find out, which is a violation of the principle of *semantic focus*.) We can certainly improve on this. Let's think about what the business rules might be for the `BillingDetails` type:

- There *must* always be a billing address.

- There *might* be a different delivery address but…

- There *must* be *no* delivery address if the product isn't a physically deliverable one, such as a download.

A good way to model this kind of thing is to express the rules as Discriminated Union cases. Listing 3-15 shows how this might play out.

Listing 3-15. Modeling delivery address possibilities using a DU

```
type Delivery =
| AsBilling
| Physical of string
| Download

type BillingDetails = {
    name : string
    billing : string
    delivery : Delivery }
```

In the new Delivery type, we've enumerated the three business possibilities: that the delivery address is the same as the billing address, that the delivery address is a separate physical address, or that the product is a download that does not need a physical address. Only in the Physical case do we need a string in which to store the address. In Listing 3-16, I've shown how it feels to consume the revamped BillingDetails type.

Listing 3-16. Consuming the improved BillingDetails type

```
let tryDeliveryLabel (billingDetails : BillingDetails) =
    match billingDetails.delivery with
    | AsBilling ->
        billingDetails.billing |> Some
    | Physical address ->
        address |> Some
    | Download -> None
    |> Option.map (fun address ->
        sprintf "%s\n%s" billingDetails.name address)

let deliveryLabels (billingDetails : BillingDetails seq) =
    billingDetails
    |> Seq.choose tryDeliveryLabel

let myOrder = {
    name = "Kit Eason"
    billing = "112 Fibonacci Street\nErehwon\n35813"
    delivery = AsBilling }
```

```
let hisOrder = {
    name = "John Doe"
    billing = "314 Pi Avenue\nErewhon\n15926"
    delivery = Physical "16 Planck Parkway\nErewhon\n62291" }

let herOrder = {
    name = "Jane Smith"
    billing = "9 Gravity Road\nErewhon\n80665"
    delivery = Download }

// seq
//      [ "Kit Eason
//          112 Fibonacci Street
//          Erehwon
//          35813";
//         "John Doe
//          16 Planck Parkway
//          Erewhon
//          62291"]
[ myOrder; hisOrder; herOrder ]
|> deliveryLabels
```

In Listing 3-16, I've imagined that we want a function that generates delivery labels only for those orders that require physical delivery. I've divided the task up into two parts.

- The tryDeliveryLabel function uses a match expression to extract the relevant address, then Option.map to combine this (when it exists) with the customer name to form a complete label.

- The deliveryLabels function takes a sequence of billingDetails items and applies tryDeliveryLabel to each item. Then it uses Seq. choose both to pick out those items where Some was returned, and to extract the payloads of these Some values. (I go into more detail about Seq.choose and related functions in Chapter 4.)

Viewed in the light of the principles I laid out in Chapter 1, the code in Listings 3-15 and 3-16 is much better:

- It has good *semantic focus*. You can tell without looking elsewhere what functions such as tryDeliveryLabel will do and why.

- It has good *revisability*. Let's say you realize that you want to support an additional delivery mechanism: so-called "Click and Collect," where the customer comes to a store to collect their item. You might start by adding a new case to the `Delivery` DU, maybe with a store ID payload. From then on, the compiler would tell you all the points in existing code that you needed to change; and it would be pretty obvious how to add new features such as a function to list click-and-collect orders and their store IDs.

- It has good *motivational transparency*. You aren't left wondering why a particular delivery address is `None`. The reasons why an address might or might not exist are right there in the code. Other developers both "above you" in the stack (e.g., someone designing a view model for a UI) and "below you" (e.g., someone consuming the data to generate back-end fulfilment processes) can be clear about when and why certain items should and should not be present.

Modeling like this, where we use DUs to provide storage of the requisite type (as the "payload" of a DU case) only in instances where it is required, brings us toward the nirvana of "Making Illegal State Unrepresentable," an approach that I believe does more to eliminate bugs than any other coding philosophy I've come across.

Interoperating with the Nullable World

In this section, I'll talk a bit about the implications of nullability when interoperating between F# and C#. There shouldn't be anything too unexpected here, but when working in F# it's always worth bearing in mind the implications of interop scenarios.

Leaking In of Null Values

If you're of a skeptical frame of mind, you'll realize that there is a pretty big hole in my suggestion so far in this chapter (i.e., the claim that you can protect against null values by wrapping things in option types or Discriminated Unions). The hole is that (if it is a reference type like a string), the wrapped type could still have a value of `null`. So, for example, the code in Listing 3-17 will compile fine, but it will fail with a null reference exception at runtime.

Listing 3-17. A null hiding inside an option type

```
type BillingDetails = {
    name : string
    billing :  string
    delivery : string option }

let printDeliveryAddress (details : BillingDetails) =
    details.delivery
    |> Option.map
        (fun address -> address.ToUpper())
    |> Option.iter
        (fun address ->
            printfn "Delivery address:\n%s\n%s"
                (details.name.ToUpper()) address)

let dangerOrder = {
    name = "Will Robinson"
    billing = "2 Jupiter Avenue\nErewhon\n199732"
    delivery = Some null }

// NullReferenceException
printDeliveryAddress dangerOrder
```

(As an aside, and perhaps a little surprisingly, doing a `printfn "%s"` null or a `sprint "%s"` null is fine – formatting a string with %s produces output as if the string was a non-null, empty string. The problem in Listing 3-17 is the call to the `ToUpper()` method of a null instance.)

Obviously, you wouldn't knowingly write code exactly like Listing 3-17, but it does indicate how we are at the mercy of anything calling our code that might pass us a null. This doesn't mean that the whole exercise of using option types or DU's is worthless. Option types and other DU wrappers are primarily useful because they make the intention of our code clear. But it does mean that, at the boundary of the code we consider to be safe, we need to validate for or otherwise deal with null values.

Defining a SafeString Type

One generalized way to deal with incoming nulls is to define a new wrapper type and perform the validation in its constructor (Listing 3-18).

Listing 3-18. Validating strings on construction

```
type SafeString (s : string) =
    do
        if s = null then
            raise <| System.ArgumentException()
    member __.Value = s
    override __.ToString() = s

type BillingDetails = {
    name : SafeString
    billing :  SafeString
    delivery : SafeString option }

let printDeliveryAddress (details : BillingDetails) =
    details.delivery
    |> Option.map
        (fun address -> address.Value.ToUpper())
    |> Option.iter
        (fun address ->
            printfn "Delivery address:\n%s\n%s"
                (details.name.Value.ToUpper()) address)

// NullReferenceException at construction time
let dangerOrder = {
    name = SafeString "Will Robinson"
    billing = SafeString "2 Jupiter Avenue\nErewhon\n199732"
    delivery = SafeString null |> Some }
```

Having done this, one would need to require all callers to provide us with a SafeString rather than a string type.

It's a tempting pattern, but frankly, things like strings are so ubiquitous in .NET code that hardly anyone bothers. The overhead of switching to and from such null-safe types so that one can consume them, and use them in .NET calls requiring string arguments, is just too much to cope with. This is particularly in the case of mixed-language codebases, where, like it or not, nullable strings are something of a *lingua franca*.

Using Option.ofObj

We can fight the battle at a different level by using some more functions from the Option module; there are several very useful functions here to help mediate from the nullable to the non-nullable world. The first of these is Option.ofObj, which takes a reference type instance and returns that same instance wrapped in an option type. It returns Some value if the input was non-null, or None if the input was null. This is invaluable at the boundaries of your system, when callers might give you nulls (Listing 3-19).

Listing 3-19. Using Option.ofObj

```
let myApiFunction (stringParam : string) =
    let s =
        stringParam
        |> Option.ofObj
        |> Option.defaultValue "(none)"

    // You can do things here knowing that s isn't null
    printfn "%s" (s.ToUpper())

// HELLO
myApiFunction "hello"

// (NONE)
myApiFunction null
```

Using Option.ofNullable

If you have an instance of System.Nullable (for example, a nullable integer), you can use Option.ofNullable to smoothly transition it into an option type (Listing 3-20).

Listing 3-20. Using Option.ofNullable

```
open System

let showHeartRate (rate : Nullable<int>) =
    rate
    |> Option.ofNullable
    |> Option.map (fun r -> r.ToString())
    |> Option.defaultValue "N/A"

// 96
showHeartRate (System.Nullable(96))

// N/A
showHeartRate (System.Nullable())
```

Incidentally, Listing 3-20 was inspired by my exercise watch, which occasionally tells me that my heart rate is null.

Leaking Option Types and DUs Out

Clearly the flipside of letting nulls leak *into* our F# code is the potential for leakage *outward* of F#-specific types such as the option type and Discriminated Unions in general. It's *possible* to create and consume these types in languages such as C#, using compiler-generated sugar such as the NewCase constructor and the .IsCase, .Tag, and .Item properties, plus a bit of casting. However, it's generally regarded as bad manners to force callers to do so, if those callers might not be written in F#. Again, some functions in the Option module come to the rescue.

Using Option.toObj

Option.toObj is the mirror image of Option.ofObj. It takes an option type and returns either the underlying value if it is Some, or null if it is None. Listing 3-21 shows how we might handle returning a nullable "location" string for a navigation UI.

Listing 3-21. Using Option.toObj

```
open System

let random = new Random()

let tryLocationDescription (locationId : int) =
    // In reality this would be attempting
    // to get the location from a database etc.
    let r = random.Next(1, 100)
    if r < 50 then
        Some (sprintf "Location number %i" r)
    else
        None

let tryLocationDescriptionNullable (locationId : int) =
    tryLocationDescription()
    |> Option.toObj

// Sometimes null, sometimes "Location number #"
tryLocationDescriptionNullable 99
```

Alternatively, you might want to reflect the kind of pattern used in functions like `System.Double.TryParse()`, which return a Boolean value indicating success or failure, and place the result of the operation (if successful) into a "by reference" parameter (Listing 3-22). This is a pattern that might feel more natural if the function is being called from C#.

Listing 3-22. Returning success or failure as a Boolean, with result in a reference parameter

```
open System

let random = new Random()

let tryLocationDescription (locationId : int, description : string
byref) : bool =
    // In reality this would be attempting
```

```
    // to get the description from a database etc.
    let r = random.Next(1, 100)
    if r < 50 then
        description <- sprintf "Location number %i" r
        true
    else
        description <- null
        false
```

Using Option.toNullable

It won't surprise you to learn that `Option.toNullable` is the counterpart of `Option.ofNullable`. It gets you from an option type to a nullable type, for example, `Nullable<int>`. Listing 3-23 shows us getting a heart rate from an unreliable sensor and returning either `null` or a heart rate value. (Clearly, unlike my exercise watch, the UI would need to know how to handle the `null` case!)

Listing 3-23. Using Option.toNullable

```
open System

let random = new Random()

let getHeartRateInternal() =
    // In reality this would be attempting
    // to get a heart rate from a sensor:
    let rate = random.Next(0, 200)
    if rate = 0 then
        None
    else
        Some rate

let tryGetHeartRate () =
    getHeartRateInternal()
    |> Option.toNullable
```

The Future of Null

At the time of writing, there is some light at the end of the tunnel regarding nulls in the .NET framework. (Hopefully, the light is not of the oncoming-train variety!) It appears that C# 8.0 will effectively change the default behavior for reference types such as strings, so that they won't be nullable by default. (This may turn out to be a switchable feature.) You'll have to use specific syntax (adding a question mark to the declaration – see Listing 3-24) to declare a reference type as nullable. (It might seem perverse, but this new feature is currently being referred to as *nullable reference types*, even though reference types are currently inherently nullable. This is to reflect the fact that reference types are becoming non-nullable by default, with nullable ones from then on being regarded as a special case you have to ask for specifically.) Anyway, in due course this should make it less likely that C# code that calls our nice clean F# code will send us null values by accident.

Listing 3-24. Expected syntax for nullable and non-nullable types from C# 8.0

```
class Person
{
    public string FirstName;    // Not null
    public string? MiddleName; // May be null
    public string LastName;     // Not null
}
```

The ValueOption Type

From F# version 4.5, there is a new type called ValueOption. This is analogous to the option type we discussed above, except that it is a value type (i.e., a struct) rather than a reference type. Listing 3-25 shows usage of the ValueOption type. Note the new voption keyword and the ValueSome and ValueNone case names.

Listing 3-25. Using the ValueOption type (requires F# 4.5 or later)

```
let valueOptionString (v : int voption) =
    match v with
    | ValueSome x ->
```

```
        sprintf "Value: %i" x
    | ValueNone ->
        sprintf "No value"

// "No value"
ValueOption.ValueNone
|> valueOptionString

// "Value: 99"
ValueOption.ValueSome 99
|> valueOptionString
```

Using `ValueOption` values can have performance benefits in some kinds of code. The only way to be sure is to experiment with realistic volumes and processing paths.

At the time of writing, there is no released functionality analogous to `Option. bind`, `Option.map`, and so forth, but I would expect the awesome F# community to add this soon.

Recommendations

Here are the key points I'd like you to take away from this chapter.

- Avoid using null values to represent things that legitimately might not be set. Instead, use Discriminated Unions to model explicit cases when a value is or is not relevant, and only have storage for the value in the cases where it is relevant. If DUs make things too complicated, or if it is obvious from the immediate context why a value might not be set, model it as an option type.

- To make your option-type handling more fluent, consider using functions from the `Option` module, such as `Option.bind`, `Option. map,` and `Option.defaultValue` to create little pipelines that get you safely through one or more processing stages, each of which might fail. But don't get hung up on this – pattern matching is also fine. What's not fine is accessing the `.isSome` and `.Value` properties of an option type!

- At the boundary of your system, consider using `Option.ofObj` and `Option.ofNull` to move incoming nullable values into the option world, and `Option.toObj` and `Option.toNullable` for option values leaving your code for other languages.

- Avoid exposing option types and DU's in APIs, if callers might be written in C# or other languages that might not understand F# types.

Summary

In this chapter you learned how to stop thinking of null values and other missing data items as rare cases to be fended off as an afterthought in your code. You found out how to embrace and handle missing data stylishly using F#'s rich toolbox, including option types, Discriminated Unions, pattern matching, and the `Option` module. These techniques may not come easily at first, but after a while you'll wonder how you managed in any other way.

In the next chapter we'll look at how to use F#'s vast range of *collection functions*, functions that allow you to process collections such as arrays, lists, and `IEnumerable` values with extraordinary fluency.

Exercises

EXERCISE 3-1 – SUPPORTING CLICK AND COLLECT

Take the code from Listing 3-16 and update it to support the following scenario:

- There is an additional delivery type called "Click and Collect."

- When a `BillingDetails` instance's `delivery` value is "Click and Collect," we need to store an integer `StoreId` value but no delivery address. (We still store a billing address as for the other cases.)

Write and try out a function called `collectionsFor`. It needs to take an integer `StoreId` and a sequence of `BillingDetails` instances, and return a sequence of "Click-and-Collect" instances for the specified store.

EXERCISE 3-2 – COUNTING NON-NULLS

You have a `BillingDetails` type and some orders in this form:

```
type BillingDetails = {
    name : string
    billing :  string
    delivery : string option }

let myOrder = {
    name = "Kit Eason"
    billing = "112 Fibonacci Street\nErehwon\n35813"
    delivery = None }

let hisOrder = {
    name = "John Doe"
    billing = "314 Pi Avenue\nErehwon\n15926"
    delivery = None }

let herOrder = {
    name = "Jane Smith"
    billing = null
    delivery = None }

let orders = [| myOrder; hisOrder; herOrder |]
```

What is the most concise function you can write to count the number of `BillingDetails` instances that have a non-null billing address? (Ignore the delivery address.)

Hint: One way to solve this is using two functions from the Option module `Option.ofObj` is one of them. The other one we only mentioned in passing, earlier in this chapter. You might also want use `Seq.map` and `Seq.sumBy`.

Exercise Solutions

This section shows solutions for the exercises in this chapter.

EXERCISE 3-1 – SUPPORTING CLICK AND COLLECT

You can achieve the requirement by adding a new case called `ClickAndCollect` of `int` to the Delivery DU (or `ClickAndCollect` of `storeId:int`).

Then your `collectionsFor` function can do a `Seq.choose`, containing a lambda that maps the `ClickAndCollect` back into `Some`, using a when clause to check the `StoreId`. All other cases can be mapped to `None`, meaning they don't appear in the results at all.

```
module Exercise_03_03 =

    type Delivery =
    | AsBilling
    | Physical of string
    | Download
    | ClickAndCollect of int

    type BillingDetails = {
        name : string
        billing :  string
        delivery : Delivery }

    let collectionsFor (storeId : int) (billingDetails : BillingDetails seq) =
        billingDetails
        |> Seq.choose (fun d ->
            match d.delivery with
            | ClickAndCollect s when s = storeId ->
                Some d
            | _ -> None)

    let myOrder = {
        name = "Kit Eason"
        billing = "112 Fibonacci Street\nErehwon\n35813"
        delivery = AsBilling }
```

```
let yourOrder = {
    name = "Alison Chan"
    billing = "885 Electric Avenue\nErewhon\n41878"
    delivery = ClickAndCollect 1 }

let theirOrder = {
    name = "Pana Okpik"
    billing = "299 Relativity Drive\nErewhon\79245"
    delivery = ClickAndCollect 2 }

// { name = "Alison Chan";
//   billing = "885 Electric Avenue
//              Erewhon
//              41878"; }
//   delivery = ClickAndCollect 1;}
[ myOrder; yourOrder; theirOrder ]
|> collectionsFor 1
|> Seq.iter (printfn "%A")
```

You'll also have to add a new case to the pattern match in the tryDeliveryLabel function to ensure it ignores Click and Collect instances.

```
| ClickAndCollect _
    -> None
```

EXERCISE 3-2 – COUNTING NON-NULLS

There are many ways to do this. You can, for example, use Seq.map to pick out the billing address, another Seq.map with an Option.ofObj to map from nulls to None and non-nulls to Some, and Seq.sumBy with an Option.count to count the Some values. Remember, Option.count returns 1 when there is a Some and 0 when there is a None.

```
let countNonNullBillingAddresses (orders : seq<BillingDetails>) =
    orders
    |> Seq.map (fun bd -> bd.billing)
    |> Seq.map Option.ofObj
    |> Seq.sumBy Option.count

countNonNullBillingAddresses orders
```

CHAPTER 4

Working Effectively with Collection Functions

I'm an intuitive musician. I have no real technical skills. I can only play six chords on the guitar.

—Patti Smith, Musician

Collection functions are central to productive F# coding. Trying to code without them is as crazy as trying to play the guitar without learning chords. Though you don't need to know *all* the chords to be a decent guitarist, you do need the basic ones, and to be able to use them instinctively. The same is true for using collection functions when coding in F#.

But how to start with this seemingly mountainous task? There are about 70 collection functions in the `Array` module alone! This chapter will get you familiar with the most useful collection functions, and show you how to combine them to achieve complex processing tasks with just a few lines of code. I'll also show you how to spot and recover from mistakes commonly made when using collection functions.

Anatomy of a Collection Function

If you've coded at all in F#, you're probably already familiar with the concept of *collection functions*, at least through examples such as `Array.map` and `Array.filter`. Likewise, if you're primarily a C# developer, you'll be familiar with the equivalents in LINQ: `Select` and `Where`. But just in case you aren't familiar with collection functions, here's a quick primer.

© Kit Eason 2018
K. Eason, *Stylish F#*, https://doi.org/10.1007/978-1-4842-4000-7_4

The collection functions in F# are a set of functions that are always available in F# (you don't have to bring in any extra dependencies), and which let you "do something" with a collection. A collection in this context is a grouping of values of the same type, such as an array, an F# list, or any type that implements IEnumerable. The kinds of operations you can perform are things like filtering, sorting, or transforming. Listing 4-1 shows an example of filtering.

Note   In the numeric literals such as 250_000m in Listing 4-1, the underscores are just a readability aid, equivalent to the commas we might use when handwriting the numbers.[1] The m suffix specifies that these are decimal values, which is a good choice when handling money amounts.

Listing 4-1. Filtering example

```
module Filtering =

    type House = { Address : string; Price : decimal }

    let houses =
        [|
            { Address = "1 Acacia Avenue"; Price = 250_000m }
            { Address = "2 Bradley Street"; Price = 380_000m }
            { Address = "1 Carlton Road"; Price = 98_000m }
        |]

    let cheapHouses =
        houses |> Array.filter (fun h -> h.Price < 100_000m)

    // [|{Address = "1 Carlton Road"; Price = 98000M;}|]
    printfn "%A" cheapHouses
```

Note   In the C# LINQ and SQL worlds, this is known as a where operation rather than a filter operation – it's the same thing.

---

[1]The underscore feature was introduced in F# 4.1.

The collection functions come in a number of flavors, based on the collection type to which they are applicable. Each flavor lives in its own module, so there is an `Array` module for working on .NET arrays, a `Seq` module for working on `IEnumerables` (known as "sequences" in the F# world), and a `List` module for working on F# lists. (There are some other flavors that I'll come to later.) Typically, a collection function takes at least two arguments:

- *A function that defines details of the operation we want to perform.*

    For example, the `Array.filter` function takes a function that itself takes a collection element and returns a `Boolean` value. Elements where that function returns `true` are returned in the result of the filter operation.

    In the example in Listing 4-1, we defined the element-processing function anonymously, by saying (`fun h -> h.Price < 100_000m`). When defined anonymously in this way, the function is known as a *lambda function*.

- *An instance of the collection we want to work on – for example, an array.*

This is a different approach from the one in C#, where collection functions are normally defined as extension methods on the type. For example, using LINQ in C#, we would do a `houses.Where` to perform filtering, `"Where"` being an extension method on the type of `houses`.

Collection functions that take and use a function argument are "higher order functions." But some collection functions, such as `Array.sort`, don't take a function argument (in the case of `sort` because the sorting is done using default comparison). These ones *are* collection functions but *aren't* higher order functions.

Some of the collection functions need additional arguments. For instance, `Array.init`, which creates an array, needs to be told how many elements to create.

Typically, here is how the ordering of the parameters of a collection function goes:

1. Any parameters that don't fall into the other two categories – for example, the length of the required collection.

2. The function to be applied.

3. The collection itself.

This ordering makes collection functions "pipeline friendly," because the forward-pipe operator passes the result of the *preceding* operation (typically in this context, a collection) into the last parameter of the *next* operation. Hence, we want the collection to be processed to be the last argument of a collection function so that it can be passed in by forward piping.

Note   When you define your own collection functions, use the same parameter ordering style as the built-in functions, so that yours will also be pipeline friendly.

The other essential property of collection functions is that they are designed to be used in an immutable way. For example, if you filter a collection, you end up with a *new* collection containing only the desired elements. The *original* collection is unaffected. The one slight exception is `iter`, which returns `unit` and therefore doesn't convey any useful information back to the caller. Instead you would use `iter` to do something in the "outside world" like printing output or sending messages.

Picking the Right Collection Function

I personally find lists that show the signature of the function, for example (`'T -> 'Key`) `-> 'T [] -> 'T []`, not particularly useful in finding the right function, so in Table 4-1, I have put together a more human-friendly reference, which should help you identify the right tool for the job.

Table 4-1. *Commonly Used Collection Functions*

	Begin with	End up with	Functions
	Many	Equally Many	`map, mapi, sort, sortBy, rev`
	Many	Fewer	`filter, choose, distinct, take, truncate, tail, sub`
	Many	One	`length, fold, reduce, average, head, sum, max, maxBy, min, minBy, find, pick`
	Many	Boolean	`exists, forall, isEmpty`
	Nothing	Many	`init, create, unfold`
	Many	Nothing (except side-effects)	`iter, iteri`
	Many of Many	Many	`concat, collect`
	Many	Groupings	`groupBy`
	2 of Many	Many	`append, zip`
	Many	2 of Many	`partition`

To use this table, you need to think about just two things:

- How many elements do I want to start off with?

- How many elements do I want to end up with?

We're not talking absolute numbers here, but in terms of options such as *no elements, exactly one element (or value),* or *one-to-n elements.* In the table, I've called these *cardinalities* "*Nothing,*" "*One,*" and "*Many.*" When I say *Many-to-Equally Many* I mean that the number of elements returned is the same as the number provided. In cases where the function will return *at most* the same number of elements (but probably fewer), I've called the cardinality "*Fewer.*"

Oddly enough, thinking first about the cardinality of the operation you want is better than thinking first about the specific operation.

Table 4-1 doesn't cover all the collection functions, just the ones that are most widely used. Once you get used to thinking in terms of collection operations by practicing with the common ones listed above, you'll find it relatively easy to scan the documentation for the more exotic functions, such as `Array.sortInPlaceWith`.

As an example of using Table 4-1, say we have a collection of houses, and we want to retrieve just those houses that have a sale price of less than $100,000. Our "Begin with" cardinality is *Many* and our "End up with" cardinality is *Fewer*. A quick glance at Table 4-1 shows us that the functions that fit this profile are `filter`, `choose`, `distinct,` and `sub`. At this point, it's probably pretty obvious from the name which one of these we need (it's `filter`) but if it isn't, at least we only have four functions to consider. How do we choose between these? In Tables 4-2 through 4-11, I give a breakdown of the commonly used functions in each classification. The table you would use for the house example is Table 4-3 because that is the one for *Many-to-Fewer* operations.

Detailed Collection Function Tables

Just skim these detail tables for now, and come back to them as reference when you do the exercises that follow.

Table 4-2. *Many-to-Equally Many Collection Functions*

Function	Description	Useful Variants
map	Takes each of the input values, applies the provided function to it, and returns all the results.	Array.Parallel. map
mapi	As map, but the provided function is called with two arguments: an index value starting with 0 and ending with *n*-1, and the current element.	Parallel.mapi
rev	Returns a collection containing the original elements in reverse order.	
sort	Returns a collection containing all the elements, but sorted using the default comparer for the element type.	sortBy
sortBy	As sort, but compares using not the elements, but the results of sending the elements to the provided function.	sortByDescending, sortWith

Table 4-3. *Many-to-Fewer Collection Functions*

Function	Description	Useful variants and alternatives
filter	Returns only those elements that return `true` when the provided filtering function is applied to them.	
choose	Applies the provided function to each element, and returns the values of function results when those function results were `Some(value)`.	
distinct	Returns the elements after eliminating any duplicates, where duplicates are identified using the default comparer for the element type.	distinctBy
sub	Returns a subset of the elements, starting with the element at the specified index and continuing for the specified length. (Available for arrays only.)	Array slicing syntax, e.g.: `let arr2 = arr.[3..5]`
take	Returns the first n elements.	takeWhile, truncate
truncate	Returns at most the first *n* elements (fewer if the collection contains fewer than *n* elements).	
tail	Returns all elements after the first element.	

Table 4-4. *Many-to-One Collection Functions*

Function	Description	Useful variants
length	Calculates the number of elements in the collection.	Also available as a property on arrays and F# lists, for example, `arr.Length`
fold	Starts with an initial value, applies the provided function to that value and the first element of the collection, then applies the function to the previous result and the second element of the collection, and so forth until all the elements have been used. Returns the final accumulated result of all these operations.	foldBack
reduce	Like `fold`, but takes its initial state from the first element.	reduceBack
average	Computes the average value of the elements.	averageBy
head	Gets the first element.	
sum	Computes the total value of the elements.	sumBy
max	Gets the maximum element.	maxBy
min	Gets the minimum element.	minBy
find	Gets the first element for which the provided function returns `true`.	tryFind, pick
pick	Returns the first result for which the provided function returns Some.	tryPick, find

Table 4-5. *Many-to-Boolean Collection Functions*

Function	Description	Useful variants
exists	Returns true if any of the elements returns true when passed into the provided function.	
forall	Returns true if all the elements return true when passed into the provided function.	
isEmpty	Returns true if the collection has no elements.	

Table 4-6. *Nothing-to-Many Collection Functions*

Function	Description	Useful variants and alternatives
init	Creates a collection with *n* elements, where each element value is created by calling the provided function. An index parameter (starting at 0 and ending at *n*-1) is provided to each call to the function.	initInfinite (for sequences)
create	Creates a collection with *n* elements, whose elements are initially the specified single value. (Available for arrays only.)	zeroCreate
unfold	Creates a collection by taking a specified initial value and passing it to the provided "generator" function. If the generator function returns, say Some(x,y), then x is added to the sequence and y is passed into the next iteration. If the function returns None then the sequence ends.	Array and List comprehensions

Table 4-7. *Many-to-Nothing Collection Functions*

Function	Description	Useful variants and alternatives
iter	Takes each collection element in turn and executes the provided function using the element. The provided function needs to return nothing (in F# terms unit, denoted by the literal ()). Thus the only way iter can affect the outside world is via "side effects," such as writing files, printing lines to the console, or updating mutable values.	
iteri	As iter, but the provided function is called with two arguments: the current element and an index value starting with 0 and ending with n-1.	

Table 4-8. *Many-of-Many to Many Collection Functions*

Function	Description	Useful variants and alternatives
concat	Takes a collection of collections and returns a single collection of all the input elements. Note the distinction between concat and append. concat takes a collection of collections, whereas append takes exactly two collections.	
collect	Takes a collection, applies the provided function to each of the elements (where the function itself returns a collection), and returns a single collection of all the results. Strictly speaking this isn't a "Many-of-Many to Many" operation, but it feels most natural to put it in this category.	

Table 4-9. *Many-to-Groupings Collection Functions*

Function	Description	Useful variants and alternatives
groupBy	Takes a collection, applies the provided function to each of the elements, and returns the distinct values of the results, together with all the elements that resulted in each key result.	

Table 4-10. *2-of-Many to Many Collection Functions*

Function	Description	Useful variants and alternatives
append	Creates a collection consisting of all the elements from both the input collections.	
zip	Takes two collections and returns a single collection, each of whose elements is a tuple of the corresponding values from each of the input collections.	zip3

Table 4-11. *Many to 2-of-Many Collection Functions*

Function	Description	Useful variants and alternatives
partition	Takes a collection and returns a tuple of two collections, the first of which contains elements that returned true when the provided function was applied, and the second contains those which returned false. (Available for arrays and F# lists only.)	

Practicing with Collection Functions

Much of the productivity gain from programming in F# comes from effective use of collection functions. So I want to spend a little time practicing how to choose and combine them in a variety of situations. This section contains some exercises that will let you do just that. They get progressively more difficult, so please make sure you take the time to go through them in order, so that your skills in this area are really secure.

Remember to refer back to Tables 4-1 through 4-11 to help you find the right collection function in each case. All the exercises in this section can be solved with a call to a single collection function. We'll explore tasks needing several collection functions in the next section.

Exercise Setup

You'll need a little code to provide data and useful functions to work with. Create an F# script file and add the code from Listing 4-2, replacing anything the creation template added for you.

Listing 4-2. Setup code for exercises

```
module Houses =

    type House = { Address : string; Price : decimal }
    type PriceBand = | Cheap | Medium | Expensive

    /// Make an array of 'count' random houses.
    let getHouses count =
        let random = System.Random(Seed = 1)
        Array.init count (fun i ->
            { Address = sprintf "%i Stochastic Street" (i+1)
              Price = random.Next(50_000, 500_000) |> decimal })

    let random = System.Random(Seed = 1)

    /// Try to get the distance to the nearest school.
    /// (Results are simulated)
    let trySchoolDistance (house : House) =
        // Because we simulate results, the house
```

```
    // parameter isn't actually used.
    let dist = random.Next(10) |> double
    if dist < 8. then
        Some dist
    else
        None

// Return a price band based on price.
let priceBand (price : decimal) =
    if price < 100_000m then
        Cheap
    else if price < 200_000m then
        Medium
    else
        Expensive
```

Take a moment to read the code in Listing 4-2. It provides a type called House, which has an address and a price. (This is a very naïve model but will do for the topics covered in this chapter.) There is also a function called getHouses, which will create some House instances for you, with random prices and ascending street numbers. I've hardwired the seed of the random number generator so you always get the same results, which will make debugging some of your exercise solutions easier. The usage of the trySchoolDistance and priceBand functions will become apparent as you go through the exercises.

As you tackle the exercises, structure your code as I do when I go through Exercise 4-1 with you. This will help you concentrate on the logic of the collection functions. Solutions for the exercises are at the end of the chapter.

Single Collection Function Exercises

Each of the exercises in this section can be solved using just one collection function.

```
                 EXERCISE 4-1 – TRANSFORMING DATA ITEMS
```

Note   I'll do this exercise with you, to help you get used to working with the
provided code and the collection functions tables.

Take a sample of 20 houses and for each house produce a string in the form:

```
Address: 1 Stochastic Street - Price: 123456.00000
```

The number of decimal places displayed for the price doesn't matter.

To tackle this exercise, first make sure you have the code from Listing 4-2 in
an F# script. Below that code, in the same script, make yourself a module called
Exercise04_01 and open the Houses module (Listing 4-3).

Listing 4-3. Creating an exercise module and opening the Houses module

```
module Exercise04_01 =

    open Houses
```

Now take a careful look at the exercise requirements. It doesn't require you to write
a general-purpose function, just to take one sample of 20 houses and produce some
results. That means you can just make a value (not a function) using a let binding with
no arguments. You can start to define the required value by getting the sample of 20
houses, using the getHouses function I provide in the Houses module (Listing 4-4).

Listing 4-4. Getting the houses sample

```
module Exercise04_01 =

    open Houses

    let housePrices =
        getHouses 20
```

Looking back at the exercise requirement again, you are required to produce one
string for each input house. In terms of Table 4-1, this is clearly a *Many-to-Equally Many*
operation. There are only a few collection functions in the table that match this profile:
map, mapi, sort, sortBy, and rev. It's probably obvious which of these are definitely

not the one we need, as this isn't a sorting or reversing operation. You can refine your choice further by looking at Table 4-2 to review what each function does. The map function looks promising, since its description, *"Takes each of the input values, applies the specified function to it, and returns all the results"* looks very similar to what you want to achieve. You *don't* want the `mapi` function, as there is no need for the index value it provides. To use `Array.map` you can continue your code as in Listing 4-5.

Listing 4-5. Calling the map function

```
module Exercise04_01 =

    open Houses

    let housePrices =
        getHouses 20
        |> Array.map (fun h -> ) // Still needs a body...
```

Note   In Listing 4-5 I've typed the final closing bracket for the map's lambda function, even though the function doesn't yet have a body. Doing this helps to ensure that Intellisense works correctly while you type the body of the lambda function.

Now you need a body for the lambda function, which needs to take a `house` instance and produce a string in the required format. That's easy using the `sprintf` function (Listing 4-6).

Listing 4-6. Providing a lambda body for the map function

```
module Exercise04_01 =

    open Houses

    let housePrices =
        getHouses 20
        |> Array.map (fun h ->
            sprintf "Address: %s - Price: %f" h.Address h.Price)
```

To test the function, select all the code in your F# script (including the Houses module) and send it to F# interactive. Your output should look something like Listing 4-7. Your house prices might vary from the listing, depending on the implementation of System.Random in your environment.

Listing 4-7. Output from a successful run of the exercise code

```
module Exercise04_01 = begin
  val housePrices : string [] =
    [|"Address: 1 Stochastic Street - Price: 161900.000000";
      ...
      "Address: 20 Stochastic Street - Price: 365808.000000"|]
end
```

Exercise solved!

Now tackle the remaining exercises on your own. You can solve each of them with a single collection function, and the code in each case can be structured in a very similar way to Listing 4-6.

EXERCISE 4-2 – CALCULATING AN AVERAGE

Take a sample of 20 houses and calculate the average of their prices.

You can assume the list isn't empty (you know it has 20 houses!).

EXERCISE 4-3 – SELECTING BASED ON A CONDITION

Take a sample of 20 houses and get all the houses that cost over $250,000.

EXERCISE 4-4 – ATTEMPTING A CALCULATION AND CHOOSING SUCCESSES

Take a sample of 20 houses and return an array of tuples, each tuple containing a house and the distance to the nearest school. Use the trySchoolDistance function in the Houses module to calculate the distance. Exclude houses for which this function returns None.

Sample output:

```
val housesNearSchools : (Houses.House * double) [] =
    [|({Address = "1 Stochastic Street";
        Price = 161900M;}, 2.0); ({Address = "3 Stochastic Street";
                                   Price = 99834M;}, 2.0); ...
```

Clue: Although you can achieve this in a single collection function, the lambda it uses will need to do some pattern matching on the Some/None cases coming back from trySchoolDistance.

Multiple Collection Function Exercises

By now you should be pretty slick at selecting and using an individual collection function to solve a problem. Now it's time to practice *combining* collection functions to solve slightly more complex problems. You'll need to use more than one collection function for each of the exercises in this section. When tackling these exercises, remember to think about the cardinality (for example, *Many-to-Fewer*) of each step you need to achieve the goal.

EXERCISE 4-5 – FILTERING AND ITERATING

Note I'll do this exercise with you, to help you get used to combining collection functions.

Take a sample of 20 houses, find the ones that cost over $100,000, and iterate over the results printing (not returning) their addresses and prices. The exact format doesn't matter, as long as the address and price are printed in some form.

You should be able to complete this exercise using two collection functions.

If you remember the previous section, you'll know immediately that the first function you'll need is the *Many-to-Fewer* function filter.

You can begin coding by getting the house sample and calling filter (Listing 4-8).

Listing 4-8. Filtering the sample

```
module Exercise04_05 =

    open Houses

    getHouses 20
    |> Array.filter (fun h -> h.Price > 100_000m)
```

Reading the second part of the exercise, you might notice that you aren't required to create (in F# terms *bind*) an actual value, but merely to print results. (In functional programming terms, we are using side effects.) This means that we need a *Many-to-None* operation, which should help you quickly narrow your choice down to the `iter` function.

To implement this second operation, simply use the forward-pipe operator (|>) to send the results from the filtering operation to the iteration operation (Listing 4-9).

Listing 4-9. Iterating over an array

```
module Exercise04_05 =

    open Houses

    getHouses 20
    |> Array.filter (fun h -> h.Price > 100_000m)
    |> Array.iter (fun h ->
        printfn "Address: %s Price: %f" h.Address h.Price)
```

If you run this you should get output that looks something like this.

```
Address: 1 Stochastic Street Price: 161900.000000
Address: 3 Stochastic Street Price: 260154.000000
...
Address: 20 Stochastic Street Price: 365808.000000
```

Now go on to complete the other multifunction exercises yourself. In each case, you should be able to solve the exercise by using two or more collection functions, piped together as we did here.

EXERCISE 4-6 – ORDERING

Extend the previous exercise, this time ensuring that the houses are printed in descending order of price.

You should be able to complete this exercise using three collection functions.

EXERCISE 4-7 – FILTERING AND AVERAGING

Take a sample of 20 houses and find the average price of all the houses that cost over $200,000.

You can assume for this exercise that there will be at least one house that fulfills the criterion.

You should be able to complete this exercise using two collection functions.

EXERCISE 4-8 – FINDING A SINGLE ELEMENT

Take a sample of 20 houses and find the first house that costs less than $100,000 *and* for which we can calculate the distance to a school. The results should include the house instance and the calculated distance to school.

You can assume for this exercise that there will be at least one house that fulfills the criteria.

You should be able to complete this exercise using two collection functions.

Clue: You can reuse some of the solution code from Exercise 4-4 to help complete this exercise.

EXERCISE 4-9 – GROUPING

Take a sample of 20 houses, and create an array of tuples, where the first element of each tuple is a price band (created using the provided `priceBand` function), and the second is a sequence of all the houses that fall into the band.

It's OK if a band is omitted when there are no houses in that band. Within a grouping, the houses should be in ascending order of price.

Example output:

```
val housesByBand : (Houses.PriceBand * Houses.House []) [] =
  [|(Medium,
    [|{Address = "12 Stochastic Street";
       Price = 161613M;};
  ...
      {Address = "13 Stochastic Street";
       Price = 194049M;}|]);
   (Cheap,
    [|{Address = "11 Stochastic Street";
       Price = 62886M;};
  ...
      {Address = "2 Stochastic Street";
       Price = 99834M;}|]);
   (Expensive,
    [|{Address = "7 Stochastic Street";
       Price = 209337M;};
  ...
      {Address = "14 Stochastic Street";
       Price = 495395M;}|])|]
```

You should be able to complete this exercise using three collection functions.

Partial Functions

There's another attribute of collection functions that I omitted from the tables and exercises above for simplicity, but which you must always bear in mind. That attribute is whether the collection function is *partial*. (This is a separate concept from the concept of *partial application*, which I tackle in Chapter 9.)

In this context, a function is *partial* if it can cause an error rather than return a value, even when given a logically possible input. We're talking here about errors which are inherent to the input and the function in question, not externally induced conditions such as running out of memory or having one's network connection fall over. A good example of a function that is partial in this sense is the head function (e.g., `Array.head`). Using head on an empty collection will cause an `ArgumentException`. An empty collection doesn't have a "first" element.

Another example is the zip function, but here the situation is a little trickier. It's an error to perform an Array.zip when the input arrays are different lengths. But it's fine to use Seq.zip when the input sequences are different lengths: the leftover elements in the longer sequence will just be ignored.

Table 4-12 gives a list of the functions from Table 4-1 that are partial. Whenever you use a function from this list, think carefully about whether the input could ever cause an error condition.

Table 4-12. *Partial Collection Functions to Watch Out For*

Function	Error Condition	Ways to Avoid
average, max, maxBy, min, minBy	Collection is empty.	Check length first and define a suitable value (e.g., 0 or None) in that situation.
find	No elements matched the condition (or the collection was empty).	Use tryFind and handle the Some() and None cases when consuming the result.
pick	No elements matched the condition (or the collection was empty).	Use tryPick and handle the Some() and None cases when consuming the result.
reduce	Collection is empty, so there is no way to get an initial state for the accumulator.	Use fold and provide an explicit initial state.
sub	Collection doesn't have enough elements.	Check ranges first. Use filter to select elements instead.
zip (Array and List versions)	Collections are different lengths.	Check lengths are equal. Use Seq.zip and accept that "leftover" elements will be lost.
head and last	Collection is empty.	Use tryHead or tryLast. Check length first and define a suitable value in that situation.
tail	Collection is empty.	Check length first and define a suitable value in that situation.

By the way, any kind of function can be partial. The issue doesn't just affect collection functions, but it does crop up most commonly in practice when using collection functions.

Note   Get in the habit of thinking about partiality whenever using a collection function, and handle the failure cases explicitly.

Don't think about a function being partial as a bug in the function: all these cases are inherent in the nature of the function. How can you possibly get the maximum value in an empty list?

Incidentally, a function that isn't *partial* in this sense is known as a *total function*, though you will hardly ever hear this term used outside a Math or Computer Science context (I had to look it up).

Coding Around Partial Functions

As you can see from Table 4-12, many built-in collection functions have `try...` equivalents (e.g., `tryFind`), which return `None` if there is no value to return, or `Some(value)` if there is, thus making them nice safe *total* functions. When no such function is available (or you don't want to use it), there are several other things you can do.

For example, let's say you have some transaction values and a business rule that says, "When there are no transactions, the average transaction value is considered to be zero." Listing 4-10 shows how you might define an averaging function that meets this requirement.

Listing 4-10. A function to compute an array average, or zero when the array is empty

```
module Average =

    let averageValue (values : decimal[]) =
        if values.Length = 0 then
            0.m
        else
            values |> Array.average
```

```
// 370.m
let ex1 = [|10.m; 100.m; 1000.m|] |> averageValue

// 0.m
let ex2 = [||] |> averageValue
```

This would work fine in the specific case of an array of decimal values, but since this is a book on style, I probably ought to mention a couple of alternatives. The first (Listing 4-11) takes an array of any type (not just decimal) and uses the GenericZero function to return a suitably-typed zero value.

Listing 4-11. A generic function to compute an array average, or zero when the array is empty

```
module Average =

    let inline averageOrZero (a : 'T[]) =
        if a.Length = 0 then
            LanguagePrimitives.GenericZero<'T>
        else
            a |> Array.average

    // 370.m
    let ex3 = [|10.m; 100.m; 1000.m|] |> averageOrZero
    // 370.f
    let ex3f = [|10.f; 100.f; 1000.f|] |> averageOrZero

    // 0.m
    let ex4:decimal = [||] |> averageOrZero<decimal>
    // 0.f
    let ex4f:decimal = [||] |> averageOrZero<float32>
```

Another possibility (Listing 4-12) is to allow the caller to specify what should be returned when the collection is empty.

Listing 4-12. A function to compute an array average, or a default when the array is empty

```
module Average =

    let inline averageOr (dflt : 'T) (a : 'T[]) =
        if a.Length = 0 then
            dflt
        else
            a |> Array.average

    // 370.m
    let ex5 = [|10.m; 100.m; 1000.m|] |> averageOr 0.m
    // 370.f
    let ex5f = [|10.f; 100.f; 1000.f|] |> averageOr 0.f

    // 0.m
    let ex6 = [||] |> averageOr 0.m
    // 0.f
    let ex6f = [||] |> averageOr 0.f
```

Note that in both Listings 4-11 and 4-12, I've had to "inline" the functions using the `inline` keyword, because they call `Array.average`, which has a static parameter.

Note   Remember the principle of *semantic focus*: the place to handle (for example) the empty collection case is *right here* in the code where it could occur. Don't rely on the caller to condition your inputs to prevent conditions such as an empty collection. The calling code might get changed, or your function might get used in new code, and in either case the input pre-checking might be forgotten about.

Using the "try" Idiom for Partial Functions

Another way of coding around partial functions is to define your own `try...` version that returns `Some(value)` when a sensible value can be returned, and `None` when it cannot. For example, at the time of writing, there is no built-in `Array.tryAverage` function. Listing 4-13 shows how to code your own in just a few lines.

Listing 4-13. Defining an idiomatic tryAverage function

```
module Array =

    let inline tryAverage (a : 'T[]) =
        if a.Length = 0 then
            None
        else
            a |> Array.average |> Some
```

Note   Notice that in the averageOr and tryAverage example in Listings 4-12 and 4-13, I put the function in a module called Array. This means that, for example, tryAverage will be available elsewhere as Array.tryAverage and can thus be used in exactly the same way as the built-in functions such as Array.tryFind.

I definitely prefer this final approach: defining your own try... function. This is because it is in line with a couple of our coding principles:

- It displays good *semantic focus*, because everything about the process of calculating an average (and returning None when not possible) is handled in one place in the code. The decision as to what to do when the result is None (use a default, raise an error, or whatever) is delegated back to where it should be, in the caller, which is likely to have more "knowledge" about the particular case where the averaging is required.

- It displays good *motivational transparency*: you are saying to the reader, "Here I intend to define a function which behaves like other, similarly named functions such as tryHead." This leverages the reader's existing knowledge of how such functions behave, making the code a lot easier to read.

Consuming Values from try... Functions

Whether you use a built-in `try...` function like `tryFind`, or one you defined yourself, you must explicitly handle both the Some and None possibilities when consuming the result. Listing 4-14 shows the one simple way of calling the `tryAverage` function and dealing with the return value. Here we use an explicit match statement on the Some and None cases.

Listing 4-14. Consuming option type results using match expressions

```
// "The average was 370.000000"
match [|10.m; 100.m; 1000.m|] |> Array.tryAverage with
| Some av -> printfn "The average was %f" av
| None -> printfn "There was no average."

// "There was no average."
match [||] |> Array.tryAverage with
| Some av -> printfn "The average was %f" av
| None -> printfn "There was no average."
```

There are arguably nicer alternatives to this, which are discussed in Chapters 3 and 11.

Try... Function Exercises

These exercises are variations on some of the exercises above, except here we remove the assumption that the relevant collection is non-empty.

EXERCISE 4-10 – FILTERING, AVERAGING, AND TRY

Take a sample of 20 houses and find the average price of all the houses that cost over $200,000.

You'll need to make sure you handle the case where no houses in the sample cost over $200,000. (You will need to change the price criterion a little to test this.)

You should be able to complete this exercise using two collection functions, but you may need to define one of these functions yourself.

EXERCISE 4-11 – FINDING A SINGLE ELEMENT IF ANY

Take a sample of 20 houses and find the first house that costs less than $100,000 *and* for which we can calculate the distance to a school. The results should include the house instance and the calculated distance to school.

You'll need to make sure you handle the case where no houses meet the criteria. (You will need to change the price criterion a little to test this.)

You should be able to complete this exercise using two collection functions.

Clue: You can reuse some of the solution code from previous exercises to help complete this exercise.

Functions for Other Kinds of Collections

Although most F# developers are familiar with the most widely used modules of collection functions, the `Array`, `Seq,` and `List` modules, they sometimes forget that similar functions are available for more specialized collections. You can find these in modules in the `Microsoft.FSharp.Collections` namespace (Table 4-13).

Table 4-13. *Less-Well-Known Collection Functions*

Module	Purpose
`Array2D, Array3D, Array4D`	Basic operations on n-dimensional arrays.
`Map`	Basic operations on the Map type.
`Set`	Basic operations on the Set type.

For example, let's say you have a word list generated from some natural language text (like the text of a novel), and this word list is stored as a `Set` to guarantee uniqueness. Now you want to create another set that contains only lowercased versions of the inputs. Listing 4-15 shows how you might do that.

Listing 4-15. Using Set.map

```
module WordList =

    let novelWords = Set ["The";"the";"quick";"brown";"Fox";"fox"]

    // set ["brown"; "fox"; "quick"; "the"]
    let lowerWords =
        novelWords
        |> Set.map (fun w -> w.ToLowerInvariant())
```

Note that the `Set.map` operation is strictly speaking a *Many-to-Fewer* operation, since it produces a Set, and sets inherently eliminate duplicates. For example, if the input set contained "The" and "the," the output set would contain only "the."

When the Collection Function Is Missing

Collection functions normally exist in all the flavors you are likely to need – that is, for arrays, F# lists, and sequences. However, in some cases the one you might want is missing: for example, there is an `Array.partition` and a `List.partition`, but no `Seq.partition`. When you need such a missing function, simply convert the collection you are working with into a collection type for which the function you need *is* available, using either the `Collection.ofOtherCollection` or `Collection.toOtherCollection` functions. For instance, `Array.ofSeq` or `Seq.toArray`. See Listing 4-16.

Listing 4-16. Using Array.partition on a sequence

```
    open Houses

    // Function which creates some random houses as a sequence:
    let getHousesSeq count =
        let random = System.Random(Seed = 1)
        Seq.init count (fun i ->
            { Address = sprintf "%i Stochastic Street" (i+1)
              Price = random.Next(50_000, 500_000) |> decimal })

    // Convert a sequence of houses into an array, so that we
    // can use Array.partition to divide them into affordable and
    // unaffordable. (There is no Seq.partition.)
```

```
let affordable, unaffordable =
    getHousesSeq 20
    |> Array.ofSeq
    |> Array.partition (fun h -> h.Price < 150_000m)
```

You can convert the result back to the original collection type if necessary. For example, you could add `|> Seq.ofArray` to the end of Listing 4-16.

Common Mistakes

There are a few mistakes that are commonly made when using collection functions. Quite often these don't really matter as the output is the same, but it's worth watching out for them, so as to keep your code as robust and stylish as possible.

- *Forgetting which functions are partial.* I covered this in the section on partial functions above. Always handle the error cases (such as an empty collection) explicitly, typically by using the `try...` version of the function.

- *Not using the* `choose` *function.* In my early days with F#, I would often write pipelines that called a function that might return None, then filtered for the Some cases, and finally recovered the underlying values by using pattern matching or the `Option.Value` property. When you catch yourself doing this, use the `choose` function instead. It does the Some filtering and the value recovery for you. See Listing 4-17.

- *Not using the* `collect` *function.* You may find yourself writing a pipeline that produces a collection of collections, and then immediately joins these into a single collection using the `concat` function. Instead use the `collect` function to achieve this in a single step.

- *Long lambda bodies.* If the body of a lambda function gets beyond two or three lines, consider pulling it out into a separate, named function and calling that. This will help you mentally isolate the logic of the function from the logic of the pipeline as a whole. It'll also reduce indenting! See Listing 4-18.

- *Lambdas that could be direct calls.* Whenever your code contains code like (fun x -> doSomething x), it can be replaced simply with doSomething. Listing 4-17 contains an example of this more concise approach, where we do |> Array.map trySchoolDistance instead of |> Array.map (fun h -> trySchoolDistance h).

- *Over-long pipelines.* Pipelines that contain more than a handful of forward-pipe operations can be hard to read and debug. Consider breaking them up, perhaps by binding an intermediate value and then passing this into a separate pipeline.

- *Over-long or obscure tuples.* Certain operations naturally produce tuples, which you will then want to pattern match back into individual values, for processing in the next step of your pipeline. That's fine when there are only two or at most three elements in the tuple. Beyond that, the code can get unreadable, so consider declaring a local record type so that you can label the elements. See Listing 4-19.

Listing 4-17. Using the choose function

```
module Array =
    let inline tryAverage (a : 'T[]) =
        if a.Length = 0 then
            None
        else
            a |> Array.average |> Some

module UsingChoose =

    open Houses

    // Calculate the average known distance to school
    // in a sample of 20 houses.
    let averageDistanceToSchool =
        getHouses 20
        |> Array.map trySchoolDistance
        |> Array.filter (fun d -> d.IsSome)
        |> Array.map (fun d -> d.Value)
        |> Array.tryAverage
```

```
// As previous function, but use Array.choose instead
// of map, filter and map.
let averageDistanceToSchool2 =
    getHouses 20
    |> Array.choose trySchoolDistance
    |> Array.tryAverage
```

Listing 4-18. Avoiding long lambda functions

```
module LongLambdaFunction =

    open Houses

    // Get houses with their price bands the long-winded way:
    let housesWithBands =
        getHouses 20
        |> Array.map (fun h ->
            let band =
                if h.Price < 100_000m then
                    Cheap
                else if h.Price < 200_000m then
                    Medium
                else
                    Expensive
            h, band)

    // Most of the code above could be pulled into a priceBand function:
    // (Here we use the one that is already defined in the Houses module.)
    let housesWithBands2 =
        getHouses 20
        |> Array.map (fun h ->
            h, h.Price |> priceBand)
```

Listing 4-19. Replacing tuples with records

```
module HousePriceReport =

    open Houses

    let bandOrder = function
    | Cheap -> 0 | Medium -> 1 | Expensive -> 2

    // A report of price bands and the houses that fall into them:
    getHouses 20
    |> Seq.groupBy (fun h -> h.Price |> priceBand)
    |> Seq.sortBy (fun (band, _) -> band |> bandOrder)
    |> Seq.iter (fun (band, houses) ->
        printfn "---- %A ----" band
        houses
        |> Seq.iter (fun h -> printfn "%s - %f" h.Address h.Price))

    // Like the previous report, but using an explicit type to
    // minimise use of tuples:
    type PriceBandGroup = {
        PriceBand : PriceBand
        Houses : seq<House> }

    getHouses 20
    |> Seq.groupBy (fun h -> h.Price |> priceBand)
    |> Seq.map (fun (band, houses) ->
        { PriceBand = band; Houses = houses })
    |> Seq.sortBy (fun group -> group.PriceBand |> bandOrder)
    |> Seq.iter (fun group ->
        printfn "---- %A ----" group.PriceBand
        group.Houses
        |> Seq.iter (fun h -> printfn "%s - %f" h.Address h.Price))
---- Cheap ----
2 Stochastic Street - 99834.000000
9 Stochastic Street - 95569.000000
...
```

```
---- Medium ----
1 Stochastic Street - 161900.000000
12 Stochastic Street - 161613.000000
...
---- Expensive ----
3 Stochastic Street - 260154.000000
4 Stochastic Street - 397221.000000
...
```

Recommendations

Here are some key points to take away from this chapter:

- Become familiar with the many collection functions available to you in modules such as `Array`, `List`, and `Seq`, and the more specialized modules such as `Map` and `Set`.

- Learn how to map from the problem you are trying to solve (e.g., "I have an array of numbers and I want the average of largest three") to the type signatures that are likely to help solve them (e.g. `'T []` `-> 'T []` for the sorting, `'T [] -> 'T []` for the top-three selection and `^T [] -> ^T` for the average), and from there to the specific collections you are going to need (`Array.sort`, `Array.truncate`, and `Array.average`).

- If you find type signatures a little inaccessible, refer back to Tables 4-2 through 4-11 for a more visual reference to the most useful collection functions.

- Beware of collection functions that are *partial*, such as `Array.head`, which raises an exception when the array is empty. Use the `try...` version (e.g., `Array.tryHead`), or if there isn't one, consider writing one using the `try...` naming style.

- Think of explicit looping, especially using mutable values, as a last resort. There's usually a collection function or a combination of them that will do the job more simply.

- Use pipelines of collection functions, but don't let them get too long, and beware of passing values around using tuples of more than about three values. A local record type can be a more readable alternative to long tuples.

Summary

Collection functions are the guitar chords of the F# world. You simply can't get by without a good working knowledge of the basic functions, and how to fit them together. In most domains, a large proportion of your F# code should consist of pipelines of collection functions that map, filter, summarize, and group data to get from the inputs you have, to the outputs you want. Enjoy the feeling of using collection functions to achieve F#'s enduring goal: *to solve complex problems with simple code*.

In the next chapter we'll look at *immutability*, the curious notion that we should write programs that don't change anything; and we'll also learn when to break back out of this mindset and use *mutation*.

Exercise Solutions

This section shows solutions for the exercises in this chapter. For the code shown here to run, you'll also need the code for the Houses module in Listing 4-2.

EXERCISE 4-1 – TRANSFORMING DATA ITEMS

```
module Exercise04_01 =

    open Houses

    let housePrices =
        getHouses 20
        |> Array.map (fun h ->
            sprintf "Address: %s - Price: %f" h.Address h.Price)
```

EXERCISE 4-2 – CALCULATING AN AVERAGE

```
module Exercise04_02 =

    open Houses

    let averagePrice =
        getHouses 20
        |> Array.averageBy (fun h -> h.Price)
```

EXERCISE 4-3 – SELECTING BASED ON A CONDITION

```
module Exercise04_03 =

    open Houses

    let expensive =
        getHouses 20
        |> Array.filter (fun h -> h.Price > 250_000m)
```

EXERCISE 4-4 – ATTEMPTING A CALCULATION AND CHOOSING SUCCESSES

```
module Exercise04_04 =

    open Houses

    let housesNearSchools =
        getHouses 20
        |> Array.choose (fun h ->
            // See also the "Missing Data" chapter
            match h |> trySchoolDistance with
            | Some d -> Some(h, d)
            | None -> None)
```

EXERCISE 4-5 – FILTERING AND ITERATING

```
module Exercise04_05 =

    open Houses

    getHouses 20
    |> Array.filter (fun h -> h.Price > 100_000m)
    |> Array.iter (fun h ->
        printfn "Address: %s Price: %f" h.Address h.Price)
```

EXERCISE 4-6 – ORDERING

```
module Exercise04_06 =

    open Houses

    getHouses 20
    |> Array.filter (fun h -> h.Price > 100_000m)
    |> Array.sortByDescending (fun h -> h.Price)
    |> Array.iter (fun h ->
        printfn "Address: %s Price: %f" h.Address h.Price)
```

EXERCISE 4-7 – FILTERING AND AVERAGING

```
module Exercise04_07 =

    open Houses

    let averageOver200K =
        getHouses 20
        |> Array.filter (fun h -> h.Price > 200_000m)
        |> Array.averageBy (fun h -> h.Price)
```

EXERCISE 4-8 – FINDING A SINGLE ELEMENT

```
module Exercise04_08 =

    open Houses

    let cheapHouseWithKnownSchoolDistance =
        getHouses 20
        |> Array.filter (fun h -> h.Price < 100_000m)
        |> Array.pick (fun h ->
            match h |> trySchoolDistance with
            | Some d -> Some(h, d)
            | None -> None)
```

EXERCISE 4-9 – GROUPING

```
module Exercise04_09 =
    open Houses

    let housesByBand =
        getHouses 20
          |> Array.groupBy (fun h -> priceBand h.Price)
          |> Array.map (fun group ->
             let band, houses = group
             band, houses |> Array.sortBy (fun h -> h.Price))
```

You can also "pattern match" in the lambda declaration of the Array.map call for a more concise solution:

```
    let housesByBand =
        getHouses 20
          |> Array.groupBy (fun h -> priceBand h.Price)
          |> Array.map (fun (band, houses) ->
             band, houses |> Array.sortBy (fun h -> h.Price))
```

EXERCISE 4-10 – FILTERING, AVERAGING, AND TRY

To test this solution, you'll need to increase the price criterion so that the sample is empty.

```
module Array =

    let inline tryAverageBy f (a : 'T[]) =
        if a.Length = 0 then
            None
        else
            a |> Array.averageBy f |> Some

module Exercise04_10 =

    open Houses

    let averageOver200K =
        getHouses 20
        |> Array.filter (fun h -> h.Price > 200_000m)
        |> Array.tryAverageBy (fun h -> h.Price)
```

EXERCISE 4-11 – FINDING A SINGLE ELEMENT IF ANY

To test this solution, you'll need to decrease the price criterion so that the sample is empty.

```
module Exercise04_11 =

    open Houses

    let cheapHouseWithKnownSchoolDistance =
        getHouses 20
        |> Array.filter (fun h -> h.Price < 100_000m)
        |> Array.tryPick (fun h ->
            match h |> trySchoolDistance with
            | Some d -> Some(h, d)
            | None -> None)
```

CHAPTER 5

Immutability and Mutation

Nothing is so painful to the human mind as a great and sudden change.

—Mary Wollstonecraft Shelley, from the novel *Frankenstein*

These Folks Are Crazy!

Most software developers, for most of the history of programming, have been entirely comfortable with *mutation*. Code that uses mutation *declares* a variable (perhaps with some initial value, perhaps uninitialized), then *updates* its value one or more times until some final result is achieved. It's so natural of an approach (at least for those of us who came to programming via languages such as BASIC, JavaScript, and C) that we didn't really feel the need to name it. Mutable programming *was* programming.

For people with that kind of background, the first encounter with immutable style is disorientating to say the least. I still clearly remember seeing an early presentation on F# and thinking "these folks are crazy." The only reason I stayed with it was because the presenter was particularly engaging. It was beyond me at the time to think that immutable style programming might actually be useful. I certainly wouldn't have entertained the notion that it could even be *easier*. How the times have changed!

My aim in this chapter is to show you how immutable style can indeed be easier. I hope by the end you'll agree that most code should be written in an immutable style, with mutation only coming into play where performance considerations, or the nature of the operation being performed, genuinely require it.

Classic Mutable Style

For most of my career, I've written code in the style exemplified in Listing 5-1. (In different languages, obviously; it's the logic that's important.)

© Kit Eason 2018
K. Eason, *Stylish F#*, https://doi.org/10.1007/978-1-4842-4000-7_5

Listing 5-1. A loop using mutation

```
open System
open System.IO

let latestWriteTime (path : string) (searchPattern : string) =
    let files = Directory.EnumerateFiles(path, searchPattern,
                                    SearchOption.AllDirectories)
    let mutable latestDate = DateTime.MinValue
    for file in files do
        let thisDate = File.GetLastWriteTime(file)
        if thisDate > latestDate then
            latestDate <- thisDate
    latestDate

latestWriteTime @"c:\temp" "*.*"
```

The pattern here is that we set some variable to an initial state (it might be null, zero, an empty string, or whatever); then we perform some kind of loop, updating the variable repeatedly; and finally, we use whatever value was set last. In this case the "variable" is the mutable value latestDate, and we keep updating it if it the write date of the current file is later than the last value we set. There are variations on the pattern – sometimes we break out of the loop when some condition is attained; sometimes the mutable thing is a collection to which we add elements; and so forth.

This kind of coding works fine when the logic is as simple as in Listing 5-1. But as soon as things get even remotely complicated, the code gets very hard to follow. For example, we might end up with nested loops, and a variety of variables being declared and updated at various different scopes. Or a variable might get updated in two successive loops, maybe having the same business meaning in each loop; or maybe having a subtly different one. You might answer that this kind of coding is bad practice whether you are writing in a mutable style or not; but the fact is that it's extremely common, and it leads to a lot of bugs. It's also somewhat verbose. And in a sense, it isn't DRY ("Don't Repeat Yourself") because, as I'll illustrate below, one is in fact repeating the same essential logic each time one does it.

Immutability Basics

So what is the immutable equivalent to Listing 5-1, and how do we get to it? The secret is to think "up" one level of abstraction, work out what we are *really* doing, and find the appropriate built-in F# functions to achieve it. Applying this method to Listing 5-1, your thought process should be:

- Oops, I'm using a mutable. Is there a better way?

- What I really want is the maximum date for a list of files.

- A list is a sequence, and there is a Seq.max function.

Following this approach, you might end up with a first cut of your immutable version looking like Listing 5-2.

Listing 5-2. First cut of an immutable latestWriteTime

```
open System.IO

let latestWriteTime (path : string) (searchPattern : string) =
    Directory.EnumerateFiles(path, searchPattern,
                                SearchOption.AllDirectories)
    // Could also just say 'Seq.map File.GetLastWriteTime' here.
    |> Seq.map (fun file -> File.GetLastWriteTime(file))
    |> Seq.max

latestWriteTime @"c:\temp" "*.*"
```

This is already a vast improvement over Listing 5-1. It's more *concise*, which is not automatically an advantage, but here, where we are plugging well-understood operations together in a completely idiomatic way, it certainly is. It follows the principle of *motivational transparency* – the use of Seq.max tells us we are looking for the largest something, and the Seq.map tells us what that something is. And it also follows the principle of *revisability*. If we suddenly decided we wanted the earliest write time instead of the latest, we'd just have to change the Seq.max to a Seq.min. Contrast that with Listing 5-1, where we'd have to change both the initial value of the mutable, and the operator of the check (less-than instead of greater-then).

There's another, subtler but more fundamental advantage. Working at this level lets us reason about our code without getting involved in the nitty gritty of intermediate values, terminating conditions, and so forth. If you were paying attention during Chapter 4, you might remember that certain functions are *partial*; that is, they don't return valid outputs for seemingly sensible inputs. If you don't immediately see the significance of this, try running the code from Listing 5-2 for a search pattern for which no file exists, for example:

```
latestWriteTime @"c:\temp" "doesnotexist.*"
```

You'll get an "input sequence is empty error." Seq.max is a partial function: you can't find the maximum value of "no values." Back in Listing 5-1, the no-files situation was dealt with by returning DateTime.MinValue. This kind of works, but it violates the principle of *motivational transparency*, because the caller isn't forced by the type signature to think about the empty-file-list case. Therefore. they may not deal properly with DateTime.MinValue. Imagine a UI saying "You last updated a file on 1st January 0001." It wouldn't look great, would it?

How do we force callers to handle empty cases? We learned in Chapter 3 that the answer is often an option type, so we start by hoping there is a built-in Seq.tryMax function to do the work for us, by returning None when there is nothing in the sequence. At the time of writing there isn't such a function, but defining one is almost trivial. Listing 5-3 shows us defining Seq.tryMax, then using it to ensure we return None when there are no files and Some date when there is at least one file.

Listing 5-3. Defining and using Seq.tryMax to handle the empty case

```
open System.IO

module Seq =
    let tryMax s =
        if s |> Seq.isEmpty then
            None
        else
            s |> Seq.max |> Some

let tryLatestWriteTime (path : string) (searchPattern : string) =
    Directory.EnumerateFiles(path, searchPattern,
                              SearchOption.AllDirectories)
    |> Seq.map File.GetLastWriteTime
    |> Seq.tryMax
```

```
// Some date
tryLatestWriteTime @"c:\temp" "*.*"
// None
tryLatestWriteTime @"c:\temp" "doesnotexist.*"
```

Now the caller is forced to think about the no-files case, and to handle it explicitly. It might do this by defaulting the value using pattern matching or `Option.defaultValue`; or it might use `Option.bind` and `Option.map` to skip subsequent processing when the return value from `trylatestWriteTime` is `None`. It doesn't matter how the caller handles `None` - it's good enough to know that it will be handled.

Common Mutable Patterns

When transitioning to an "immutable-first" coding style, it's easy to get blocked, particularly if the mutable answer to the problem is already obvious to you. If this happens, don't worry: just code the function in mutable style if that's what seems more natural, and then go look at it again to see what is needed to transform it to immutable style. Once you've done this a few times, you'll start to recognize the logical mappings between the old and new approaches, and you'll gradually find yourself able to code in immutable style by default.

To help you with the process, here's a list of common mutable-style coding patterns, together with suggestions on how to re-express them in immutable style. For each pattern, I'll first show how you might naïvely code the F# solution, then I'll give the immutable equivalent.

Linear Search

In this pattern, the aim is to search a sequence of items for the first that meets a specific condition.

Listing 5-4. Linear Search in mutable style

```
type Student = { Name : string; Grade : char }

let findFirstWithGrade (grade : char) (students : seq<Student>) =
    let mutable result = { Name = ""; Grade = ' ' }
    let mutable found = false
```

```
        for student in students do
            if not found && student.Grade = grade then
                result <- student
                found <- true
        result
```

In Listing 5-4 we set a mutable value to some arbitrary "empty" value. Then we loop over the items in the collection until we find one that meets the criterion. When we find it, we take a note of its value by updating the mutable value with the found value. When the loop is complete we return that mutable value.

In a language like C or C#, we would also break out of the loop when we found the first element. This would skip the cost of further iterations, and would avoid overwriting our mutable found value with some later matching element. In F# we don't have a `break` keyword, so we use a mutable value `found` to achieve a similar effect. (There are still some useless iterations, but at least they are cheap.)

There are several aspects of this code that shout out "refactor me as immutable":

- Use of mutable values

- Use of an arbitrary empty initialization value (often null in other languages)

- For-loops

- Use of flag values such as `found`

The good news is that the refactoring is easy (Listing 5-5).

Listing 5-5. Linear Search in immutable style

```
    type Student = { Name : string; Grade : char }

    let findFirstWithGrade2 (grade : char) (students : seq<Student>) =
        students
        |> Seq.find (fun s -> s.Grade = grade)
```

In Listing 5-5 we simply use `Seq.find` to do the work. This has a couple of advantages:

- We are letting the F# libraries do the work, so we won't introduce any of the bugs that inevitably creep in with mutable values.

- We can now reason more readily about the code. For example, the fact that Seq.find is a partial function (see Chapter 4) should immediately flag up the fact we should be handling the "not found" case explicitly, which leads us nicely onto "Guarded Linear Search."

Guarded Linear Search

This pattern is like Linear Search, except that we handle the fact that a matching element might not be found (Listing 5-6).

Listing 5-6. Guarded Linear Search in mutable style

```
type Student = { Name : string; Grade : char }

let tryFindFirstWithGrade (grade : char) (students : seq<Student>) =
    let mutable result = { Name = ""; Grade = ' ' }
    let mutable found = false
    for student in students do
        if not found && student.Grade = grade then
            result <- student
            found <- true
    if found then
        Some result
    else
        None
```

In C-like languages, it would be common to raise an exception in the "not found" case. Instead I've chosen to make the function return an option type, so the caller has a fighting chance of knowing what has happened. I've used the found mutable value to decide whether to return Some value or None.

The warning signs that this isn't great F# code are the same as they were for 5-4, and the cure is equally simple (Listing 5-7).

Listing 5-7. Guarded Linear Search in immutable style

```
type Student = { Name : string; Grade : char }

let tryFindFirstWithGrade (grade : char) (students : seq<Student>) =
    students
    |> Seq.tryFind (fun s -> s.Grade = grade)
```

`Seq.tryFind` is a *total function* (i.e., not a partial function), which gives us a warm feeling that our function will work in a predictable way from the caller's point of view, whether or not the collection is empty or an element is found.

Process All Items

In this pattern we do something "to" or "with" every element in a collection. We need to do different things in the "to" (imperative) version, versus the "with" (functional) version. Listing 5-8 shows us processing every student by doing something imperative using each element.

Listing 5-8. Process All Items, imperative version, in looping style

```
type Student = { Name : string; Grade : char }

let printGradeLabel (student : Student) =
    printfn "%s\n\nGrade: %c" (student.Name.ToUpper()) student.Grade

let printGradeLabels (students : seq<Student>) =
    for student in students do
        printGradeLabel student
```

Listing 5-8 really isn't too bad – there is no explicit mutation anywhere. The argument for the more idiomatic version (Listing 5-9) is only that it's more consistent with how we like to handle collections generally in F# code.

Listing 5-9. Process All Items, imperative version, in loop-free style

```
type Student = { Name : string; Grade : char }

let printGradeLabel (student : Student) =
    printfn "%s\n\nGrade: %c" (student.Name.ToUpper()) student.Grade
```

```
let printGradeLabels (students : seq<Student>) =
    students
    |> Seq.iter (fun student -> printGradeLabel student)
    // Alternatively:
    //|> Seq.iter printGradeLabel
```

Using Seq.iter also allows us (if we want) to avoid having an explicit value for a single student, as shown in the commented-out line in Listing 5-9. This is more concise, but it does require you to name your functions clearly, and not to have pipelines that are too long. Otherwise you risk sacrificing readability.

How about processing a collection of items by doing some calculation using each element, and returning all the results? Listing 5-10 shows a mutable-style approach.

Listing 5-10. Process All Items, returning a result for each, in mutable style

```
type Student = { Name : string; Grade : char }

let makeGradeLabel (student : Student) =
    sprintf "%s\n\nGrade: %c" (student.Name.ToUpper()) student.Grade

let makeGradeLabels (students : seq<Student>) =
    let result = ResizeArray<string>()
    for student in students do
        result.Add(makeGradeLabel student)
    result |> Seq.cast<string>
```

Here we start with an empty collection that is mutable, in the sense that it can be added to. I've used ResizeArray, which is F#'s alias for System.Collections.Generic. List. (You can actually resize an ordinary .NET array with the Array.Resize, but... well, just don't.) We call a function for each element in the input list, and add the result to the output list. Finally, we return the built-up list. I've also explicitly cast the result so that it is a sequence of strings, because it isn't the caller's concern that we used a ResizeArray to build up the result.

This "initialize-empty-then-add" style of coding is almost unthinkable when you've mentally made the transition to immutable style, but it's the pattern I see most from people who *haven't* yet made the transition. (Incidentally you may well see this style legitimately used in low-level code, but most code should avoid it.) Another common mutable approach is to initialize a collection of the right size with zero-valued elements, then mutate them to the right values (Listing 5-11).

Listing 5-11. Process All Items in mutable style, another approach

```
type Student = { Name : string; Grade : char }

let makeGradeLabel (student : Student) =
    sprintf "%s\n\nGrade: %c" (student.Name.ToUpper()) student.Grade

let printGradeLabels (students : seq<Student>) =
    let length = students |> Seq.length
    let result = Array.zeroCreate<string> length
    let mutable i = 0
    for student in students do
        result.[i] <- makeGradeLabel student
        i <- i + 1
    result |> Seq.ofArray
```

While Listings 5-10 and 5-11 may seem self-evidently ridiculous as I've presented them here, somewhat more complex instances of what is fundamentally the same thing abound. So watch out for them. Generally, when the input is a collection of known size, and the result is a collection of the same size, the answer is map (Listing 5-12).

Listing 5-12. Process All Items, returning a result for each, in immutable style

```
type Student = { Name : string; Grade : char }

let makeGradeLabel (student : Student) =
    sprintf "%s\n\nGrade: %c" (student.Name.ToUpper()) student.Grade

let printGradeLabels (students : seq<Student>) =
    students
    |> Seq.map makeGradeLabel
```

Listings 5-10 and 5-11 may be among the most common anti-patterns in beginner F# code, but they are also the easiest to rectify. Sprinkle your code with map operations!

Repeat Until

This pattern occurs when we need to repeat an operation until some condition has been reached, but there is no way to know the condition until we have executed the operation at least once. Many languages provide a "repeat until" construct to handle this, but not F#.

We also don't have the concept of "break," which would enable us to achieve the same thing by exiting from a for-loop before all elements had been exhausted. Thus, our attempt to do this in mutable style (Listing 5-13) is notably inelegant. In Listing 5-13 I've also had to add a function called tryGetSomethingFromApi that simulates a "must call once" API. The code we want to improve is listThingsFromApi.

Listing 5-13. Repeat Until in mutable style

```
// Simulate something coming from an API, which only
// tells you if you are going to get something after
// you asked for it.
let tryGetSomethingFromApi =
    let mutable thingCount = 0
    let maxThings = 10
    fun () ->
        if thingCount < maxThings then
            thingCount <- thingCount+1
            "Soup"
        else
            null // No more soup for you!

let listThingsFromApi() =
    let mutable finished = false
    while not finished do
        let thing = tryGetSomethingFromApi()
        if thing <> null then
            printfn "I got %s" thing
        else
            printfn "No more soup for me!"
            finished <- true

// I got Soup (x10)
// No more soup for me!
listThingsFromApi()
```

We can improve on this using a "sequence" expression, which calls the API, converts the result into an option type using `Option.ofObj`, and decides whether to continue based on whether the result is Some or None. Note that the sequence expression is recursive because it needs to include not only the result from "this" iteration, using `yield`, but also the results from every subsequent iteration, using `yield!` (note the exclamation mark after `yield`).

Listing 5-14. Repeat Until in immutable style using a recursive sequence expression

```
// Simulate something coming from an API, which only
// tells you if you are going to get something after
// you asked for it.
let tryGetSomethingFromApi =
    let mutable thingCount = 0
    let maxThings = 10
    fun () ->
        if thingCount < maxThings then
            thingCount <- thingCount+1
            "Soup"
        else
            null // No more soup for you!

let rec apiToSeq() =
    seq {
        match tryGetSomethingFromApi() |> Option.ofObj with
        | Some thing ->
            yield thing
            yield! apiToSeq()
        | None -> ()
    }

let listThingsFromApi() =
    apiToSeq()
    |> Seq.iter (printfn "I got %s")

// I got Soup (x10)
listThingsFromApi()
```

Find Extreme Value

In this pattern we are trying to find an extreme value, typically a maximum or minimum value. That "max-ness" or "min-ness" might be expressed in all sorts of ways; simply as the magnitude of a number; closeness to or distance from zero; time duration; alphabetical order, and so on. Focusing for a moment on numerical magnitude, here's how we might naïvely code getting the maximum of a sequence of numbers (Listing 5-15).

Listing 5-15. Naïve get-maximum function in mutable style

```
open System

let getMax (numbers : seq<float>) =
    let mutable max = Double.MinValue
    for number in numbers do
        if number > max then
            max <- number
    max
```

Listing 5-15 has several serious shortcomings. It only works for collections of floating-point values; it has no way of finding a whole object in a collection, based on some property of each element; and most seriously of all, it will return an arbitrary value (-1.797693135e+308) if the collection is empty. This is an obvious candidate for the "try" idiom, where we return Some maximum or None. At the time of writing, there isn't a Seq.tryMax nor a Seq.tryMaxBy, but it's simple to write them (Listing 5-16).

Listing 5-16. Implementing Seq.tryMax and Seq.tryMaxBy

```
module Seq =
    let tryMax s =
        if s |> Seq.isEmpty then
            None
        else
            s |> Seq.max |> Some
    let tryMaxBy f s =
        if s |> Seq.isEmpty then
            None
        else
            s |> Seq.maxBy f |> Some
```

Listing 5-16 means we don't need to write the code in Listing 5-15 at all – we'd just call Seq.tryMax. If we want to get the maximum of a collection of objects "by" some property, we'd call Seq.tryMaxBy as in Listing 5-17.

Listing 5-17. Using Seq.tryMaxBy

```
type Student = { Name : string; Grade : char }

let tryGetLastStudentByName (students : seq<Student>) =
    students
    |> Seq.tryMaxBy (fun s -> s.Name)
```

Going back to the "distance from zero" requirement, Listing 5-18 shows how we might code this, again using Seq.tryMaxBy.

Listing 5-18. Using Seq.tryMaxBy to find furthest from zero

```
// -5.3
let furthestFromZero =
    [| -1.1; -0.1; 0.; 1.1; -5.3 |]
    |> Seq.tryMaxBy abs
```

Summarize a Collection

In this pattern, we're trying to produce a single value that in some sense summarizes a collection. Straightforward summaries such as summing or averaging can easily be dealt with using appropriate collection functions such as Seq.sum, Seq.sumBy, Seq.average, and Seq.averageBy. But what about calculations that aren't directly covered by built-in functions? Let's take the example of calculating the *root mean square* (RMS) of a data series. This is a measure that expresses, for example, the effective voltage of an alternating electric current. Because it oscillates between positive and negative values, the simple average of the voltage is 0. But by calculating the average of the *squares* (converting the negative parts of each wave to positive), then taking the square root of the results, we can produce a useful figure. Listing 5-19 shows how one might be tempted to do this in a mutable style.

Listing 5-19. Calculating RMS in mutable style

```
let rms (s : seq<float>) =
    let mutable total = 0.
    let mutable count = 0
    for item in s do
        total <- total + (item ** 2.)
        count <- count + 1
    let average = total / (float count)
    sqrt average

// 120.2081528
[|0.; -170.; 0.; 170.|]
|> rms
```

Even though there is no `Seq.rms` function, it's still possible to achieve the same result with no mutation. In Listing 5-20 we average "by" the square of each sample, then we pipe the result into the built-in `sqrt` function.

Listing 5-20. Calculating RMS in immutable style

```
let rms (s : seq<float>) =
    s
    |> Seq.averageBy (fun item -> item ** 2.)
    |> sqrt

// 120.2081528
[|0.; -170.; 0.; 170.|]
|> rms
```

This is common: even if there isn't a summary collection function to do exactly what you want, you can normally combine collection functions with other calculations to get where you need to be. The presence of mutable accumulator values (such as `total` and `count` in Listing 5-19) is a sure-fire sign that you can improve your code in this way.

Sometimes you still need to thread an "accumulator" value through a collection computation, because the value at position *n* depends on the cumulative value built up at position *n-1*. Listing 5-21 shows a mutable example, in this case multiplying together all the successive elements of a collection.

Listing 5-21. Cumulative computation in mutable style

```
let product (s : seq<float>) =
    let mutable total = 1.
    for item in s do
        total <- total * item
    total

// 1.98
[| 1.2; 1.1; 1.5|]
|> product
```

This is, technically speaking, a "fold" operation, and to support it we have `Seq.fold` (and `Array.fold` etc.). Fold sometimes gets bad press because it can be confusing, but here it is a perfect fit (Listing 5-22).

Listing 5-22. Cumulative computation in immutable style

```
let product (s : seq<float>) =
    s
    |> Seq.fold (fun acc elem -> acc * elem) 1.

// 1.98
[| 1.2; 1.1; 1.5|]
|> product
```

Incidentally, I have a way of taming the confusion that can easily accompany use of `fold`. I always name the two arguments of the lambda function, which represent the accumulated value and the value of the current element, `acc` and `elem`. Somehow sticking to the *acc-elem* mantra, rather than using context-specific names like `totalSoFar` and `thisElement`, helps me remember which way round to put the values and how they are used.

Recommendations

Here are the main points you should take away from this chapter:

- Programming in immutable style is a key way to access the benefits of programming in F#.

- Watch out for the common signs of mutable or imperative programming style: use of mutable values, use of arbitrary initialization values (e.g., nulls), for-loops, and use of flag or "sentinel" values such as `found`.

- It's OK to code a first cut in mutable style. But when that is working, try to factor it into immutable style, often using collection functions such as `Seq.max` to work at a higher level of abstraction.

- As you get used to the style, it'll start feeling natural to code in immutable style from the outset.

Summary

In this chapter I've listed some of the most common coding patterns where, in C-like languages, and in the absence of wonderful technologies like LINQ, one has to resort to using mutable values and looping. I hope you're convinced that this old style of coding is hardly ever necessary.

Of course, you sometimes have to resort to mutable style for performance reasons. But I can't remember a case in the past few years where I've personally had to do so. All that said, feel free to start off in mutable style and refactor to immutable as you go along. You soon find that immutable-first becomes your natural default.

In the next chapter we'll look at *pattern matching*, a technique for flow control and data assignment that leaves `if` and `switch` statements in the dust!

Exercises

EXERCISE 5-1 – CLIPPING A SEQUENCE

Write a function "clip," which takes a sequence of values, and returns a sequence of the same length, in which the values are the same as the inputs, except elements that were higher than a defined ceiling are replaced with that ceiling.

For example:

```
// seq [1.0; 2.3; 10.0; -5.0]
[| 1.0; 2.3; 11.1; -5. |]
|> clip 10.
```

You can solve this exercise using one collection function and one other function.

EXERCISE 5-2 – MINIMUM AND MAXIMUM

You come across a function that appears to be designed to calculate the minimum and maximum values in a sequence:

```
open System

let extremes (s : seq<float>) =
    let mutable min = Double.MaxValue
    let mutable max = Double.MinValue
    for item in s do
        if item < min then
            min <- item
        if item > max then
            max <- item
    min, max

// (-5.0, 11.1)
[| 1.0; 2.3; 11.1; -5. |]
|> extremes
```

How would you rewrite the function to avoid using mutable values? You can ignore the situation where the input sequence is empty.

Given a pre-computed array of one million elements, how does the performance of your function compare with the mutable version?

You can solve this exercise using two collection functions.

Exercise Solutions

This section shows solutions for the exercises in this chapter.

EXERCISE 5-1 – CLIPPING A SEQUENCE

You can achieve the requirement by writing a function that takes a required ceiling value and a sequence. Then you can use `Seq.map` to map the input values to the lower of either the input element or the specified ceiling, using the built-in `min` function.

```
let clip ceiling (s : seq<_>) =
    s
    |> Seq.map (fun x -> min x ceiling)

// seq [1.0; 2.3; 10.0; -5.0]
[| 1.0; 2.3; 11.1; -5. |]
|> clip 10.
```

EXERCISE 5-2 – MINIMUM AND MAXIMUM

You can achieve the requirement simply by using `Seq.min` and `Seq.max`, and returning the results as a tuple by putting a comma between the calls.

```
open System

let extremes (s : seq<float>) =
    s |> Seq.max,
    s |> Seq.min

// (-5.0, 11.1)
[| 1.0; 2.3; 11.1; -5. |]
|> extremes
```

117

Basic performance can be analyzed by using code like this:

```
// Performance test:
open System.Diagnostics

let r = Random()

let big = Array.init 1_000_000 (fun _ -> r.NextDouble())
let sw = Stopwatch()
sw.Start()
let min, max = big |> extremes
sw.Stop()

// 8ms for the original, mutable version
// 12ms for the Seq.max/Seq.min version,
//    when s is specified as a seq<float>
// 272ms when is a seq<_>, i.e. as generic
// 17ms when generic, but inlined
printfn "min: %f max: %f - time: %ims" min max sw.ElapsedMilliseconds
```

As you can see from the comments, on my setup and when running through F# Interactive, the immutable version takes 50% longer than the mutable version. If s is allowed to be a generic sequence (seq<_>), the situation is much, much worse. You can gain back most of this by inlining the function (i.e., let inline extremes...). Making functions inline is a technique that you should use very selectively. We'll return to performance in Chapter 12.

CHAPTER 6

Pattern Matching

We may say most aptly, that the Analytical Engine weaves algebraical patterns just as the Jacquard-loom weaves flowers and leaves.

—Ada Lovelace, Computer Pioneer

Weaving Software with Patterns

I have many "favorite" F# features, but my *favorite* favorite is pattern matching! Perhaps this is because it's the feature that takes us furthest away from Object Oriented coding, letting us truly differentiate from legacy coding patterns. Another nice aspect is how unexpectedly pervasive it can be in well-factored codebases. Prepare to be surprised at the places where you can use pattern matching to simplify and beautify your code. But also be prepared to exercise some restraint in using your newfound superpower. Pattern matching can be overdone.

Because pattern matching tends to be completely new, conceptually, to many developers, I'm going to be more progressive in my explanations than I have been in other chapters of this intermediate book. I'll start with the very basics.

Pattern Matching Basics

At its simplest, pattern matching is analogous to the `switch` or `case` constructs found in many languages. For example Listings 6-1 and 6-2 show how we'd implement simple switching of control using C# and F#.

K. Eason, *Stylish F#*, https://doi.org/10.1007/978-1-4842-4000-7_6

Listing 6-1. Case switching in C#

```
int caseSwitch = 1;

switch (caseSwitch)
{
    case 1:
        Console.WriteLine("Case 1");
        break;
    case 2:
        Console.WriteLine("Case 2");
        break;
    default:
        Console.WriteLine("Default case");
        break;
}
```

Listing 6-2. Case switching in F#

```
let caseSwitch = 2

match caseSwitch with
| 1 -> printfn "Case 1"
| 2 -> printfn "Case 2"
| _ -> printfn "Default case"
```

This is explicit pattern matching – that is, we are using the `match` keyword - and it's super clear what is going on.

Using pattern matching to match on integer literals like this is a bit like using an expensive torque wrench as a hammer, but even here there are some surprising goodies to be had. Try commenting out the bottom line in Listing 6-2. You'll get a compiler warning (a compiler warning mind, not a linter or external tool warning) saying "`Incomplete pattern matches on this expression. For example, the value '0' may indicate a case not covered by the pattern(s).`" The F# compiler checks, at the type level, whether a value that isn't covered by the listed cases could conceivably be passed in. And just in case you don't believe it, it gives you an example! I can't tell you how many times that feature alone has saved my bacon. Incidentally, it's a good habit to have no warnings in your F# code, or even to turn on the "warnings as errors" setting in your development/build environment. F# warnings are almost always pointing you to a genuine weakness in your code, and "Incomplete pattern matches" warnings are the best example of this.

If you want to cover more than one case, and have these cases go to the same line of code, use several | *case* constructs and follow the last of them with the -> arrow, then the code to be executed (Listing 6-3).

Listing 6-3. Handling multiple match cases

```
let caseSwitch = 3

// "Maybe 3, maybe 4"
match caseSwitch with
| 1 -> printfn "Case 1"
| 2 -> printfn "Case 2"
| 3
| 4 -> printfn "Maybe 3, maybe 4"
| _ -> printfn "Default case"
```

I love how layout and syntax work together here, so that you can run your eye down the code and spot anomalies and special cases at a glance. The code is almost a diagram of what you want to happen.

Now let's start treating the torque wrench with a bit of respect. What else can it do? Well it can recover the value that actually matched at runtime, if you follow the final case with as x (Listing 6-4).

Listing 6-4. Recovering a matched value

```
let caseSwitch = 3

// "Maybe 3, maybe 4. But actually 3."
match caseSwitch with
| 1 -> printfn "Case 1"
| 2 -> printfn "Case 2"
| 3
| 4 as x -> printfn "Maybe 3, maybe 4. But actually %i." x
| _ -> printfn "Default case"
```

Using the as x construct means that an identifier of the appropriate type, called x (or whatever you want to label it), is bound with the value that matched. The scope of this identifier is limited to the code that's executed as a result of the match. In the code of other cases, and outside the match expression, it has no meaning.[1]

I like to think of a match expression as a kind of time travel, allowing you to go back and get the value that must have been assigned for this case to have matched.

When Guards

If you want a bit more branching, using the value recovered in a match case, you can use a *when guard*. A when guard is a bit like an if expression, and it uses the recovered value for some comparison. Only if the comparison returns true is the following code executed (Listing 6-5).

Listing 6-5. Matching with a when guard

```
let caseSwitch = 11

// "Less than a dozen"
match caseSwitch with
| 1 -> printfn "One"
| 2 -> printfn "A couple"
| x when x < 12 ->
    printfn "Less than a dozen"
| x when x = 12 ->
    printfn "A dozen"
| _ ->
    printfn "More than a dozen"
```

Pattern Matching on Arrays and Lists

What if the value being matched is a bit more structured – say an array? We can pattern match on arrays and pick out cases having specific element counts (Listing 6-6).

---

[1]No horrific fall-through semantics, as in C!

Listing 6-6. Pattern matching on arrays

```
let arr0 = [|||]
let arr1 = [|"One fish" |]
let arr2 = [|"One fish"; "Two fish" |]
let arr3 = [|"One fish"; "Two fish"; "Red fish"|]
let arr4 = [|"One fish"; "Two fish"; "Red fish"; "Blue fish" |]

let arr = arr1

// "A pond containing one fish: One fish"
match arr with
| [|||] ->
    "An empty pond"
| [| fish |] ->
    sprintf "A pond containing one fish: %s" fish
| [| f1; f2 |] ->
    sprintf "A pond containing two fish: %s and %s" f1 f2
| _ ->
    "Too many fish to list!"
```

This process of recovering the constituents of a structured type is often called *decomposition.*

Array decomposition is a little limited, as you have to specify either arrays of specific sizes (including size zero), or a catch-all case using an underscore. List decomposition is a bit more powerful, as befits the linked structure of a list (Listing 6-7).

Listing 6-7. Pattern matching on lists

```
let list0 = []
let list1 = ["One fish" ]
let list2 = ["One fish"; "Two fish" ]
let list3 = ["One fish"; "Two fish"; "Red fish" ]
let list4 = ["One fish"; "Two fish"; "Red fish"; "Blue fish" ]

let list = list4
```

```
// "A pond containing one fish: One fish (and 3 more fish)"
match list with
| [] ->
    "An empty pond"
| [ fish ] ->
    sprintf "A pond containing one fish only: %s" fish
| head::tail ->
    sprintf "A pond containing one fish: %s (and %i more fish)"
        head (tail |> List.length)
```

Here the first two cases are pretty much as Listing 6-6, except we use list brackets [ ] instead of "array clamps" [||]. The next case uses a cons operator ::. When *constructing* a list, you can use the cons operator to join a single element onto the beginning of a list (e.g., "One fish" :: ["Two fish"; "Red fish"]). But here we are using it in the opposite direction - to recover the first element, and all subsequent elements (if any) from an existing list. (You can see now why I referred to pattern matching as a form of time travel.)

In Listing 6-7 I've used the identifiers head and tail in the cons case, that is, head::tail. Two things to say about this. First, "head" and "tail" refer to the head (first element) and tail (remaining elements if any) of the list, not the head and tail of the fish! Second, I've found it useful to always use the names head and tail in cons matching, regardless of the business meanings of the particular values in question. (The alternative in this case might have been something like firstFish::otherFishes.) This is one of those conventions, like using acc and elem in fold functions, which helps your mind recognize common idioms with as little cognitive overhead as possible, and saves you from some unnecessary decision making. If you're feeling super concise, h::t is also a commonly used naming convention.

Incidentally, you might want to experiment a bit to prove what I said about the possibility of the tail containing zero elements. Comment out the | [fish] -> case from Listing 6-7, and its following printf line. What do you expect to happen when you send list1 into the match expression? Were you right?

Pattern Matching on Tuples

We've got a bit ahead of ourselves and missed out one of the most pervasive forms of pattern matching – so pervasive it's not that obvious that it is pattern matching at all. Consider a function that returns a tuple. You can call that function and decompose the tuple result straight into separate values like this (Listing 6-8).

Listing 6-8. Pattern matching on tuples in a let binding

```
let extremes (s : seq<_>) =
    s |> Seq.min,
    s |> Seq.max

// lowest : int = -1
// highest : int = 9
let lowest, highest =
    [1; 2; 9; 3; -1] |> extremes
```

You can also explicitly pattern match on tuples using the `match` keyword. For example, the `Int32.TryParse` function returns a tuple consisting of a Boolean flag to say whether the parsing succeeded, and the parsed integer value. (The compiler cleverly translates into a tuple result from the "real" signature of `TryParse`, in which the value is placed in a by-reference parameter.) Thus you can pattern match to recover the value and place it into an option type, which makes it more usable from the rest of your F# code (Listing 6-9).

Listing 6-9. Pattern matching on tuples using match

```
open System

let tryParseInt s =
    match Int32.TryParse(s) with
    | true, i -> Some i
    | false, _ -> None

// Some 30
"30" |> tryParseInt
// None
"3X" |> tryParseInt
```

Pattern Matching on Records

You can also use pattern matching to decompose record types. This is sometimes useful when you want to pluck one or two values out of the record and ignore the rest.

Listing 6-10. Pattern matching on record types

```
type Track = { Title : string; Artist : string }

let songs =
    [ { Title = "Summertime"
        Artist = "Ray Barretto" }
      { Title = "La clave, maraca y guiro"
        Artist = "Chico Alvarez" }
      { Title = "Summertime"
        Artist = "DJ Jazzy Jeff & The Fresh Prince" } ]

// seq ["Summertime"; "La clave, maraca y guiro"]
let distinctTitles =
    songs
    |> Seq.map (fun song ->
        match song with
        | { Title = title } -> title)
    |> Seq.distinct
```

In Listing 6-10 we pull `Title` out of the record and ignore `Artist`. (You aren't obliged to use `Artist = _` to do this; you can just omit the fields you aren't interested in.). The syntax is a little confusing at first, because `Title = title` looks almost like an assignment, but written backward, given that it is `title` (on the right) that receives the value.

There are more concise ways to achieve what we did in Listing 6-10 (e.g., `Seq.map (fun song -> song.Title)`) – but it's worth getting used to record matching in the context of a `match` expression, as it'll make things easier to understand when we start to discover record matching in other constructs. In fact, let's jump ahead a bit and look at one example of pattern matching without a match expression.

Say the `Track` type from Listing 6-10 has a few more fields, and we want to write a function that formats a track name and artist as a menu item. Clearly that function only cares about two fields from the Track type, but it would be quite nice to be able to throw whole Track instances at the function, without either the caller or the callee having to break out the fields of interest. Listing 6-11 shows how to achieve exactly that.

Listing 6-11. Pattern matching at the function call boundary

```
type Track = { Id : int
               Title : string
               Artist : string
               Length : int }

let songs =
    [ { Id = 1
        Title = "Summertime"
        Artist = "Ray Barretto"
        Length = 99 }
      { Id = 2
        Title = "La clave, maraca y guiro"
        Artist = "Chico Alvarez"
        Length = 99 }
      { Id = 3
        Title = "Summertime"
        Artist = "DJ Jazzy Jeff & The Fresh Prince"
        Length = 99 } ]

let formatMenuItem ( { Title = title; Artist = artist } ) =
    let shorten (s : string) = s.Substring(0, 10)
    sprintf "%s - %s" (shorten title) (shorten artist)

// Summertime - Ray Barret
// La clave,  - Chico Alva
// Summertime - DJ Jazzy J
songs
|> Seq.map formatMenuItem
|> Seq.iter (printfn "%s")
```

The magic happens in the argument list of `formatMenuItem`, where we say ({ Title = title; Artist = artist }). This will cause values called `title` and `artist` to be bound with the relevant fields' values from a `Track` instance, and they will be available within the function body. Other fields from the record are ignored. See how the `Seq.map` near the bottom of the listing can send in whole `Track` instances.

You could argue that this technique offers a whole new paradigm of argument declaration: an alternative to both the *curried* style, where you just list the parameters with spaces, meaning the caller can populate as many as it feels like; and the *tupled* style, where the caller must supply values for all parameters. In this new paradigm, the *caller* must supply a whole record instance, but the *callee* only sees some of the values. It can be very useful, but it's a trick to use sparingly. I've come across it *in my own code* and been confused by it!

Pattern Matching on Discriminated Unions

It's time for the yin of pattern matching to meet its yang, in the form of Discriminated Unions. As we've already said (and you probably already knew anyway), a Discriminated Union (DU) is a type that has several labeled cases, each of which may have an associated payload of any type. The payload type associated with each case can be different. Multiple types can be put into the payload of a DU case simply by tupling them together.

You can recover the payload of a DU instance using explicit pattern matching (Listing 6-12).

Listing 6-12. Pattern Matching on a DU

```
type MeterReading =
| Standard of int
| Economy7 of Day:int * Night:int

let formatReading (reading : MeterReading) =
    match reading with
    | Standard reading ->
        sprintf "Your reading: %07i" reading
    | Economy7(Day=day; Night=night) ->
        sprintf "Your readings: Day: %07i Night: %07i" day night
```

```
let reading1 = Standard 12982
let reading2 = Economy7(Day=3432, Night=98218)

reading1 |> formatReading
reading2 |> formatReading
```

In Listing 6-12 we are modeling readings for two kinds of UK domestic electricity meters. The "Standard" meter is one where your consumption is simply recorded as a single number. The "Economy 7" meter is one where daytime and nighttime consumption is recorded separately, and charged at different rates. Clearly a single "meter read" event will produce one value for standard readings, and two (which we absolutely must not mix up) for Economy 7. Given these rules, the code in Listing 6-12 should be fairly self-explanatory. The function `formatReading` takes a `MeterReading` instance of either type, and formats it appropriately for printing on a bill or web page, using pattern matching to recover the reading(s).

If you are at an intermediate level in F#, DU's and pattern matching will be pretty familiar to you. But let me point out some language features in Listing 6-12 that are little used in F# codebases generally, and which I think should be used more. First, I've assigned labels to each of the readings in the Economy7 case, that is, `Economy7 of Day:int * Night:int` rather than `Economy7 of int*int`. Second, I've used those labels when instantiating Economy 7 readings, i.e. `Economy7(Day=3432, Night=98218)` rather than `Economy7(3432, 98218)`. (F# doesn't force you to do this, even if you've given labels to the tuple elements in the case declaration.) Finally, when decomposing out the day and night values in the pattern match, I've again used the labels, that is, `| Economy7(Day=day; Night=night)` rather than `| Economy7(day, night)`. There's an oddity in the decomposition part: note how the decomposition syntax has a semicolon, while when you construct the instance, you used a comma (Table 6-1).

Table 6-1. *DU Labeled Payload Elements Construction and Decomposition Syntax*

Action	Syntax
Construction	`Economy7(Day=3432, Night=98218)`
Decomposition	`Economy7(Day=day; Night=night)`

I suspect there is a reason for this: here the decomposition isn't quite the "opposite" of the composition, because in the decomposition you can legitimately omit some of the items from the payload. For example if you just wanted to pull out the day reading, you could use the match case | `Economy7(Day=day) -> ...`.

Anyway, if you choose not to label the items in your payload, Listing 6-13 shows the same functionality as Listing 6-12, but without the labels.

Listing 6-13. DUs and pattern matching without payload labels

```
type MeterReading =
| Standard of int
| Economy7 of int * int

let formatReading (reading : MeterReading) =
    match reading with
    | Standard reading ->
        sprintf "Your reading: %07i" reading
    | Economy7(day, night) ->
        sprintf "Your readings: Day: %07i Night: %07i" day night

let reading1 = Standard 12982
let reading2 = Economy7(3432, 98218)
```

You will see code like Listing 6-13 much more often, but I prefer the style of 6-12 if there is any possibility of confusion between the elements of a DU payload, or if the nature of the payload isn't immediately obvious from context. Remember: *motivational transparency*!

Another alternative to labeling the payload elements is to have the payload as a whole be a type with some structure, for example, a record type. Thus the field labels or member names make the code self-documenting, taking the place of the payload element labels. Using a "proper" type is obviously a less minimalist approach than simply having labels in the DU payload (and generally I like minimalism); but obviously it has benefits if you have broader uses for the type anyway.

Pattern Matching on DUs in Function Parameters

If you think back to the section "Pattern Matching on Records," you might remember that we said you can pattern match in the declaration of a function, thus:

```
let formatMenuItem ( { Title = title; Artist = artist } ) = ...
```

In this way you can recover items from the incoming type and use their values within the function body. It might occur to you that the same should be possible for Discriminated Unions. And yes, you can – with certain important restrictions. Imagine you are trying to implement *complex numbers*. For this example, all you need to know about complex numbers is that each one has two components, the *real* and *imaginary* parts; and that to add two complex numbers you add each one's real parts, and each one's imaginary parts, and make a new complex number using the two results. (Incidentally there is no need, in reality, to implement complex numbers, as they are already right there in `System.Numerics`. Nonetheless they do make a useful example.) Listing 6-14 shows how you could model complex numbers using a single-case DU.

Listing 6-14. Implementing complex numbers using a single-case DU

```
type Complex =
| Complex of Real:float * Imaginary:float

let add (Complex(Real=a;Imaginary=b)) (Complex(Real=c;Imaginary=d)) =
    Complex(Real=(a+c), Imaginary=(b+d))

let (+) = add

let c1 = Complex(Real = 0.2, Imaginary = 3.4)
let c2 = Complex(Real = 2.2, Imaginary = 9.8)

// Complex (2.4,13.2)
let c3 = c1 + c2
```

Note how, as in Listing 6-12, I've opted to label the two components of the payload tuple, as it is rather critical we don't mix up the real and imaginary components! The key new concept here is the add function, where I've done pattern matching *in the parameter declaration* to pull out the actual values we need for the computation. In the body of the add function we simply construct a new `Complex` instance, doing the necessary computation at the same time. Once again, we use the slightly odd semicolon-based syntax at the decomposition stage, even though we compose the instances using commas.

Exactly as with records, this technique can be useful in certain circumstances. But it is a double-edged sword in terms of readability, particularly for non-advanced maintainers of your code. I would say I've regretted using single-case DU's in the manner outlined in Listing 6-14 about as often as I've been pleased with the results.

I mentioned "certain important restrictions" when you want to do pattern matching in a function declaration. Apart from the readability risk, the main restriction is that the DU you are using should be a single-case one, or the pattern you use should cover all the possibilities. Consider Listing 6-15, where I have extended the complex number example from Listing 6-14, so that we can have either a "real" number, which is just an everyday floating-point number, or the complex number we described earlier.

Listing 6-15. Pattern matching in function declaration, on a multi-case DU

```
type Number =
| Real of float
| Complex of Real:float * Imaginary:float

// Warning: Incomplete pattern matches on this expression.
let add (Complex(Real=a; Imaginary=b)) (Complex(Real=c; Imaginary=d)) =
    Complex(Real=(a+c), Imaginary=(b+d))
```

This immediately causes a compiler warning where the add function is declared, because the function only handles one of the two DU cases that could be sent to it. Never ignore this kind of warning: if the DU truly needs to have multiple cases, you will have to refactor any code that uses it, to handle all the cases. Failing to do so will undermine the whole edifice of type safety that using F# lets you construct.

You could extend the parameter binding to cover all the cases, as in Listing 6-16.

Listing 6-16. Handling a multi-case DU in a function parameter

```
let addReal (Complex(Real=a)|Real(a)) (Complex(Real=b)|Real(b)) =
  Real(a+b)
```

Leaving aside whether this is a mathematically valid operation, this really isn't terribly readable, and I struggle to think of a good reason to do it, except perhaps in rather specialized code.

Pattern Matching in Let Bindings

There's yet another place you can use DU pattern matching: directly in let bindings. If you have a complex number, stored as a single-case DU as in Listing 6-14, you can recover its components directly in a let binding (Listing 6-17).

Listing 6-17. Pattern matching in a let binding

```
type Complex =
| Complex of Real:float * Imaginary:float

let c1 = Complex(Real = 0.2, Imaginary = 3.4)

let (Complex(real, imaginary)) = c1

// 0.200000, 3.400000
printfn "%f, %f" real imaginary
```

You can also use the component labels if you want to, that is

```
let (Complex(Real=real; Imaginary=imaginary)) = c1
```

Note that when using labels like this, you must use a semicolon separator rather than a comma, as we saw earlier.

If you want an assign from a multi-case DU you can do so using the | character, providing you bind the same value in all cases and use _ to ignore "left over" values (Listing 6-18).

Listing 6-18. A let binding from a multi-case DU

```
let (Complex(real, _)| Real (real)) = c1
```

As I said in the previous section, the times where it is useful and advisable to do this are fairly rare.

Pattern matching in `let` bindings is a really useful trick... once you get used to it! But do bear in mind the readability implications based on the skill level of your collaborators. Don't do it just to look clever!

Pattern Matching in Loops and Lambdas

Sometimes you have a collection of tuples or records that you want to loop over, either explicitly using for-loops, or implicitly using Higher Order Functions such as `iter` and `map`. Pattern matching comes in useful here, because it lets you seamlessly transition from the collection items, to the items to be used in the body of the for-loop or lambda function (Listing 6-18).

Listing 6-19. Pattern matching in loops

```
let fruits =
    [ "Apples", 3
      "Oranges", 4
      "Bananas", 2 ]

// There are 3 Apples
// There are 4 Oranges
// There are 2 Bananas
for (name, count) in fruits do
    printfn "There are %i %s" count name

// There are 3 Apples
// There are 4 Oranges
// There are 2 Bananas
fruits
|> List.iter (fun (name, count) ->
    printfn "There are %i %s" count name)
```

In Listing 6-19 we make a list of tuples, then iterate over it in both a for-loop and a Higher Order Function style. In both cases, a pattern match in the form of (`name,` `count`) lets us recover the values from the tuple, for use in the body code.

You can also do this with Record Types, and there's an exercise showing that at the end of the chapter. And you can do it with Discriminated Unions, though normally only when they are single case.

Purely as a curiosity, Listing 6-20 shows an example of "cheating" by looping with a pattern match over a multi-case discriminated union. This code actually works (it will just iterate over the cases that are circles) but isn't great practice unless your aim is to annoy purists. You will get a compiler warning.

Listing 6-20. Pattern matching in loop over a multi-case DU (bad practice!)

```
type Shape =
| Circle of Radius:float
| Square of Length:float
| Rectangle of Length:float * Height:float
```

```
let shapes =
    [ Circle 3.
      Square 4.
      Rectangle(5., 6.)
      Circle 4. ]

// Circle of radius 3.000000
// Circle of radius 4.000000
for (Circle r) in shapes do
    printfn "Circle of radius %f" r
```

Pattern Matching and Enums

If you want a Discriminated Union to be treated more like a C# enum, you must assign each case a distinct value, where the value is one of a small set of simple types such as byte, int32, and char. Listing 6-21 shows how to combine this feature, together with the Sytem.Flags attribute, to make a simplistic model of the Unix file permissions structure.

Listing 6-21. Simple model of Unix file permissions

```
open System

[<Flags>]
type FileMode =
| None =    0uy
| Read =    4uy
| Write =   2uy
| Execute = 1uy

let canRead (fileMode : FileMode) =
    fileMode.HasFlag FileMode.Read

let modea = FileMode.Read
let modeb = FileMode.Write
let modec = modea ^^^ modeb

// True
canRead (modea)
```

```
// False
canRead (modeb)
// True
canRead (modec)
```

Here the DU `FileMode` can take one of four explicit values, each of which is associated with a bit pattern (000, 001, 010, and 100). We can use the `HasFlag` property (which is added for us because we used the `Flags` attribute) to check whether an instance has a particular bit set, regardless of the other bits. We can also bitwise-OR two instances together, using the `^^^` operator.

But beware! As soon as you make a DU into an enum, code can assign to it any value that is compatible with the underlying type, including one not supported by any specified case. For example:

```
open Microsoft.FSharp.Core.LanguagePrimitives

let naughtyMode =
    EnumOfValue<byte, FileMode> 255uy
```

For the same reason, enum pattern matching that doesn't contain a default case ('_') will always cause a compiler warning. The compiler knows, at the type level, that any value of the underlying type could be sent in, not just one covered by the specified DU cases (Listing 6-22).

Listing 6-22. Pattern matching on an enum DU without a default case

```
open System

[<Flags>]
type FileMode =
| None =     0uy
| Read =     4uy
| Write =    2uy
| Execute = 1uy
```

```
let describe (fileMode : FileMode) =
    let read =
        // Compiler warning: Incomplete pattern matches...
        match fileMode with
        | FileMode.None -> "cannot"
        | FileMode.Read -> "can"
        | FileMode.Write -> "cannot"
        | FileMode.Execute -> "cannot"

    printfn "You %s read the file"
```

Because it makes a hole in type safety, I always avoid using enum DU's except in very specific scenarios, typically those involving language interop.

Active Patterns

Pattern Matching and Discriminated Unions are exciting enough, but there's more! *Active Patterns* let you exploit the syntactical infrastructure that exists to support pattern matching, by building your own mapping between values and cases. Once again, because this is a reasonably advanced feature, I'm going to explain Active Patterns from the very beginning. Then we can discuss their stylistic implications.

Single Case Active Patterns

The simplest form of Active Pattern is the Single Case Active Pattern. You declare it by writing a case name between (| and |) (memorably termed *banana clips*), followed by a single parameter, then some code that maps from the parameter value to the case.

For instance, in Listing 6-23 we have an Active Pattern that takes a floating-point value and approximates it to a sensible value for a currency, which for simplicity we are assuming always has two decimal places.

Listing 6-23. A Single Case Active Pattern

```
open System

let (|Currency|) (x : float) =
    Math.Round(x, 2)

// true
match 100./3. with
| Currency 33.33 -> true
| _ -> false
```

With the `Currency` active pattern in place, we can pattern match on some floating-point value that has an arbitrary number of decimal places (such as 33.333333...), and compare it successfully with its approximated value (33.33).

The code is now nicely integrated with the semantics of Pattern Matching generally, especially as it regards recovering the matched value. Listing 6-24 shows us using `Currency` in the three contexts we have seen for other pattern matching: match expressions, let bindings, and function parameters.

Listing 6-24. Recovering decomposed values with Active Patterns

```
open System

let (|Currency|) (x : float) =
    Math.Round(x, 2)

// "That didn't match: 33.330000"
// false
match 100./3. with
| Currency 33.34 -> true
| Currency c ->
    printfn "That didn't match: %f" c
    false

// Cs: 33.330000
let (Currency c) = 1000./30.
printfn "Cs: %f" c
```

```
let add (Currency c1) (Currency c2) =
    c1 + c2

// 66.66
add (100./3.) (1000./30.)
```

Multi-Case Active Patterns

While Single Case Active Patterns map any value to a *single* case, Multi-Case Active Patterns map any value to one of *several* cases. Let's say you have a list of wind turbine model names (I got mine from the USGS wind turbine database here: `https://eerscmap.usgs.gov/uswtdb/`), and you want to divide these into ones made by Mitsubishi, ones made by Samsung, and ones made by some other manufacturer. (Since we are dealing with unconstrained string input data, it's wise to provide an "Other" case). Listing 6-25 shows how we might do this using a combination of regular expressions and Multi-Case Active Patterns.

Listing 6-25. Categorizing wind turbines using Multi-Case Active Patterns and Regex

```
open System.Text.RegularExpressions

let (|Mitsubishi|Samsung|Other|) (s : string) =
    let m = Regex.Match(s, @"([A-Z]{3})(\-?)(.*)")
    if m.Success then
        match m.Groups.[1].Value with
        | "MWT" -> Mitsubishi
        | "SWT" -> Samsung
        | _     -> Other
    else
        Other

// From https://eerscmap.usgs.gov/uswtdb/
let turbines = [
    "MWT1000"; "MWT1000A"; "MWT102/2.4"; "MWT57/1.0"
    "SWT1.3_62"; "SWT2.3_101"; "SWT2.3_93"; "SWT-2.3-101"
    "40/500" ]
```

```
// MWT1000 is a Mitsubishi turbine
// ...
// SWT1.3_62 is a Samsung turbine
// ...
// 40/500 is an unknown turbine
turbines
|> Seq.iter (fun t ->
    match t with
    | Mitsubishi -> printfn "%s is a Mitsubishi turbine" t
    | Samsung ->   printfn "%s is a Samsung turbine" t
    | Other ->     printfn "%s is an unknown turbine" t)
```

Listing 6-25 exploits the observation that all (and only) Mitsubishi turbines have model names starting with "MWT," and Samsung ones start with either "SWT" or "SWT-". We use a regular expression to pull out this prefix, then some string literal pattern matching to map onto one of our cases. It's important to note that the Active Pattern is defined using a `let` binding rather than a type declaration, even though the fact that it has a finite domain of cases makes it feel like a type.

Multi-Case Active Patterns have a serious limitation: the number of cases is capped at seven. Since I'm pretty sure there are more than seven wind turbine manufacturers, Multi-Case Active Patterns wouldn't be a great fit when trying to map every case in the real dataset. You'd have to be content with a more fluid data structure.

Partial Active Patterns

Partial Active Patterns divide the world into things that match by some condition and things that don't. If we just wanted to pick out the Mitsubishi turbines from the previous example, we could change the code to look like Listing 6-26.

Listing 6-26. Categorizing wind turbines using Partial Active Patterns

```
open System.Text.RegularExpressions

let (|Mitsubishi|_|) (s : string) =
    let m = Regex.Match(s, @"([A-Z]{3})(\-?)(.*)")
```

```
    if m.Success then
        match m.Groups.[1].Value with
        | "MWT" -> Some s
        | _      -> None
    else
        None

// From https://eerscmap.usgs.gov/uswtdb/
let turbines = [
    "MWT1000"; "MWT1000A"; "MWT102/2.4"; "MWT57/1.0"
    "SWT1.3_62"; "SWT2.3_101"; "SWT2.3_93"; "SWT-2.3-101"
    "40/500" ]

turbines
|> Seq.iter (fun t ->
    match t with
    | Mitsubishi m -> printfn "%s is a Mitsubishi turbine" m
    | _ as s ->       printfn "%s is not a Mitsubishi turbine" s)
```

Here we can pattern match on just two cases – `Mitsubishi` and 'not `Mitsubishi`', the latter represented by the default match '_'. Notice that in the non-matching case, although the Active Pattern doesn't return a value, you can recover the input value using the 'as' keyword and a label (here I used 'as s').

Parameterized Active Patterns

You can parameterize Active Patterns, simply by adding extra parameters before the final one. (The last parameter is reserved for the primary input of the Active Pattern.) Say, for example, you had to validate postal codes for various regions. US postal codes (zip codes) consist of five digits, while UK ones have a rather wacky format consisting of letters and numbers (e.g., "RG7 1DP"). Listing 6-27 uses an active pattern, parameterized using a regular expression to define a valid format for the region in question.

Listing 6-27. Using parameterized Active Patterns to validate postal codes

```
open System
open System.Text.RegularExpressions

let zipCodes = [ "90210"; "94043"; "10013"; "10013" ]
let postCodes = [ "SW1A 1AA"; "GU9 0RA"; "PO8 0AB"; "P 0AB" ]

let regexZip = @"^\d{5}$"
// Simplified: the official regex for UK postcodes is much longer!
let regexPostCode = @"^(\d|[A-Z]){2,4} (\d|[A-Z]){3}"

let (|PostalCode|) pattern s =
    let m = Regex.Match(s, pattern)
    if m.Success then
        Some s
    else
        None

// None
let (PostalCode regexZip z) = "WRONG"

// ["90210"; "94043"; "10013"]
let validZipCodes =
    zipCodes
    |> List.choose (fun (PostalCode regexZip p) -> p)

// ["SW1A 1AA"; "GU9 0RA"; "PO8 0AB"]
let validPostCodes =
    postCodes
    |> List.choose (fun (PostalCode regexPostCode p) -> p)
```

In Listing 6-27 I've had to simplify the regular expression used for UK postcodes as the real (government endorsed!) as one is too long to fit into book-listing form.

One important point to note about Listing 6-27 is that although the active pattern we have defined is a "Complete" one (declared using (|PostalCode|) rather than (|PostalCode|_)), it can still return Some or None as values.

Pattern Matching with '&'

Occasionally it's useful to be able to 'and' together items in a pattern match. Imagine, for example, your company is offering a marketing promotion that is only available to people living in 'outer London' (in the United Kingdom), as identified by their postcode. To be eligible, the user needs to provide a valid postcode, and that postcode must begin with one of a defined set of prefixes. Listing 6-28 shows one approach to coding this using active patterns.

Listing 6-28. Using & with Active Patterns

```
open System.Text.RegularExpressions

let (|PostCode|) s =
    let m = Regex.Match(s, @"^(\d|[A-Z]){2,4} (\d|[A-Z]){3}")
    if m.Success then
Some s
    else
        None

let outerLondon =
    ["BR";"CR";"DA";"EN";"HA";"IG";"KT";"RM";"SM";"TW";"UB";"WD"]

let (|OuterLondon|) (s : string) =
    outerLondon
    |> List.tryFind (s.StartsWith)

let promotionAvailable (postcode : string) =
    match postcode with
    | PostCode(Some p) & OuterLondon(Some o) ->
        printfn "We can offer the promotion in %s (%s)" p o
    | PostCode(Some p) & OuterLondon(None) ->
        printfn "We cannot offer the promotion in %s" p
    | _ ->
        printfn "Invalid postcode"
```

```
let demo() =
    // "We cannot offer the promotion in RG7 1DP"
    "RG7 1DP" |> promotionAvailable
    // "We can offer the promotion in RM3 5NA (RM)"
    "RM3 5NA" |> promotionAvailable
    // "Invalid postcode"
    "Hullo sky" |> promotionAvailable
```

In Listing 6-28 we have two active patterns, a `PostCode` one that validates UK postcodes, and an `OuterLondon` one that checks whether a postcode has one of the defined prefixes (and also returns which prefix matched). In the `promotionAvailable` function we use & to match on both `PostCode` and `OuterLondon` for the main switching logic.

Note   The symbol to 'and' together items in a pattern match is a single &, in contrast to && that is used for logical 'and' in, for example, `if` expressions.

Incidentally it might look as though `PostCode` and `OuterLondon` would each be called twice for each input string, but this is not the case. The code is more efficient than it appears at first glance.

Pattern Matching on Types

Occasionally even functional programmers have to deal with type hierarchies! Sometimes it's because we are interacting with external libraries like `System.Windows.Forms`, which make extensive use of inheritance. Sometimes it's because inheritance is genuinely the best way to model something, even in F#. Whatever the reason, this can place us in a position where we need to detect whether an instance is of a particular type, or is of a descendent of that type. You won't be surprised to learn that F# achieves this using pattern matching.

In Listing 6-29 we define a two-level hierarchy with a top-level type of `Person`, and one lower-level type `Child`, which inherits from `Person` and adds some extra functionality, in this case just the ability to print the parent's name. (For simplicity I'm assuming one parent per person.)

Listing 6-29. Pattern matching on type

```
type Person (name : string) =
    member __.Name = name

type Child(name, parent : Person) =
    inherit Person(name)
    member __.ParentName =
        parent.Name

let alice = Person("Alice")
let bob = Child("Bob", alice)

let people = [ alice; bob :> Person ]

// Person: Alice
// Child: Bob of parent Alice
people
|> List.iter (fun person ->
    match person with
    | :? Child as child ->
        printfn "Child: %s of parent %s" child.Name
        child.ParentName
    | _ as person ->
        printfn "Person: %s" person.Name)
```

With this little hierarchy in place, we define a list called `people`, and put both `alice` and `bob` into the list. Because collections require elements to all be the same type, we must shoehorn (*upcast*) `bob` back into a plain old `Person`. Then when we iterate over the list, we must use pattern matching to identify whether each element is 'really' a `Child`, using the `:?` operator, or is just a `Person`. I use a wildcard pattern '_' to cover the `Person` case, otherwise I will get a compiler warning. This is because the operation ':? `Person`' is redundant, since all the elements are of type `Person`.

Pattern matching on types is indispensable when dealing with type hierarchies in F#, and I use it unhesitatingly when hierarchies crop up.

Pattern Matching on Null

Remember back in Chapter 3 we used `Option.ofObj` and `Option.defaultValue` to process a nullable string parameter? Listing 6-30 shows an example of that approach.

Listing 6-30. Using Option.ofObj

```
let myApiFunction (stringParam : string) =
    let s =
        stringParam
        |> Option.ofObj
        |> Option.defaultValue "(none)"

    // You can do things here knowing that s isn't null
    sprintf "%s" (s.ToUpper())

// HELLO
myApiFunction "hello"

// (NONE)
myApiFunction null
```

Well there is an alternative, because you can pattern match on the literal `null`. Here's Listing 6-30, redone using null pattern matching (Listing 6-29).

Listing 6-31. Pattern matching on null

```
let myApiFunction (stringParam : string) =

    match stringParam with
    | null -> "(NONE)"
    | _ -> stringParam.ToUpper()

// HELLO
myApiFunction "hello"

// (NONE)
myApiFunction null
```

How do you choose between these alternatives? On stylistic grounds I prefer the original version (Listing 6-31) because – at least for code that is going to be maintained by people with strong F# skills – sticking everywhere to functions from the `Option` module feels more consistent. But there's no doubt that the new version (Listing 6-30) is slightly more concise, and more likely to be readable to maintainers who are earlier in their F# journey. You might also want to experiment with performance in your use case, since it looks as though the null-matching version creates no intermediate values, and may therefore allocate/de-allocate less memory. In performance-critical code, this could make quite a difference.

Recommendations

Get used to pattern matching almost everywhere in your code. To help you remember the breadth of its applicability, here's a table both to remind you of what pattern matching features are available, and to help you decide when to use them (Table 6-2).

***Table 6-2.** Pattern Matching Features and When to Use Them*

Feature	Example	Suggested Usage
match keyword	`match x with` `| Case payload -> code...`	Use widely. Consider `Option` module (e.g., `Option.map`) when dealing with option types.

Default case ('wildcard')	`match x with`
	`| Case payload -> code...`
	`| _ -> code ...`
		With caution. Could this cause you to ignore important cases added in the future?

when guards	`| x when x < 12 -> code...`	Use freely when applicable. Complicated schemes of when-guarding may indicate another approach is needed, for example, Active Patterns.

(continued)

Table 6-2. (*continued*)

Feature	Example	Suggested Usage

On arrays	```match arr with```
	```| [||] -> code...```
	```| [|x|] -> code...```
	```| [|x;y|] -> code...```
		With caution. The cases can never be exhaustive, so there will always be a wildcard (default) case. Would lists and the cons operator :: be a better fit?

On lists	```match l with```
	```| [] -> code...```
	```| acc::elem -> code...```
		Use freely when applicable. Indispensable in recursive list-processing code.

In let bindings on tuples	```let a, b =``` ```GetNameVersion(...)```	Use widely.

On records	```match song with```
	```| { Title = title } ->```
	```code...```
		Use freely when collaborators are reasonably skilled in F#.

On Discriminated Unions with match keyword.	```match shape with``` ```| Circle r -> code...```	Use widely.

On DUs using payload item labels.	```match reading with```
	```| Economy7(Day=day;```
	```Night=night) -> code...```
		Use where it improves readability or avoids mixing elements up.

On records in parameter declarations	```let formatMenuItem ({ Title```
	```= title; Artist = artist })```
	```= code...```
		With caution. May be confusing if collaborators are not highly skilled.

On Single-Case Discriminated unions in parameter declarations	```let add```
	```(Complex(Real=a;Imaginary=b))```
	```(Complex(Real=c;Imaginary=d))```
	```= code...```
		With caution. May be confusing if collaborators are not highly skilled. Need to be sure the DU will remain single-case or at worst that all cases are handled. Very useful in specialized situations.

(*continued*)

Table 6-2. (*continued*)

Feature	Example	Suggested Usage
In let bindings on Discriminated Unions	`let (Complex(real, imaginary)) = c1`	With caution. May be confusing if collaborators are not highly skilled.
In Loops and Lambdas	`for (name, count) in fruits do code...`	Use freely when applicable, especially on tuples.

On Enums	`match fileMode with`
	`| FileMode.Read -> "can"`
	`| FileMode.Write -> "cannot"`
	`| ...`
		With caution. The matching can never be exhaustive unless there is a wildcard case, so new cases added later can cause bugs.

Active Patterns	`let (|PostalCode|) pattern s = code...`	Use where applicable and collaborators are reasonably skilled in F#. Beware of the limitation of 7 cases.
On Types	`match person with` `| :? Child as child -> code...`	Use freely where forced to deal with OO inheritance.
On Null	`match stringParam with` `| null -> code...`	Use freely, but also consider mapping to an option type and using, for example, `Option.map` and `Option.bind`.

Summary

If you aren't pattern matching heavily, you aren't writing good F# code. Remember that you can pattern match explicitly using the `match` keyword, but you can also pattern match in `let` bindings, loops, lambdas, and function declarations. Active Patterns add a whole new layer of power, letting you map from somewhat open-ended data like strings or floating-point values, to much more strongly-typed classifications.

But pattern matching can be overdone, leading to code that is unreadable to collaborators who may not have the very highest skill level. Doing this violates the principle of *motivational transparency*.

In the next chapter, we'll look more closely at F#'s primary mechanism for storing groups of labeled values: *record types*.

Exercises

EXERCISE 6-1 – PATTERN MATCHING ON RECORDS WITH DUS

Exercise: Let's say you want to amend the code from Listing 6-12 so that a meter reading can have a date. This is the structure you might come up with:

```
type MeterValue =
| Standard of int
| Economy7 of Day:int * Night:int

type MeterReading =
    { ReadingDate : DateTime
      MeterValue : MeterValue }
```

How would you amend the body of the formatReading function so that it formats your new MeterReading type in the following form?

```
"Your readings on: 24/02/2019: Day: 0003432 Night: 0098218"
"Your reading on: 23/03/2019 was 0012982"
```

You can use DateTime.ToShortDateString() to format the date.

EXERCISE 6-2 – RECORD PATTERN MATCHING AND LOOPS

Exercise: Start with this code from Listing 6-19:

```
let fruits =
    [ "Apples", 3
      "Oranges", 4
      "Bananas", 2 ]
```

```
// There are 3 Apples
// There are 4 Oranges
// There are 2 Bananas
for (name, count) in fruits do
    printfn "There are %i %s" count name

// There are 3 Apples
// There are 4 Oranges
// There are 2 Bananas
fruits
|> List.iter (fun (name, count) ->
    printfn "There are %i %s" count name)
```

Add a record type called `FruitBatch` to the code, using field names `Name` and `Count`. How can you alter the `fruits` binding to create a list of `FruitBatch` instances, and the `for` loop and `iter` lamba so that they have the same output as they did before you added the record type?

EXERCISE 6-3 – ZIP+4 CODES AND PARTIAL ACTIVE PATTERNS

Exercise: In the United States, postal codes can take the form of simple 5-digit Zip codes, or 'Zip+4' codes, which have five digits, a hyphen, then four more digits. Here is some code that defines active patterns to identify Zip and Zip+4 codes, but with the body of the Zip+4 pattern omitted. The exercise is to add the body.

```
open System
open System.Text.RegularExpressions

let zipCodes = [
    "90210"
    "94043"
    "94043-0138"
    "10013"
    "90210-3124"
    "10013" ]
```

```
let (|USZipCode|_|) s =
    let m = Regex.Match(s, @"^(\d{5})$")
    if m.Success then
        USZipCode s |> Some
    else
        None

let (|USZipPlus4Code|_|) s =
    raise <| NotImplementedException()

zipCodes
|> List.iter (fun z ->
    match z with
    | USZipCode c ->
        printfn "A normal zip code: %s" c
    | USZipPlus4Code(code, suffix) ->
        printfn "A Zip+4 code: prefix %s, suffix %s" code suffix
    | _ as n ->
        printfn "Not a zip code: %s" n)
```

Hint: a regular expression to match Zip+4 codes is "`^(\d{5})\-(\d{4})$`". When this
expression matches, you can use `m.Groups.[1].Value` and `m.Groups.[2].Value` to
pick out the prefix and suffix digits.

Exercise Solutions

This section shows solutions for the exercises in this chapter.

EXERCISE 6-1 – PATTERN MATCHING ON RECORDS WITH DUS

I tackled this exercise in two passes. In the first pass, I pattern matched on the whole
`MeterReading` structure, using a combination of record pattern matching and DU pattern
matching to pull out the date and reading or readings:

```
open System

type MeterValue =
| Standard of int
| Economy7 of Day:int * Night:int
```

```
type MeterReading =
    { ReadingDate : DateTime
        MeterValue : MeterValue }

let formatReading (reading : MeterReading) =
    match reading with
    | { ReadingDate = readingDate
        MeterValue = Standard reading } ->
        sprintf "Your reading on: %s was %07i"
            (readingDate.ToShortDateString()) reading
    | { ReadingDate = readingDate
        MeterValue = Economy7(Day=day; Night=night) } ->
        sprintf "Your readings on: %s were Day: %07i Night: %07i"
            (readingDate.ToShortDateString()) day night

let reading1 = { ReadingDate = DateTime(2019, 3, 23)
                    MeterValue = Standard 12982 }

let reading2 = { ReadingDate = DateTime(2019, 2, 24)
                    MeterValue = Economy7(Day=3432, Night=98218) }

reading1 |> formatReading
reading2 |> formatReading
```

The salient lines are these:

```
    | { ReadingDate = readingDate
        MeterValue = Standard reading }
...
    | { ReadingDate = readingDate
        MeterValue = Economy7(Day=day; Night=night) }
```

Note how the curly braces {...} indicate that we are pattern matching on records, but within this we also have <DUCase>(Label=value) syntax to decompose the DU field of the record.

This worked, but I wasn't happy with it, because of the repetition of the reading date pattern match, and of the date formatting ((readingDate.ToShortDateString())).

In a second pass I eliminated the repetition. I used pattern matching in the parameter declaration to pick out the date and value fields. I also created a formatted date string in one place rather than two.

```
let formatReading { ReadingDate = date; MeterValue = meterValue }  =
    let dateString = date.ToShortDateString()
    match meterValue with
    | Standard reading ->
        sprintf "Your reading on: %s was %07i"
            dateString reading
    | Economy7(Day=day; Night=night) ->
        sprintf "Your readings on: %s were Day: %07i Night: %07i"
            dateString day night
```

EXERCISE 6-2 – RECORD PATTERN MATCHING AND LOOPS

In the fruits binding, you just need to use standard record-construction syntax:

```
type FruitBatch = {
    Name : string
    Count : int }

let fruits =
    [ { Name="Apples"; Count=3 }
      { Name="Oranges"; Count=4 }
      { Name="Bananas"; Count=2 } ]
```

In the for loop and List.iter lambda, you can use record pattern matching in the form { FieldName1=label1; FieldName2=label2...} to recover the name and count values.

```
// There are 3 Apples
// There are 4 Oranges
// There are 2 Bananas
for { Name=name; Count=count } in fruits do
    printfn "There are %i %s" count name

// There are 3 Apples
// There are 4 Oranges
// There are 2 Bananas
fruits
|> List.iter (fun { Name=name; Count=count } ->
    printfn "There are %i %s" count name)
```

EXERCISE 6-3 – ZIP+4 CODES AND PARTIAL ACTIVE PATTERNS

The body of the Zip+4 active pattern should look something like this:

```
let (|USZipPlus4Code|_|) s =
    let m = Regex.Match(s, @"^(\d{5})\-(\d{4})$")
    if m.Success then
        USZipPlus4Code(m.Groups.[1].Value,
                        m.Groups.[2].Value)
        |> Some
    else
        None
```

See how when the regular expression matches, we return a USZipPlus4Code case whose payload is a tuple of the two matching groups.

CHAPTER 7

Record Types

Proper storage is about creating a home for something so that minimal effort is required to find it and put it away.

—Geralin Thomas, Organizing Consultant

Winning with Records

Record types are a simple way of recording small groups of values. You define a set of names and corresponding types, then you can create, compare, and amend instances of these groupings with some extremely simple syntax. But behind this simplicity lies some powerful and well-thought-out functionality. Learn to wield record types effectively and you'll be well on the way to becoming an expert F# developer. It's also worth knowing when *not* to use record types, and what the alternatives are in these circumstances.

Record Type Basics

Declaring and instantiating a record type could hardly be easier. You define the names (field labels) of the items you want the record to contain, together with their types, all in curly braces (Listing 7-1).

Listing 7-1. Declaring a record type

```
open System

type FileDescription = {
    Path : string
    Name : string
    LastModified : DateTime }
```

© Kit Eason 2018
K. Eason, *Stylish F#*, https://doi.org/10.1007/978-1-4842-4000-7_7

Then you create instances simply by binding values to each name, again in curly braces (Listing 7-2).

Listing 7-2. Instantiating record type instances

```
open System.IO

let fileSystemInfo (rootPath : string) =
    Directory.EnumerateFiles(rootPath, "*.*",
                             SearchOption.AllDirectories)
    |> Seq.map (fun path ->
        { Path = path |> Path.GetDirectoryName
          Name = path |> Path.GetFileName
          LastModified = (FileInfo(path)).LastWriteTime })
```

Note that at instantiation time, you don't have to mention the name of the record type itself, just its fields. The exception to this is when two record types have field names in common, in which case you may have to prefix the first field name in the binding with the name record type you want, for example, `{ FileDescription.Path = ...`.

You can access the fields of record type instances using dot-name notation, exactly as if they were C# class members (Listing 7-3).

Listing 7-3. Accessing record type fields using dot notation

```
// Name: ad.png Path: c:\temp Last modified: 15/08/2017 22:07:34
// Name: capture-1.avi Path: c:\temp Last modified: 27/02/2017 22:04:31
// ...
fileSystemInfo @"c:\temp"
|> Seq.iter (fun info -> // info is a FileDescription instance
    printfn "Name: %s Path: %s Last modified: %A"
        info.Name info.Path info.LastModified)
```

Record Types and Immutability

Like most things in F#, record types are immutable by default. You can in principle bind the whole record instance as mutable using `let mutable` (Listing 7-4), but this means that the entire record instance can be replaced with a new and different record using the `<-` operator. It does not make the individual fields mutable. In practice, I can't remember ever declaring an entire record to be mutable.

Listing 7-4. Declaring a record instance as mutable

```
type MyRecord = {
    String : string
    Int : int }

let mutable myRecord =
    { String = "Hullo clouds"
      Int = 99 }

// {String = "Hullo clouds";
//   Int = 99;}
printfn "%A" myRecord

myRecord <-
    { String = "Hullo sky"
      Int = 100 }

// {String = "Hullo sky";
//   Int = 100;}
printfn "%A" myRecord
```

What about making the *fields* of the record mutable? This is certainly possible (Listing 7-5), and having done this you can assign into fields using <-. This isn't quite as unheard of as declaring whole records mutable, but it's still rare. I guess there might be performance-related cases where this might be desirable, but again I can't recall doing it myself.

Listing 7-5. Declaring record fields as mutable

```
type MyRecord = {
    mutable String : string
    mutable Int : int }

let myRecord =
    { String = "Hullo clouds"
      Int = 99 }

// {String = "Hullo clouds";
//   Int = 99;}
printfn "%A" myRecord
```

```
myRecord.String <- "Hullo sky"

// {String = "Hullo sky";
//   Int = 99;}
printfn "%A" myRecord
```

By far the most common and idiomatic way of "amending" record types is using the not-very-snappily-named *copy-and-update record expression* (Listing 7-6).

Listing 7-6. "Amending" a record using copy and update

```
type MyRecord = {
    String : string
    Int : int }

let myRecord =
    { String = "Hullo clouds"
      Int = 99 }

// {String = "Hullo clouds";
//   Int = 99;}
printfn "%A" myRecord

let myRecord2 =
    { myRecord with String = "Hullo sky" }

// {String = "Hullo sky";
//   Int = 99;}
printfn "%A" myRecord2
```

In a copy-and-update operation, all the fields of the new record are given the values from the original record, except those given new values in the with clause. Needless to say, the original record is unaffected. This is the idiomatic way to handle "changes" to record type instances.

Default Constructors, Setters, and Getters

One downside to immutability by default: you may occasionally have problems with external code (particularly serialization and database code) failing to instantiate record types correctly, or throwing compilation errors about default constructors. In these cases, simply add the [<CLIMutable>] attribute to the record declaration. This causes the record to be compiled with a default constructor and getters and setters, which the external framework should find easier to cope with.

Records versus Classes

Records offer a nice, concise syntax for grouping values, but surely they aren't *that* different from the conventional "object" of object orientation (which are known in F# as *class types* or just *classes*). After all, if we make a class-based version of Listings 7-1 and 7-2, the code doesn't look all that different, and seems to behave exactly the same (Listing 7-7).

Listing 7-7. F# Object Oriented class types versus records

```
open System

type FileDescriptionOO(path:string, name:string, lastModified:DateTime) =
    member __.Path = path
    member __.Name = name
    member __.LastModified = lastModified

open System.IO

let fileSystemInfoOO (rootPath : string) =
    Directory.EnumerateFiles(rootPath, "*.*",
                             SearchOption.AllDirectories)
    |> Seq.map (fun path ->
        FileDescriptionOO(path |> Path.GetDirectoryName,
                          path |> Path.GetFileName,
                          (FileInfo(path)).LastWriteTime))
```

We'll look properly at classes in Chapter 8, but it's fairly easy to see what is going on here. The class we make is even immutable. So do we really need to bother with record types? In the next few sections I'll discuss some of the advantages (and a few disadvantages!) of using record types.

Structural Equality by Default

Consider the following attempt to represent a position on the Earth's surface, using latitude and longitude (Listing 7-8).

Listing 7-8. Representing latitude and longitude using a class

```
type LatLon(latitude : float, longitude : float) =
    member __.Latitude = latitude
    member __.Longitude = longitude
```

You might think that if two positions have the same latitude and longitude values, they would be considered equal. But they are not![1] (Listing 7-9).

Listing 7-9. Some types are less equal than others!

```
let waterloo = LatLon(51.5031, -0.1132)
let victoria = LatLon(51.4952, -0.1441)
let waterloo2 = LatLon(51.5031, -0.1132)

// false
printfn "%A" (waterloo = victoria)
// true
printfn "%A" (waterloo = waterloo)
// false!
printfn "%A" (waterloo = waterloo2)
```

This is because classes in both F# and C# have what is called *reference* - or *referential equality* by default, which means that to be considered equal, two values need to represent the same physical object in memory. Sometimes, as in the LatLon example, this is very much not what you want.

The conventional way around this in C# (and you can do the same for classes in F#) is to write custom code that decides whether two instances are equal in some meaningful sense. The trouble is, in practice this is quite a palaver, requiring you to override Object.Equals, implement System.IEquatable, override Object.GetHashCode, and (admittedly optionally) override the equality and inequality operators. Who has time for all that? (I will show how to do it in Chapter 8, just in case you *do* have time!)

---

[1] In this example I'm ignoring the perils of comparing floating point values (which even if they are different by a tiny amount are still different) for exact equality.

Record types, by contrast, have what is called *structural equality*. (I think that's a terrible name, so I always mentally translate this to *content equality*.) With structural equality, two items are considered equal if all their fields are equal. Listing 7-10 shows the LatLon issue being solved simply by using a record instead of a class.

Listing 7-10. Default structural (content) equality with record types

```
type LatLon = {
    Latitude : float
    Longitude : float }

let waterloo = { Latitude = 51.5031; Longitude = -0.1132 }
let victoria = { Latitude = 51.4952; Longitude = -0.1441 }
let waterloo2 = { Latitude = 51.5031; Longitude = -0.1132 }

// false
printfn "%A" (waterloo = victoria)
// true
printfn "%A" (waterloo = waterloo)
// true
printfn "%A" (waterloo = waterloo2)
```

You can mess things up again, though, if one of the fields of your record is itself of a type that implements referential equality. This is because, under those circumstances, the records' fields aren't all equal by their own types' definitions of "equal" - so the records won't be considered equal. Listing 7-11 shows an example of this happening.

Listing 7-11. Do all the fields of your record implement the right equality?

```
type Surveyor(name : string) =
    member __.Name = name

type LatLon = {
    Latitude : float
    Longitude : float
    SurveyedBy : Surveyor }

let waterloo =
    { Latitude = 51.5031
```

```
            Longitude = -0.1132
            SurveyedBy = Surveyor("Kit") }

    let waterloo2 =
        { Latitude = 51.5031
            Longitude = -0.1132
            SurveyedBy = Surveyor("Kit") }

    // true
    printfn "%A" (waterloo = waterloo)
    // false
    printfn "%A" (waterloo = waterloo2)
```

Because they use different instances of the Surveyor class, the instances waterloo and waterloo2 aren't considered equal, even though from a content point of view the surveyors have the same name. If we had created one Surveyor instance in advance, and used that same instance when creating each of the LatLon instances, waterloo and waterloo2 would have been equal again! The general solution to this would be either to use a record for the Surveyor type, or to ensure that the Surveyor class implements structural (content) equality. Although worth bearing in mind, this issue rarely comes up in practice.

Another edge case is when you actually *want* records to have referential equality. That's easy: add the [<ReferenceEquality>] attribute (Listing 7-12).

Listing 7-12. Forcing reference equality for record types

```
    [<ReferenceEquality>]
    type LatLon = {
        Latitude : float
        Longitude : float }

    let waterloo = { Latitude = 51.5031; Longitude = -0.1132 }
    let waterloo2 = { Latitude = 51.5031; Longitude = -0.1132 }

    // true
    printfn "%A" (waterloo = waterloo)
    // false
    printfn "%A" (waterloo = waterloo2)
```

Once again, I can't ever recall having to use the `ReferenceEquality` attribute in real code. If you do use it, remember you won't be able to sort instances using default sorting, because the attribute disables greater than/less than comparison. While we are on the subject, you can also add the `NoEquality` attribute to disable "equals" and "greater/less than" operations on a record type; or you can even disable "greater/less than" operations while *allowing* "equals" operations using the `NoComparison` attribute. I have seen the `NoEquality` attribute used precisely once in real code. Stylistically, I would say that – given what records are for – use of `ReferenceEquality`, `NoEquality,` and `NoComparison` attributes in general "line of business" code is probably a code smell, though they no doubt have their place in highly technical realms.

Be aware that the `ReferenceEquality`, `NoEquality`, and `NoComparison` attributes are all F# specific. Other languages are under no obligation to respect them (and probably won't).

Records as Structs

Another possible reason to favor records is that, subject to certain restrictions, they can easily be marked as *structs*. This affects the way they are stored. To quote the official documentation:

> *Structures are value types, which means that they are stored directly on the stack or, when they are used as fields or array elements, inline in the parent type.*

You make a record a struct simply by adding the [`<Struct>`] attribute. As Listing 7-13 shows, this can have a substantial effect on performance. (Timings performed in F# Interactive.)

Listing 7-13. Marking a record type as a Struct

```
type LatLon = {
    Latitude : float
    Longitude : float }

[<Struct>]
type LatLonStruct = {
    Latitude : float
    Longitude : float }

#time "on"
```

```
// Real: 00:00:00.159, CPU: 00:00:00.156, GC gen0: 5, gen1: 3, gen2: 1
let llMany =
    Array.init 1_000_000 (fun x ->
        { LatLon.Latitude = float x
          LatLon.Longitude = float x } )

// Real: 00:00:00.046, CPU: 00:00:00.046, GC gen0: 0, gen1: 0, gen2: 0
let llsMany =
    Array.init 1_000_000 (fun x ->
        { LatLonStruct.Latitude = float x
          LatLonStruct.Longitude = float x } )

#time "off"
```

Scenarios vary widely in regard to creating, accessing, copying. and releasing instances, so you should experiment diligently in your use case, rather than blindly assuming that using the Struct attribute will solve any performance woes.

There is one significant implication of using struct records: if you want any field of the record type to be mutable, you must declare the whole instance as mutable too, as in Listing 7-14.

Listing 7-14. Struct Records must be mutable instances to mutate fields

```
[<Struct>]
type LatLonStruct = {
    mutable Latitude : float
    mutable Longitude : float }

let waterloo = { Latitude = 51.5031; Longitude = -0.1132 }

// Error: a value must be mutable in order to mutate the contents.
waterloo.Latitude <- 51.5032

let mutable waterloo2 = { Latitude = 51.5031; Longitude = -0.1132 }
waterloo2.Latitude <- 51.5032
```

You also can't declare struct records as being mutually referential, but this is such an obscure use case, I'm not even going to offer a code sample for it.

Mapping from Instantiation Values to Members

The final, and for me. clinching advantages of records over classes is the direct and complete mapping *from* what you provide when creating instances *to* what you get back when consuming instances. If you create a `LatLon` record instance by providing a latitude and longitude, then you automatically know the following facts when you later consume the instance:

- You can get all the values back that you originally provided, and in their original form.

- You can't get anything else back other than what you provided (unless you define members on the record type, which is possible but rare).

- You can't create an instance without providing *all* the necessary values.

- Nothing can change the values you originally provided – unless you declare fields as mutable, which generally is unwise.

These may seem like small points, but they contribute greatly to the *motivational transparency* and *semantic focus* of your code. As an example, consider the third point: *You can't create an instance without providing all the necessary values.* Contrast that with the coding pattern that any experienced OO developer has seen, where you need to both construct an object instance *and* set some properties in order for the object to become usable. (Any place you use object-initializer syntax to get to a usable state is an example.) Sometimes the create-and-amend approach is unavoidable, but F# ushers you politely away from that route, like a discreet waiter subtly discouraging you from making an unwise menu choice.

The fact that, in order to create a record, you have to provide values for all its fields has an interesting consequence: if you add a field, you'll have to make code changes everywhere that record is instantiated. This is true even if you make the field an option type – there is no concept in record instantiation of default values for fields, even ones that are option types. At first this can seem annoying, but it is actually a very good thing. All sorts of subtle bugs can creep in if it's possible to add a property to a type without making an explicit decision about what that property should contain, everywhere the type is used. Those compiler errors are telling you something!

167

Records Everywhere?

If the case for record types is so compelling, why don't we use them everywhere? Why does F# even bother to offer OO-style class types? Are these just a sop to C# programmers, to be avoided by the cool kids?

The answer is "no"; class types definitely have a place in F# code. I'll go into detail on class types in Chapter 8, but just to balance all the positive things I've said about record types, Table 7-1 shows the reasons why you might *not* want to use them, together with some suggestions for alternatives.

Table 7-1. *When to Consider Not Using Record Types*

Scenario	Consider instead
External and internal representations of data need to differ.	Class types.
Need to participate in an inheritance hierarchy – either to inherit from or be inherited from in a traditional OO sense.	Class types.
Need to represent a standard set of functions, with several realizations that share function names and signatures, but have different implementations.	F# interfaces and/or abstract types, inherited from by class types.

The last of these points bears a little elaboration. From time to time I have come across codebases where records of functions have been used as a supposedly more functional alternative to interfaces. In principle this does have a few advantages:

- Unlike code that uses interfaces, you don't have to upcast to the interface type whenever you want to use the interface. (I give a few more details of this in Chapter 8.)

- It can make it easier to use partial application when using the "pretend interface."

- It's sometimes claimed to be more concise.

The MSDN F# Style Guide comes out firmly *against* records-as-interfaces, and, having worked with a substantial codebase where records were used in this way, so do I! To quote the guide:

> *Use interface types to represent a set of operations. This is preferred to other options, such as tuples of functions or records of functions… Interfaces are first-class concepts in .NET.…*

In my experience, use of records-as-interfaces leads to unfriendly, incomprehensible code. When editing, one rapidly gets into the situation where *everything* has to compile before *anything* will compile. In concrete terms, your screen fills with red squiggly lines, and it's very hard to work out what to do about it! With true interfaces, by contrast, the errors resulting from incomplete or slightly incorrect code are more contained, and it's much easier to work out if an error results, for example, from a wrongly implemented method, or from a completely missing one. Interfaces play more nicely with Intellisense as well. As for the supposed advantage of partial application – well, I'd much rather maintainers (including my future self) have some idea of what is going on, than save a few characters by not repeating a couple of function parameters.

I'm not saying, by the way, that records shouldn't *implement* interfaces, which they can do in exactly the same way as I show with classes in Chapter 8. If you find that useful, it's fine.

Pushing Records to the Limit

Now you're familiar with how and when to use basic record types, it's time to look at some of the more exotic features and usages that are available. Don't take this section as encouragement to use the all the techniques it describes. Some (not all) of these tricks really are rarities, and when it's truly necessary to use them, you'll know.

Generic Records

Records can be generic – that is you can specify the type (or types) of the fields, as a kind of meta-property of the record type. The meta-property is called a *type parameter*. Listing 7-15 shows a `LatLon` record that could use any type for its `Latitude` and `Longitude` fields.

Listing 7-15. A generic record type

```
type LatLon<'T> = {
    mutable Latitude : 'T
    mutable Longitude : 'T }

// LatLon<float>
let waterloo = { Latitude = 51.5031; Longitude = -0.1132 }

// LatLon<float32>
let waterloo2 = { Latitude = 51.5031f; Longitude = -0.1132f }

// Error: Type Mismatch...
printfn "%A" (waterloo = waterloo2)
```

Note that we don't have to specify the type to use at construction time. The simple fact that we say { Latitude = 51.5031f... versus { Latitude = 51.5031... (note the 'f', which specifies a single-precision constant) is enough for the compiler to create a record that has single-precision instead of double-precision fields. Also notice that, since waterloo and waterloo2 are different types, we can't directly compare them using the equals operator.

What if you don't want to leave type inference to work out the type of the generic parameter? (Very occasionally type inference can even find it impossible to work this out.) Clearly in this case we can't use the trick of prefixing the first field binding with the record type name to disambiguate, as the name will be the same in each case. Instead – as in any let binding – you can specify the type of the bound value, in this case LatLon<float> or LatLon<float32> (Listing 7-16).

Listing 7-16. Pinning down the generic parameter type of a record type

```
type LatLon<'T> = {
    mutable Latitude : 'T
    mutable Longitude : 'T }

// LatLon<float>
let waterloo : LatLon<float> = {
    Latitude = 51.5031
    Longitude = -0.1132 }
```

```
// Error: The expression was expected to have type 'float32'
// but here has type 'float'.
let waterloo2 : LatLon<float32> = {
    Latitude = 51.5031f
    Longitude = -0.1132 }
```

In this case, as shown in the final lines of Listing 7-16, it's an error to try and bind a field using a value of a different type (note the missing 'f' in the Longitude binding).

Recursive Records

Record types can also be *recursive* – that is, the type can have a field that is its own type. Not easy to put into words, so jump straight to Listing 7-17, where we define a type to represent some imaginary user interface.

Listing 7-17. A recursive Record Type

```
type Point = { X : float32; Y : float32 }

type UiControl = {
    Name : string
    Position : Point
    Parent : UiControl option }

let form = {
    Name = "MyForm"
    Position = { X = 0.f; Y = 0.f }
    Parent = None }

let button = {
    Name = "MyButton"
    Position = { X = 10.f; Y = 20.f }
    Parent = Some form }
```

Each UiControl instance can have a parent that is itself a UiControl instance. It's important that the recursive field (in this case Parent) is an option type. Otherwise we are implying either that the hierarchy goes upward infinitely (making it impossible to instantiate), or that it is circular.

Oddly enough, it *is* possible to instantiate circular hierarchies, using `let rec` and `and` (Listing 7-18). I present this mainly as a curiosity – if you need to do it in practice, either you are doing something very specialized, or something has gone terribly wrong in your domain modeling!

Listing 7-18. Instantiating a circular set of recursive records

```
// You probably don't want to do this!

type Point = { X : float32; Y : float32 }

type UiControl = {
    Name : string
    Position : Point
    Parent : UiControl }

let rec form = {
    Name = "MyForm"
    Position =  { X = 0.f; Y = 0.f }
    Parent = button }
and button = {
    Name = "MyButton"
    Position =  { X = 10.f; Y = 20.f }
    Parent = form }
```

Records with Methods

Anyone with an Object Oriented programming background will be wondering whether it's possible for records to have methods. And the answer is… yes, but it may not always be a great idea.

Instance Methods

Listing 7-19 shows us adding a `Distance` instance method to our familiar `LatLon` record, then calling it exactly as one would a class method.

Listing 7-19. Adding an instance method to a Record Type

```
type LatLon = {
    Latitude : float
    Longitude : float }
with
    // Naive, straight-line distance
    member this.DistanceFrom(other : LatLon) =
        let milesPerDegree = 69.
        ((other.Latitude - this.Latitude) ** 2.)
        +
        ((other.Longitude - this.Longitude) ** 2.)
        |> sqrt
        |> (*) milesPerDegree

let coleman = {
    Latitude = 31.82
    Longitude = -99.42 }

let abilene = {
    Latitude = 32.45
    Longitude = -99.75 }

// Are we going to Abilene? Because it's 49 miles!
printfn "Are we going to Abilene? Because it's %0.0f miles!"
    (abilene.DistanceFrom(coleman))
```

Note that the distance calculation I do here is extremely naïve. In reality, you'd want to use the *haversine formula*, but that's rather too much code for a book listing.

Instance methods like this work fine with record types, and are quite a nice solution where you want structural (content) equality for instances, and also to have instance methods to give you fluent syntax like `abilene.DistanceFrom(coleman)`.

Static Methods

You can also add static methods. If you do this, it's probably because you want to construct a record instance using something other than standard record construction syntax. For example, Listing 7-20 adds a `TryFromString` method to `LatLon`, which tries to parse a comma-separated string into two elements, and then tries to parse these as floating-point numbers, before finally constructing a record instance in the usual curly-bracket way.

Listing 7-20. Adding a static method to a Record Type

```
open System

type LatLon = {
    Latitude : float
    Longitude : float }
    with
        static member TryFromString(s : string) =
            match s.Split([|','|]) with
            | [|lats; lons|] ->
                match (Double.TryParse(lats),
                       Double.TryParse(lons)) with
                | (true, lat), (true, lon) ->
                    { Latitude = lat
                      Longitude = lon } |> Some
                | _ -> None
            | _ -> None

// Some {Latitude = 50.514444;
//        Longitude = -2.457222;}
let somewhere = LatLon.TryFromString "50.514444, -2.457222"

// None
let nowhere = LatLon.TryFromString "hullo trees"
```

This is quite a nice way of effectively adding constructors to record types. It might be especially useful it you want to perform validation during construction.

Method Overrides

Sometimes you want to change one of the (very few) methods that a record type has by default. The most common one to override is ToString(), which you can use to produce a nice printable representation of the record (Listing 7-21).

Listing 7-21. Overriding a method on a Record

```
type LatLon = {
    Latitude : float
    Longitude : float }
    with
        override this.ToString() =
            sprintf "%f, %f" this.Latitude this.Longitude

// 51.972300, 1.149700
{ Latitude = 51.9723
  Longitude = 1.1497 }
|> printfn "%O"
```

In Listing 7-21 I've used the "%O" format specifier, which causes the input's ToString() method to be called.

Records with Methods – A Good Idea?

I don't think there is anything inherently wrong with adding methods to record types. You should just beware of crossing the line into territory where it would be better to use a class type. If you are using record methods to cover up the fact that the internal and external representations of some data do in fact need to be different, you've probably crossed the line!

There is an alternative way of associating behavior (functions or methods) with types (sets of data): group them in F# *modules*. We looked at this back in Chapter 2, for example, in Listing 2-9, where we placed a MilesYards type, for representing British railroad distances, in a MilesYards module. The module also contained functions to work with the type. In my opinion, the modules approach is generally better than gluing the functions to the record in the form of methods.

Record Layout

I cover spacing and layout in general in Chapter 13, but there are few code formatting points that are specific to record types.

- Use Pascal case for both record type names, and for the individual field labels. All the listings in this chapter follow that approach.

- Where a record type definition or instantiation doesn't fit comfortably into a single line, break it into multiple lines, left-aligning the field labels. If you put fields on separate lines, omit the separating semicolons. Don't mix single and multiline styles. (Listing 7-22.)

- Use the field names in the same order in the record type definition as in any instantiations and with... operations.

Listing 7-22. Good and bad Record Type layout

```
// Declaration:
// Good
type LatLon1 = { Lat : float; Lon : float }

// Good
type LatLon2 =
    { Latitude : float
      Longitude : float }

// Good
type LatLon3 = {
    Latitude : float
    Longitude : float }

// Bad - needless semi-colons
type LatLon4 = {
    Latitude : float;
    Longitude : float }

// Bad - mixed newline style
type Position = { Lat : float; Lon : float
                  Altitude : float }

// Instantiation:
// Good
let ll1 = { Lat = 51.9723; Lon = 1.1497 }
```

```
// Good
let ll2 =
    { Latitude = 51.9723
      Longitude = 1.1497 }

// Bad - needless semi-colons
let ll3 =
    { Latitude = 51.9723;
      Longitude = 1.1497 }

// Bad - mixed newline style
let position = { Lat = 51.9723; Lon = 1.1497
                    Altitude = 22.3 }
```

Recommendations

Here are my suggestions to help you make great code with record types:

- Prefer records to class types unless you need the internal and external representations of data to differ, or the type needs to have "moving parts" internally.

- Think long and hard before making record fields or (worse still!) whole records mutable; instead get comfortable using *copy-and-update record expressions* (i.e., the `with` keyword).

- Make sure you understand the importance of "structural" (content) equality in record types, but make sure you also know when it would be violated. (When a field doesn't itself have content equality.)

- Sometimes it's useful to add instance methods, static methods, or overrides to record types, but don't get carried away: having to do this a lot might indicate that a class type would be a better fit.

- Consider putting record types on the stack with `[<Struct>]` if this gives you performance benefits across the whole life cycle of the instance.

- Lay your record type definitions and instantiations out carefully and consistently.

Summary

Effective use of records is core to writing great F# code. It's certainly my go-to data structure when I want to store small groups of labeled values. I only switch to classes (Chapter 8) when I find that I'm adorning my record types to the extent they might as well be classes – which is rarely. Once my tuples get above three items, or beyond a few lines in scope, I also move straight to records. And any day I find that I'm using the `with` keyword with record types is a good day!

All that said – classes have their place, even in F# code, so in the next chapter we'll talk about them in considerable detail.

Exercises

EXERCISE 7-1 – RECORDS AND PERFORMANCE

You need to store several million items, each consisting of X, Y, and Z positions (single precision) and a `DateTime` instance. For performance reasons, you want to store them on the stack. How might you model this using an F# record?

How can you prove, in the simple case, that instantiating a million records works faster when the items are placed on the stack than when they are allowed to go on the heap?

EXERCISE 7-2 – WHEN TO USE RECORDS

You have an idea for a novel cache that stores expensive-to-compute items when they are first requested, and periodically evicts the 10% of items that were least accessed over a configurable time period. Is a record a suitable basis for implementing this? Why or why not?

Don't bother to actually code this – it's just a decision-making exercise.

EXERCISE 7-3 – EQUALITY AND COMPARISON

A colleague writes a simple class to store music tracks but is disappointed to discover that
they can't deduplicate a list of tracks by making a Set instance from them:

```
type Track (name : string, artist : string) =
    member __.Name = name
    member __.Artist = artist

let tracks =
    [ Track("The Mollusk", "Ween")
      Track("Bread Hair", "They Might Be Giants")
      Track("The Mollusk", "Ween") ]
    // Error: The type 'Track' does not support the
    // comparison constraint
    |> Set.ofList
```

What's the simplest way to fix the problem?

EXERCISE 7-4 – MODIFYING RECORDS

Start off with the struct record from Exercise 7-1. Write a function called translate that takes a
Position record and produces a new instance with the X, Y, and Z positions altered by specified
amounts, but the Time value unchanged.

```
open System

[<Struct>]
type Position = {
    X : float32
    Y : float32
    Z : float32
    Time : DateTime }
```

Exercise Solutions

EXERCISE 7-1 – RECORDS AND PERFORMANCE

You need to create a record type with suitably typed fields X, Y, Z, and Time. Mark the record with the [<Struct>] attribute to force instances to be placed on the stack. Note that DateTime is also a value type (struct) so the Time field should not interfere with the storage.

```
open System

[<Struct>]
type Position = {
    X : float32
    Y : float32
    Z : float32
    Time : DateTime }
```

You can do a simple performance check by turning on timing in F# Interactive with the #time directive, and using Array.init to create a million-element array.

```
#time "on"

let test =
    Array.init 1_000_000 (fun i ->
        { X = float32 i
          Y = float32 i
          Z = float32 i
          Time = DateTime.MinValue } )

#time "off"
```

On my system the instantiation took 24ms with the [<Struct>] attribute and 147ms without it. In reality, you'd need to check the whole life cycle of the items (instantiation, access, and release) in the context of the real system and volumes you were working on.

EXERCISE 7-2 – WHEN TO USE RECORDS

This sounds like something with a number of moving parts, including storage for the cached items, a timer for periodic eviction, and members allowing values to be retrieved independently of how they are stored internally. There is also, presumably, some kind of locking going on for thread safety. This clearly fulfills the criteria of "internal storage differs from external representation" and "has moving parts," which means that one or more class types is almost certainly a more suitable approach than a record type.

EXERCISE 7-3 – EQUALITY AND COMPARISON

Simply change the class type to a record type. Now your type will have structural (content) equality and Set.ofList can be used successfully to deduplicate a collection of tracks.

```
type Track = {
    Name : string
    Artist : string }

// set [{Name = "Bread Hair";
//       Artist = "They Might Be Giants";};
//      {Name = "The Mollusk";
//       Artist = "Ween";}]
let tracks =
    [ { Name = "The Mollusk"
        Artist = "Ween" }
      { Name = "Bread Hair"
        Artist = "They Might Be Giants" }
      { Name = "The Mollusk"
        Artist = "Ween" } ]
    |> Set.ofList
```

EXERCISE 7-4 – MODIFYING RECORDS

Use the with keyword to assign new values for the X, Y, and Z values. Note that you can access the old values from the original instance using dot notation. Make sure you have the instance to be "modified" as the last function parameter, to make your function pipeline friendly.

```
open System

[<Struct>]
type Position = {
    X : float32
    Y : float32
    Z : float32
    Time : DateTime }

let translate dx dy dz position =
    { position with
        X = position.X + dx
        Y = position.Y + dy
        Z = position.Z + dz }

let p1 =
    { X = 1.0f
      Y = 2.0f
      Z = 3.0f
      Time = DateTime.MinValue }

// val p2 : Position = {X = 1.5f;
//                      Y = 1.5f;
//                      Z = 4.5f;
//                      Time = 01/01/0001 00:00:00;}
let p2 = p1 |> translate 0.5f -0.5f 1.5f
```

CHAPTER 8

Classes

It's a curious thing about our industry: not only do we not learn from our mistakes, we also don't learn from our successes.

—Keith Braithwaite, Software Engineer

The Power of Classes

F# *classes* give you the full power of object oriented programming. When you need to go beyond record types, for example, when the external and internal representations of data need to differ, or when you need to hold or even mutate state over time, classes are often the answer. They are also a great solution when you need to interact closely with an OO codebase, for instance, by participating in a class hierarchy. F# classes can inherit from C# classes and can implement C# interfaces, and vice versa.

By the way, I'm avoiding using the phrase *class types* (although that is what we are talking about), because there also exists a rather different concept, confusingly called *type classes*. Type classes aren't supported in F# at the time of writing, although there is work going on in that area so perhaps someday they will be. I'm not going to talk about them at all in this book, and I'll stick to the term *class* for object oriented F# types and their C# equivalents.

Asymmetric Representation

One place where you may want to use a class is where the internal and external data representations need to be *asymmetric*. In other words, the set of values you see when you *use* an instance isn't the same set you provided when you *created* the instance.

Let's say you want to encapsulate the concept of an input prompt for use in a script or console program. Listing 8-1 shows a simple implementation.

© Kit Eason 2018
K. Eason, *Stylish F#*, https://doi.org/10.1007/978-1-4842-4000-7_8

Listing 8-1. A console input prompt class

```
open System

type ConsolePrompt(message : string) =
    member this.GetValue() =
        printfn "%s:" message
        let input = Console.ReadLine()
        if not (String.IsNullOrWhiteSpace(input)) then
            input
        else
            Console.Beep()
            this.GetValue()

let firstPrompt = ConsolePrompt("Please enter your first name")
let lastPrompt = ConsolePrompt("Please enter your last name")

let demo() =

    let first, last = firstPrompt.GetValue(), lastPrompt.GetValue()

    printfn "Hello %s %s" first last

// > demo();;
// Please enter your first name:
// Kit
// Please enter your last name:
// Eason
// Hello Kit Eason
```

Note   In Listing 8-1, I've used `printfn` rather than `printf` to output the prompt message. This is simply because F# Interactive doesn't work well with `printf`.

ConsolePrompt is a great example of asymmetry: when you create an instance, you provide a prompt message, but there is no property that lets you get that message back. (Why would there be? It's sufficient for that message to be printed out when prompting for input.) Conversely, the class's one member, GetValue(), returns something that is independent of anything that was provided on construction, because what it returns was typed in by the user.

In case you aren't already familiar with F# class syntax, let me point out some key aspects of the `ConsolePrompt` declaration in Listing 8-1.

- The class declaration (up to any member definitions) and the primary constructor are one and the same thing. In a moment we'll say how to do things in the constructor body – in this first example, there isn't really a body at all.

- Values provided in the constructor arguments (in this case, `message`) are available throughout the rest of the class. Thus when the input prompt is printed, we can access the `message` value without further ceremony. Constructor arguments don't *have* to be exposed as members, though they can be, if their values need to be accessible outside the class definition.

- Members are declared simply by saying

  `member <self-identifier>.Name(<parameters>) = <body>`

  The self-identifier, in this case `this`, can be any non-reserved identifier, though you might as well stick to `this` if you are going to use it in the member body, as we do here. People often use __ (double underscore) as the self-identifier if they aren't going to reference the current instance in the member body. This is just a convention to avoid having obvious unused identifiers, and doesn't affect behavior.

- It's also interesting to note that members can call themselves recursively, as we do here when no correct input is entered. You don't have to use any special keyword like `rec`, as you do when making stand-alone functions recursive.

Constructor Bodies

Our initial cut of `ConsolePrompt` (Listing 8-1) had no constructor body, but you can add one by placing code immediately after the first line of the class definition (Listing 8-2).

Listing 8-2. A class with code in its constructor

```
open System

type ConsolePrompt(message : string) =

    do
        if String.IsNullOrWhiteSpace(message) then
            raise <| ArgumentException("Null or empty", "message")
    let message = message.Trim()

    member this.GetValue() =
        printfn "%s:" message
        let input = Console.ReadLine()
        if not (String.IsNullOrWhiteSpace(input)) then
            input
        else
            Console.Beep()
            this.GetValue()

let demo() =

    // System.ArgumentException: Null or empty
    // Parameter name: message
    let first = ConsolePrompt(null)
    printfn "Hello %s" (first.GetValue())
```

There are two kinds of operations you can conduct in a constructor body. One is imperative operations: actions that *do* something but which don't *return* anything. Imperative actions commonly performed here include validation of the constructor arguments, and possibly logging. In this case we validate the prompt message to make sure it isn't null or blank. Imperative actions in F# class constructor bodies must be contained within a code block beginning with the keyword do.

The other kind of thing we can do in the constructor is to bind values using the let keyword. In Listing 8-2 we bind a new value for message, containing the original message value but with any leading or trailing spaces trimmed. This is an example of *shadowing*, not mutation. The original value for message isn't overwritten, it's just hidden because there is a new thing in the same scope with the same name. In this case, because the cleaned-up message is the definitive version, and we don't want any later code to access the original input, it's reasonable to use the same name. Again, as with constructor arguments, values bound with let in the constructor body are available throughout the body of the class, including in all its methods. You don't use a self-identifier like this to access them, as they aren't properties.

Values as Members

If you want to publish constructor values (or values derived from them) as members, you can do so as in Listing 8-3.

Listing 8-3. Values as members

```
open System

type ConsolePrompt(message : string) =

    do
        if String.IsNullOrWhiteSpace(message) then
            raise <| ArgumentException("Null or empty", "message")
    let message = message.Trim()

    member __.Message =
        message

    member this.GetValue() =
        printfn "%s:" message
        let input = Console.ReadLine()
        if not (String.IsNullOrWhiteSpace(input)) then
            input
        else
            Console.Beep()
            this.GetValue()

let first = ConsolePrompt("First name")
// First name
printfn "%s" first.Message
```

Here we publish the cleaned-up version of message as a property called Message. Callers can access the value using dot notation. No brackets are needed after the definition or call, because it's a read-only property that simply gets the value of message, which itself never changes.

Getters and Setters

If you want simple properties that can be retrieved and set, but without any logic to compute the values or validate or process input, you can use member val syntax with default getters and setters. For example, in Listing 8-4 I've amended ConsolePrompt so that you can control whether there is a "beep" when the user enters invalid input (for example, an empty string). There's a settable BeepOnError property that GetValue consults to decide whether to beep.

Listing 8-4. Adding a mutable property with member val and default getter and setter

```
open System

type ConsolePrompt(message : string) =

    do
        if String.IsNullOrWhiteSpace(message) then
            raise <| ArgumentException("Null or empty", "message")
    let message = message.Trim()

    member val BeepOnError = true
        with get, set
    member __.Message =
        message
    member this.GetValue() =
        printfn "%s:" message
        let input = Console.ReadLine()
        if not (String.IsNullOrWhiteSpace(input)) then
            input
        else
            if this.BeepOnError then
```

```
            Console.Beep()
        this.GetValue()

let demo() =
    let first = ConsolePrompt("First name")
    first.BeepOnError <- false
    let name = first.GetValue()
    // No beep on invalid input!
    printfn "%s" name
```

Using a so-called *auto-implemented property* is a reasonable thing to do here: BeepOnError is not an important enough thing to have as a constructor parameter, and a default value is fine; but one would also like to have the flexibility to change it. And as a Boolean it hardly needs validation!

Additional Constructors

You might disagree with my assertion above that BeepOnError isn't an important enough property to have in a constructor parameter. After all, by making it a member val we have cracked open the door to mutability, something we could have avoided by making beepOnError a constructor parameter. Luckily you can dodge the whole issue by declaring *additional constructors* (Listing 8-5).

Listing 8-5. An additional constructor

```
open System

type ConsolePrompt(message : string, beepOnError : bool) =

    do
        if String.IsNullOrWhiteSpace(message) then
            raise <| ArgumentException("Null or empty", "message")
    let message = message.Trim()

    new (message : string) =
        ConsolePrompt(message, true)

    member this.GetValue() =
        printfn "%s:" message
```

```
            let input = Console.ReadLine()
            if not (String.IsNullOrWhiteSpace(input)) then
                input
            else
                if beepOnError then
                    Console.Beep()
                this.GetValue()

    let demo() =
        let first = ConsolePrompt("First name", false)
        let last = ConsolePrompt("Second name")
        // No beep on invalid input!
        let firstName = first.GetValue()
        // Beep on invalid input!
        let lastName = last.GetValue()
        printfn "Hello %s %s" firstName lastName
```

In Listing 8-5 we've added a beepOnError parameter to the primary constructor, and accessed its value in GetValue() when deciding whether to beep. Then we've added an additional constructor after the body of the primary constructor (i.e., after the validation and trimming of message). Secondary constructors are always declared using the new keyword (you don't use the name of the class), and must always call the primary constructor. In this case we call the primary constructor with whatever message value was passed in, and a hardwired default value of true for beepOnError.

Additional constructors are useful, but having more than a very small number of them may be a code smell. If you need so many permutations of construction values, does your class really have a "single responsibility," as it should?

Explicit Getters and Setters

Going back to mutable properties: sometimes auto-implemented properties aren't sufficient for your needs. What do you do if, for instance, you want to validate the value that is being set, or calculate a value on demand? For these kinds of operations, you can use explicit getters and setters. Let's extend the ConsolePrompt class so that you can set the foreground and background colors of the prompt, and let's also make a rule that the foreground and background colors can't be the same (Listing 8-6).

Listing 8-6. Explicit getters and setters

```
open System

type ConsolePrompt(message : string) =

    let mutable foreground = ConsoleColor.White
    let mutable background = ConsoleColor.Black

    member __.ColorScheme
        with get() =
            foreground, background
        and set(fg, bg) =
            if fg = bg then
                raise <| ArgumentException(
                            "Foreground, background can't be same")
            foreground <- fg
            background <- bg

    member this.GetValue() =
        Console.ForegroundColor <- foreground
        Console.BackgroundColor <- background
        printfn "%s:" message
        Console.ResetColor()
        let input = Console.ReadLine()
        if not (String.IsNullOrWhiteSpace(input)) then
            input
        else
            this.GetValue()

let demo() =
    let first = ConsolePrompt("First name")
    // System.ArgumentException: Foreground, background can't be same
    first.ColorScheme <- (ConsoleColor.Red, ConsoleColor.Red)
```

Note   For simplicity, in Listing 8-6 I've omitted some of the features we added to ConsolePrompt in previous listings.

In contrast to BeepOnError in Listing 8-4, the ColorScheme property in Listing 8-6 has the following extras:

- There are mutable *backing stores* to store the current state of the foreground and background colors. We declare these and bind their initial values in the class constructor.

- The getter has a unit parameter (), and a body that returns something: in this case a tuple of the currently set colors.

- The setter has a parameter that is used to provide a new value. In this case it's a tuple of colors. The setter body validates that the new colors are different, and if so updates the mutable backing values.

Note   You can test out the validation in F# Interactive, but if you want to see the colors in action, you'll have to incorporate the Listing 8-6 code into a console program. At the time of writing, F# Interactive doesn't support console colors.

Internal Mutable State

A mutable state doesn't have to be accessible from outside. You can declare and initialize a mutable value in the class constructor, and update it anywhere in the body. Listing 8-7 shows a version of ConsolePrompt that limits the number of attempts to enter a valid input.

Listing 8-7. A class with internal mutable state

```
open System

type ConsolePrompt(message : string, maxAttempts : int) =

    let mutable attempts = 1

    member this.GetValue() =
        printfn "%s:" message
        let input = Console.ReadLine()
        if not (String.IsNullOrWhiteSpace(input)) then
            input
```

```
            elif attempts < maxAttempts then
                attempts <- attempts + 1
                this.GetValue()
            else
                raise <| Exception("Max attempts exceeded")

    let demo() =
        let first = ConsolePrompt("First name", 2)
        let name = first.GetValue()
        // Exception if you try more than twice:
        printfn "%s" name
```

There's nothing inherently evil about a mutable state, especially, as here, where nothing else can directly see or change it. That said, you do have to be a bit canny about thread safety. It's hardly likely in the case of `ConsolePrompt`, but what would happen if two threads were to call `GetValue()` and both happened to check `attempts < maxAttempts` simultaneously? *Both* might pass the check before *either* of them incremented `attempts`. Both threads would then perform the recursive `GetValue()` call, meaning that the total attempts could exceed the specified limit. Whenever there is mutation, you should always consider thread safety, even if it's only to document "this method is not thread safe."

Generic Classes

`ConsolePrompt` would be much more useful if it could produce typed results: a string for a name, an integer for an age, and so forth. The first step to doing this is to make the class generic, by adding a type parameter after the name in the declaration, thus:

```
type ConsolePrompt<'T>(message : string...
```

Then we need to think about how to convert from what the user enters into the type we want (string, integer, floating point, or whatever). We also need to take into account that the user might not type in what we expect: if they type "abc" or just press Enter, we won't be able to convert that into an integer, so we must build in the possibility of failure.

A great way to do all this is to require a conversion function as one of the constructor parameters. We pretty much defined the necessary function signature in the previous paragraph: we need to go *from* a string *to* a value of some type - and we might fail. So the conversion signature needs to be `string -> 'T option`. Putting all that together leads to a type signature like this:

```
type ConsolePrompt<'T>
    (message : string, maxAttempts : int, tryConvert : string -> 'T option) =
```

(I've kept the `maxAttempts` parameter from the previous section as it's relevant to how we'll need to use the converter.)

Now we're ready to update `GetValue()` to use the converter. In rough pseudocode the logic needs to be:

- Get the user input.

- Pass it to the supplied conversion function.

- If that succeeds, return the converted value.

- If it fails, increment attempts and if the maximum isn't exceeded, try again.

Listing 8-8 contains an initial implementation of that logic.

Listing 8-8. Using an injected conversion function

```
open System

type ConsolePrompt<'T>
    (message : string, maxAttempts : int,
     tryConvert : string -> 'T option) =

    let mutable attempts = 1

    member this.GetValue() =
        printfn "%s:" message
        let input =  Console.ReadLine()
        match input |> tryConvert with
        | Some v -> v
        | None ->
```

```
            if attempts < maxAttempts then
                attempts <- attempts + 1
                this.GetValue()
            else
                raise <| Exception("Max attempts exceeded")
```

It's interesting to note that we don't need to change the signature of GetValue to make it return 'T rather than a string. The fact that it uses tryConvert to generate a return value, and that tryConvert returns 'T, is enough for type inference to do its job.

Now we need some code to exercise our nice generic class. Listing 8-9 shows us using it to get a name as a string, and an age as an integer. We define suitable conversion functions and provide them to ConsolePrompt instances. Note incidentally how the string validation logic we had earlier (checking the string isn't null or whitespace) has moved to the string conversion function.

Listing 8-9. Using the generic ConsolePrompt class

```
let tryConvertString (s : string) =
    if String.IsNullOrWhiteSpace(s) then
        None
    else
        Some s

let tryConvertInt (s : string) =
    match Int32.TryParse(s) with
    | true, x -> Some x
    | false, _ -> None

let demo() =
    let namePrompt = ConsolePrompt("Name", 2, tryConvertString)
    let agePrompt = ConsolePrompt("Age", 2, tryConvertInt)
    let name = namePrompt.GetValue()
    let age = agePrompt.GetValue()
    printfn "Name: %s Age: %i" name age
```

This works absolutely fine, and I would be strongly tempted to leave the code at that. But you might remember from Chapter 3 that there is often a better alternative to explicitly pattern matching on option types. In Listing 8-10 I've restated the body of GetValue() to use Option.defaultWith, thus avoiding explicit pattern matching.

Listing 8-10. The GetValue function using Option.defaultWith

```
member this.GetValue() =
    printfn "%s:" message
    Console.ReadLine()
    |> tryConvert
    |> Option.defaultWith (fun () ->
        if attempts < maxAttempts then
            attempts <- attempts + 1
            this.GetValue()
        else
            raise <| Exception("Max attempts exceeded"))
```

This works as well as Listing 8-9, but I personally think it is slightly less readable. On the other hand, if one needed to perform additional operations on the `tryConvert` result, then there would be more of a case for using `Option.defaultValue`, as the functions in the Option module pipe together nicely.

Named Parameters and Object Initializer Syntax

One problem for the reader of any code is working out, at the call site, what the various arguments going into a constructor or method actually mean. This is particularly acute for Boolean flags, where a value of `true` or `false` gives no clue, at the call site, to what the value might do. It's time to demonstrate our commitment to the principle of *semantic focus* by looking at some alternative construction styles (Listing 8-11).

Listing 8-11. Alternative construction styles

```
// Requires the version of ConsolePrompt from Listing 8-4.
// No argument names:
let namePrompt1 =
    ConsolePrompt("Name", 2, tryConvertString)

// With argument names:
let namePrompt2 =
    ConsolePrompt(
        message = "Name",
```

```
            maxAttempts = 2,
            tryConvert = tryConvertString)

    // No argument names, but with object initialization:
    let namePrompt3 =
        ConsolePrompt(
            "Name",
            2,
            tryConvertString,
            BeepOnError = false)

    // With argument names and object initialization:
    let namePrompt4 =
        ConsolePrompt(
            message = "Name",
            maxAttempts = 2,
            tryConvert = tryConvertString,
            BeepOnError = false)
```

In Listing 8-11, I show four variations on constructor calling. (I've separated the arguments onto separate lines because of page width limitations; you don't have to do this unless you want to.)

- The namePrompt1 instance is constructed in the default manner, giving arguments in the same order that the parameters are declared in the constructor. To work out what the arguments mean, you'd have to guess from their values or look at the class definition. (Or if you are lucky, the author may have documented the parameters in a /// comment, meaning that the definitions would appear in a tool tip in most IDEs.)

- The namePrompt2 instance is constructed using named argument syntax. It's a little more verbose but much more readable.

- The namePrompt3 instance assumes that the ConsolePrompt class has the BeepOnError mutable property we introduced in Listing 8-4. You can set this at construction time using *object initialization syntax*. Just include assignments for mutable properties after you've provided values for all constructor arguments, all within the same pair of brackets. Here we do this without using named argument syntax (`namePrompt3`)

- The `namePrompt4` instance combines named argument syntax with an object initializer syntax.

In my opinion, named argument syntax isn't used enough in F# code. Object initialization syntax is more well-used, particularly when interacting with C#-based APIs, which tend to make extensive use of mutable properties. In fact, I would say: if you find yourself creating instances and immediately setting their properties, always change this to object initializer style.

Make sure you give some thought to which style you adopt. Naming at the call site can be very helpful to the reader, especially when you are calling APIs that require you to set lots of constructor arguments and mutable properties.

Indexed Properties

We've already learned how to provide simple properties in a class by providing default or explicit getters and setters. That's fine if the properties are single values, but what if you want a class to provide a collection property: one that you can access with the syntax `property.[index]`? For example, let's implement a ring buffer: a structure that contains a collection of length n. When we access elements beyond the last, we circle back to element number (*index* modulus *length*). For instance, in Figure 8-1, element [8] is actually the same item as element [0].

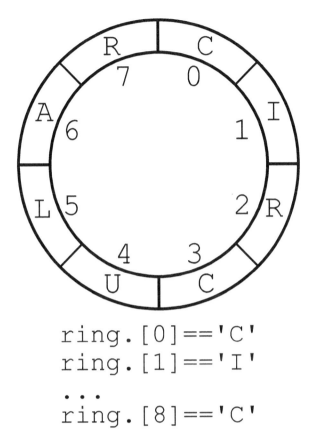

```
ring.[0]=='C'
ring.[1]=='I'
...
ring.[8]=='C'
```

Figure 8-1. *A Ring Buffer*

Listing 8-12 shows a simple ring buffer implementation that is initialized with values from a sequence.

Listing 8-12. A ring buffer implementation

```
type RingBuffer<'T>(items : 'T seq) =

    let _items = items |> Array.ofSeq
    let length = _items.Length

    member __.Item i =
        _items.[i % length]

let demo() =
    let fruits = RingBuffer(["Apple"; "Orange"; "Pear"])
```

```
// Apple Orange Pear Apple Orange Pear Apple Orange
for i in 0..7 do
    printfn "%s" fruits.[i]

// Invalid assignment
// fruits.[4] <- "Grape"
```

The important part here is the member called Item. When a property has the name Item and an index argument (here we used i), it describes a read-only, indexed property that can be accessed by the caller using array-like syntax. Notice that I used the name _items for the array backing store. I could instead have shadowed the original items sequence by reusing the name items for the backing store array. I used a private backing store to avoid potentially slow indexed access into the provided sequence.

If you want indexed properties to be settable, you need to use a slightly different syntax, one with an explicit getter and setter (Listing 8-13).

Listing 8-13. Settable indexed properties

```
type RingBuffer<'T>(items : 'T seq) =

    let _items = items |> Array.ofSeq
    let length = _items.Length

    member __.Item
        with get(i) =
            _items.[i % length]
        and set i value =
            _items.[i % length] <- value

let demo() =
    let fruits = RingBuffer(["Apple"; "Orange"; "Pear"])
    fruits.[4] <- "Grape"
    // Apple Grape Pear Apple Grape Pear Apple Grape
    for i in 0..7 do
        printfn "%s" fruits.[i]
```

You can also have multidimensional indexed properties. Listing 8-14 implements a (slightly mind-bending) two-dimensional ring buffer. Maybe this could be used to represent a 2D gaming environment with wrap-around when a player went beyond the finite bounds.

Listing 8-14. A two-dimensional ring buffer

```
type RingBuffer2D<'T>(items : 'T[,]) =

    let leni = items.GetLength(0)
    let lenj = items.GetLength(1)
    let _items = Array2D.copy items

    member __.Item
        with get(i, j) =
            _items.[i % leni, j % lenj]
        and set (i, j) value =
            _items.[i % leni, j % lenj] <- value

let demo() =
    let numbers = Array2D.init 4 5 (fun x y -> x * y)
    let numberRing = RingBuffer2D(numbers)
    // 0 0 -> 0
    // 0 1 -> 0
    // ...
    // 1 1 -> 1
    // 1 2 -> 2
    // ..
    // 9 8 -> 3
    // 9 9 -> 4
    for i in 0..9 do
        for j in 0..9 do
            printfn "%i %i -> %A" i j (numberRing.[i,j])
```

The one subtlety here is that the dimension index parameters (i and j in this case) *must* be tupled together. But the value parameter in the set declaration is curried – that is, it's outside the brackets that surround i and j.

Interfaces

Interfaces are a key concept of the Object Oriented world. An interface lets you define a set of members in terms of their names and type signatures, but without any actual behavior. Classes may then *implement* the interface, in other words, provide member implementations that have the same names and type signatures as the members defined in the interface.

Let's imagine we want to have an interface that defines a simple media player. The player needs to know how to open, play, stop playing, and eject media items. We want to specify these behaviors in abstract terms, without worrying about whether a player implementation plays audio, video, or something else (smell?); or thinking about how it does so. Listing 8-15 shows an interface definition that meets these requirements.

Listing 8-15. Simple interface definition for a media player

```
type MediaId = string
type TimeStamp = int

type Status =
    | Empty
    | Playing of MediaId * TimeStamp
    | Stopped of MediaId

type IMediaPlayer =
    abstract member Open : MediaId -> unit
    abstract member Play : unit -> unit
    abstract member Stop : unit -> unit
    abstract member Eject : unit -> unit
    abstract member Status : unit -> Status
```

Listing 8-15 starts with a couple of type aliases, which give new names for the `string` and `int` types. I'm not a huge fan of littering code with type aliases, but when defining interfaces, they make a lot of sense. They help *motivational transparency* by incorporating meaningful names for both parameters and results in the type signature. Next we have a Discriminated Union called `Status`, which embodies the states that the media player can be in. Finally, there is the actual interface definition. It starts with `type <Name>`, just like a class definition, but since there can be no constructor, the name isn't followed by brackets or constructor parameters.

The definition of the interface consists of a series of abstract member definitions, each of which must have a *name*, such as Open, and a *type signature*, such as MediaId -> unit. Use the keyword unit if you need to express the fact that the member doesn't require any "real" parameters, or that it doesn't return anything "real."

The beauty of this approach is that you can start to think about the design of your classes (the ones that will implement this interface) without getting distracted by implementation details. For example, the fact that Open has a signature of MediaId -> unit tells you that implementations of Open aren't going to return any feedback to the caller about whether they successfully opened the requested media item. This further implies that any failures are either swallowed and not reported back, or are signaled in the form of exceptions. That might or might not be the best design: the point is that you can think about it here, before committing to a lot of coding in either the implementation of classes or their consuming code. If you have become accustomed to designing systems based on function signatures, you could think of an interface as a sort of big, multi-headed function signature.

Now we have an interface definition, it's time to start implementing the interface: in other words, writing at least one class that provides actual code to execute for each of the abstract members in the interface. To implement an interface, start by defining a class in the usual way, providing a name and a constructor body (Listing 8-16).

Listing 8-16. Implementing an Interface

```
type DummyPlayer() =

    let mutable status = Empty

    interface IMediaPlayer with

        member __.Open(mediaId : MediaId) =
            printfn "Opening '%s'" mediaId
            status <- Stopped mediaId

        member __.Play() =
            match status with
            | Empty
            | Playing(_, _) -> ()
            | Stopped(mediaId) ->
                printfn "Playing '%s'" mediaId
                status <- Playing(mediaId, 0)
```

```
member __.Stop() =
    match status with
    | Empty
    | Stopped(_) -> ()
    | Playing(mediaId, _) ->
        printfn "Stopping '%s'" mediaId
        status <- Stopped(mediaId)

member __.Eject() =
    match status with
    | Empty -> ()
    | Stopped(_)
    | Playing(_, _) ->
        printfn "Ejecting"
        status <- Empty

member __.Status() =
    status
```

Implement the interface by adding `interface <Interface Name> with`, followed by implementations for each member in the interface. Each member declaration replaces the abstract member from the interface with a concrete member containing real code. The implementation needs to have the same function signature as the interface member it is implementing.

In Listing 8-16 I've called the implementation `DummyPlayer` because this class doesn't really do very much – it certainly doesn't actually play media! But you can see how a real implementation would fit into the same interface/implementation pattern.

Now we have a class that implements the interface, we can use it in code. There is one minor complication, which always trips people up, because it is a different behavior from that in C#. To access any interface members, you must cast the concrete class instance to the interface type, which you do with the `:>` (upcast) operator (Listing 8-17).

Listing 8-17. Accessing interface members

```
let demo() =

    let player = new DummyPlayer() :> IMediaPlayer

    // "Opening 'Dreamer'"
    player.Open("Dreamer")

    // "Playing 'Dreamer'"
    player.Play()

    // "Ejecting"
    player.Eject()

    // "Empty"
    player.Status() |> printfn "%A"
```

To help me remember which operator to use, I visualize the upcast operator `:>` as a sort of sarcastic emoticon, saying "Haha, you forgot to cast to the interface... again!"

In Listing 8-17 I cast to the interface as soon as I've constructed the class instance. This is appropriate here because I am only accessing members that were part of the interface. You can't get away with this if you need to access members that *aren't* part of the interface – either direct members of the class itself, or members from some other interface that the class also implements. In those cases, you'll need to cast the interface just before you access the relevant members (Listing 8-18).

Listing 8-18. Accessing instance and interface members

```
type MediaId = string
type TimeStamp = int

type Status =
    ...code as Listing 8-17...

type IMediaPlayer =
    ...code as Listing 8-17...

open System
open System.IO
```

```
type DummyPlayer() =

    let uniqueId = Guid.NewGuid()
    let mutable status = Empty
    let stream = new MemoryStream()

    member __.UniqueId =
        uniqueId

    interface IMediaPlayer with

        member __.Open(mediaId : MediaId) =
            printfn "Opening '%s'" mediaId
            status <- Stopped mediaId

        member __.Play() =
            match status with
            | Empty
            | Playing(_, _) -> ()
            | Stopped(mediaId) ->
                printfn "Playing '%s'" mediaId
                status <- Playing(mediaId, 0)

        member __.Stop() =
            match status with
            | Empty
            | Stopped(_) -> ()
            | Playing(mediaId, _) ->
                printfn "Stopping '%s'" mediaId
                status <- Stopped(mediaId)

        member __.Eject() =
            match status with
            | Empty -> ()
            | Stopped(_)
            | Playing(_, _) ->
                printfn "Ejecting"
                status <- Empty
```

```
        member __.Status() =
            status

    interface IDisposable with

        member __.Dispose() =
            stream.Dispose()

let demo() =
    let player = new DummyPlayer()
    (player :> IMediaPlayer).Open("Dreamer")
    // 95cf8c51-ee29-4c99-b714-adbe1647b62c
    printfn "%A" player.UniqueId
    (player :> IDisposable).Dispose()
```

The class in Listing 8-18 implements two interfaces: IMediaPlayer and IDisposable, and it also creates a memory stream in the class constructor, just as an example of a resource that the class might want to dispose promptly when it itself is disposed. It also has a member of its own, called UniqueId. In the demo() function, we create a player, open a media item, then explicitly dispose the player. (By the way it would be better generally to create the player with the use keyword or the using function, meaning that the player instance would be disposed on going out of context. I've coded in this way so you can see the casting in action.)

Notice how, to call the Open() method, we cast to IMediaPlayer; to call the Dispose method we cast to IDisposable; and to use the UniqueId property we don't cast at all, because this is a member of the class itself. You might wonder why I didn't have to cast the stream instance to IDisposable when calling its Dispose() method. The answer is that the C# code for MemoryStream didn't implement the IDisposable interface explicitly. F# *always* implements interfaces explicitly; in C# you have the choice.

Object Expressions

You can use an object expression to create a "something," which inherits from a class or implements one or more interfaces, but which is not a new named type. It's a great way of creating ad hoc objects for specific tasks, without actual, named types proliferating in your codebase.

Let's say you are testing some class that takes a logger as one of its constructor arguments, and uses that logger throughout its implementation. You don't want the overhead of creating a real logger instance; you just want a simple dummy logger that writes to the console or even does nothing. Listing 8-19 shows how to do that for the MediaPlayer example, without creating any new types.

Listing 8-19. Using Object Expressions

```
type ILogger =
    abstract member Info : string -> unit
    abstract member Error : string -> unit

type MediaId = string
type TimeStamp = int

type Status =
    ...code as Listing 8-18...

type IMediaPlayer =
    ...code as Listing 8-18...

type LoggingPlayer(logger : ILogger) =

    let mutable status = Empty

    interface IMediaPlayer with

        member __.Open(mediaId : MediaId) =
            logger.Info(sprintf "Opening '%s'" mediaId)
            status <- Stopped mediaId

        member __.Play() =
            match status with
            | Empty ->
                logger.Error("Nothing to play")
            | Playing(_, _) ->
                logger.Error("Already playing")
            | Stopped(mediaId) ->
                logger.Info(sprintf "Playing '%s'" mediaId)
                status <- Playing(mediaId, 0)
```

```
        member __.Stop() =
            match status with
            | Empty
            | Stopped(_) ->
                logger.Error("Not playing")
            | Playing(mediaId, _) ->
                logger.Info(sprintf "Playing '%s'" mediaId)
                status <- Stopped(mediaId)

        member __.Eject() =
            match status with
            | Empty ->
                logger.Error("Nothing to eject")
            | Stopped(_)
            | Playing(_, _) ->
                logger.Info("Ejecting")
                status <- Empty

        member __.Status() =
            status

let demo() =

    let logger = {
        new ILogger with
            member __.Info(msg) = printfn "%s" msg
            member __.Error(msg) = printfn "%s" msg }

    let player = new LoggingPlayer(logger) :> IMediaPlayer

    // "Nothing to eject"
    player.Eject()

    // "Opening 'Dreamer'"
    player.Open("Dreamer")

    // "Ejecting"
    player.Eject()
```

In Listing 8-19 we make a new implementation of `IMediaPlayer` that requires a logger as a constructor argument. The logger needs to be of type `ILogger`, which I've also declared here but could just as easily be defined externally. The `LoggingPlayer` implementation calls the logger's `Info` and `Error` methods at various points.

The object expression part comes in the `demo()` function, where we create a value called logger that implements `ILogger` but is not a new, named type. The curly brackets `{}` are important here: they are part of the object expression. When various members of the `LoggingPlayer` instance are called, these call the methods we defined in the logger binding.

I personally don't use object expressions very often, but they can certainly be useful. The times I have used them have been in writing tests in F# for highly coupled C# codebases. There they really have been a boon.

Abstract Classes

An abstract class is, broadly speaking, a class that allows at least some of its members to be implemented by derived classes. The concept in F# is not precisely the same as it is in C#, so if you are going to use abstract classes, it's good to be clear about F#'s interpretation of "abstract":

- A *method* is abstract if it is marked with the keyword `abstract`, meaning that it can be overridden in a derived class.

- Abstract members can have *default definitions*, meaning that they *can* be, but don't *have to be* overridden.

- A *class* is only considered abstract if it contains at least one abstract member that doesn't have a default implementation. Classes that fall into this category *must* be annotated with the `[<AbstractClass>]` attribute.

- Thus a class's members can all be abstract without the class being considered abstract: that's when all the class's abstract members have default implementations. Classes that fall into this category *must not* be annotated with the `[<AbstractClass>]` attribute.

Confused yet? Let's look at some examples.

Abstract Members

Listing 8-20 shows a simple class hierarchy with one abstract class and one derived class.

Listing 8-20. A simple abstract class

```
[<AbstractClass>]
type AbstractClass() =
    abstract member SaySomething : string -> string

type ConcreteClass(name : string) =
    inherit AbstractClass()
    override __.SaySomething(whatToSay) =
        sprintf "%s says %s" name whatToSay

let demo() =
    let cc = ConcreteClass("Concrete")
    // "Concrete says hello"
    cc.SaySomething("hello")
```

The abstract class's member SaySomething is defined using the same kind of syntax as we used when defining an interface: we specify the *name* of the member and its *signature* (in this case string -> string). Importantly, we use the [<AbstractClass>] attribute because this truly is an abstract class: it has at least one abstract member that doesn't have a default definition. The error message you get if you omit the [<AbstractClass>] attribute is a little confusing:

```
error FS0365: No implementation was given for 'abstract member
AbstractClass.SaySomething : string -> string'
```

So don't forget the attribute!

Default Member Implementations

Sometimes we want to provide a *default implementation* for an abstract member: one that will be used if a derived class doesn't bother to override that member. Default implementations are defined separately from the abstract definition. You use the same syntax as for ordinary members, except by using the keyword default instead of member (Listing 8-21).

Listing 8-21. Default abstract member implementation

```
type ParentClass() =
    abstract member SaySomething : string -> string
    default __.SaySomething(whatToSay) =
        sprintf "Parent says %s" whatToSay

type ConcreteClass1(name : string) =
    inherit ParentClass()

type ConcreteClass2(name : string) =
    inherit ParentClass()
    override __.SaySomething(whatToSay) =
        sprintf "%s says %s" name whatToSay

let demo() =
    let cc1 = ConcreteClass1("Concrete 1")
    let cc2 = ConcreteClass2("Concrete 2")
    // "Parent says hello"
    printfn "%s" (cc1.SaySomething("hello"))
    // "Concrete 2 says hello"
    printfn "%s" (cc2.SaySomething("hello"))
```

See how SaySomething is defined twice in ParentClass, once as an abstract member and again as the default implementation of that member.

It's important to notice that, because SaySomething now has a default implementation, its class is no longer considered abstract. This is why I've renamed the class ParentClass and removed the [<AbstractClass>] attribute. It *would* still be abstract if there was at least one other abstract member that *didn't* have a default implementation.

Moving on to the derived classes: one of them, ConcreteClass1, doesn't override SaySomething, so the default implementation takes over. The other one, ConcreteClass2, does override SaySomething, and it is the overriding implementation that we see in operation.

Class Equality and Comparison

Although many F# developers don't use inheritance or interfaces a great deal, there are a few standard interfaces that we often have to support. One is IDisposable, which we dealt with briefly above. The others are IEquatable and IComparable, which are used to determine if two instances are *equal* in some meaningful sense, and whether one is *larger* or *smaller* than another.

Implementing Equality

Back in Chapter 7 we dodged the issue of latitude/longitude equality by storing positions as F# records, which by default implement *structural* (content) equality. Now it's time to revisit the issue in the world of classes, where *reference* equality is the default. Consider the code in Listing 8-22, and note how two instances of LatLon, landsEnd, and landsEnd2, are considered unequal even though they refer to the same geographical position.

Listing 8-22. Two identical geographical positions might be "unequal"

```
type LatLon(latitude : float, longitude : float) =

    member __.Latitude = latitude
    member __.Longitude = longitude

let landsEnd = LatLon(50.07, -5.72)
let johnOGroats = LatLon(58.64, -3.07)
let landsEnd2 = LatLon(50.07, -5.72)

// false
printfn "%b" (landsEnd = johnOGroats)
// false
printfn "%b" (landsEnd = landsEnd2)
```

> **Note**   Comparing floating-point values is always a dangerous thing to do: two
> GPS positions might only differ by the width of an atom and still be considered
> different on the basis of floating-point comparison. To keep things simple, I'm
> going to ignore that aspect and assume that instances like `landsEnd` and
> `landsEnd2` come from some completely repeatable source. I'm also ignoring
> what goes on at the North and South Poles, and what happens if someone sends in
> an out-of-range value like 181.0 for longitude!

In the world of classes, the standard way to represent equality is to implement the
.NET interface IEquatable. There are some gotchas in doing this though, so I'll take it a
step at a time and make a few deliberate mistakes.

Let's start by simply making our class implement IEquatable, which is just a matter
of overriding the Equals method (Listing 8-23).

Listing 8-23. Just implementing IEquatable isn't enough

```
open System

type LatLon(latitude : float, longitude : float) =

    member __.Latitude = latitude
    member __.Longitude = longitude

    interface IEquatable<LatLon> with
        member this.Equals(that : LatLon) =
            this.Latitude = that.Latitude
            && this.Longitude = that.Longitude

let demo()  =

    let landsEnd = LatLon(50.07, -5.72)
    let johnOGroats = LatLon(58.64, -3.07)
    let landsEnd2 = LatLon(50.07, -5.72)

    // false
    printfn "%b" (landsEnd = johnOGroats)
    // false
    printfn "%b" (landsEnd = landsEnd2)
```

This compiles absolutely fine, and you might be forgiven for relaxing at that point. Except that it doesn't work! In the last line of Listing 8-23, landsEnd = landsEnd2 still returns false. Confusingly, in the case of IEquatable, it isn't enough just to implement the interface. For a start, you must also override the Equals() method of System.Object. (All classes are derived ultimately from System.Object, and for low-level operations like equality you do sometimes have to override its methods.) Listing 8-24 shows us doing everything needed to make basic equality work.

Listing 8-24. Overriding Object.Equals

```
open System

[<AllowNullLiteral>]
type LatLon(latitude : float, longitude : float) =

    let eq (that : LatLon) =
        if isNull that then
            false
        else
            latitude = that.Latitude
            && longitude = that.Longitude

    member __.Latitude = latitude
    member __.Longitude = longitude

    override this.GetHashCode() =
        hash (this.Latitude, this.Longitude)

    override __.Equals(thatObj) =
        match thatObj with
        | :? LatLon as that ->
            eq that
        | _ ->
            false

    interface IEquatable<LatLon> with
        member __.Equals(that : LatLon) =
            eq that
```

We've made a number of changes between Listings 8-23 and 8-24, and to make equality work correctly, you'll often need to do all of these things:

- The [<AllowNullLiteral>] attribute has been added to the class. This allows other languages to create null instances. If we are implementing LatLon as a class instead of an F# record, this is a likely use case.

- There's now a private eq function that does the real work of comparing instances. This includes a null check, which is now necessary as a result of adding [<AllowNullLiteral>].

- We've overridden the Object.Equals() method. Since this takes an obj instance as its argument, this needs to pattern match on type before calling eq.

- The IEquatable implementation also calls eq.

- We've also overridden the Object.GetHashCode() method.

The GetHashCode() aspect of these changes needs a little more explanation. If you don't override GetHashCode(), equality for the class will work correctly, but you'll get a compiler warning:

```
Warning FS0346: The struct, record or union type 'LatLon' has an explicit
implementation of 'Object.Equals'. Consider implementing a matching
override for 'Object.GetHashCode()'
```

In case you didn't already know, GetHashCode() is a method that returns a "magic number" that has the following qualities:

- If two objects are considered equal they must have the same hash code. (Within one Application Domain that is – the underlying hash code generator can vary between platforms and versions.)

- If two objects are considered not equal, they will *usually* have different hash codes, though this is far from guaranteed.

The purpose of hash codes is to provide a quick way to check for likely equality in, for example, dictionary implementations. You wouldn't normally use hash codes directly – unless you were implementing some special collection type of your own – but you are encouraged to override GetHashCode so that your class can be placed into hash-based collections efficiently. Luckily this is often easy to do: just tuple together the items that embody equality (in this case, the latitude and longitude values) and apply the built-in hash function to them, as we did in Listing 8-24.

With all these changes in place, Listing 8-25 demonstrates that equality now works correctly from F#, including directly comparing instances with the = operator and adding them to a dictionary, which requires equality.

Listing 8-25. Exercising equality

```fsharp
// Requires code from Listing 8-25
let demo() =

    let landsEnd = LatLon(50.07, -5.72)
    let johnOGroats = LatLon(58.64, -3.07)
    let landsEnd2 = LatLon(50.07, -5.72)

    // false
    printfn "%b" (landsEnd = johnOGroats)
    // true
    printfn "%b" (landsEnd = landsEnd2)

    let places = [ landsEnd; johnOGroats; landsEnd2 ]

    let placeDict =
        places
        |> Seq.mapi (fun i place -> place, i)
        |> dict

    // 50.070000, -5.720000 -> 2
    // 58.640000, -3.070000 -> 1
    placeDict
    |> Seq.iter (fun kvp ->
        printfn "%f, %f -> %i"
            kvp.Key.Latitude kvp.Key.Longitude kvp.Value)
```

See how we use LatLon instances as keys in a dictionary. (The dictionary values here are integers and aren't meaningful beyond being something to put in the dictionary.) The first instance (landsEnd, i=0) isn't represented when we print out the dictionary contents, because it was replaced by another item with the same key (landsEnd2, i=2).

There is one final thing we need to do in regard to equality: ensure that the `==` operator works correctly from C# and VB.NET. To do this, add another override for the `op_Equality` method (Listing 8-26).

Listing 8-26. Overriding op_Equality

```
// static member ( = ) : this:LatLon * that:LatLon -> bool
static member op_Equality(this : LatLon, that : LatLon) =
    this.Equals(that)
```

Add the lines from Listing 8-26 after the latitude and longitude members. `op_Equality` is a static member. As in C# this means that it isn't associated with any particular `LatLon` instance.

Implementing Comparison

Sometimes you get can away with only implementing equality and not comparison, as we did in the previous section. In fact, it doesn't seem particularly meaningful to implement comparison (greater than/less than) for `LatLon` instances. Which is genuinely "greater" – `LatLon(1.0, 3.0)` or `LatLon(2.0, 0.0)`? But there's a catch: some collections, such as F# sets, *require* their elements to be comparable, not just equatable, because they rely on ordering to search for items efficiently. And, of course, other classes might have an obvious sort order, which you might need to implement, so it's important to know how.

Here's how to implement `IComparable` for our `LatLon` class (Listing 8-27).

Listing 8-27. Implementing IComparable

```
open System

[<AllowNullLiteral>]
type LatLon(latitude : float, longitude : float) =

    ...code as Listing 8-24...

    interface IComparable with
        member this.CompareTo(thatObj) =
            match thatObj with
```

```
  | :? LatLon as that ->
      compare
          (this.Latitude, this.Longitude)
          (that.Latitude, that.Longitude)
  | _ ->
      raise <| ArgumentException("Can't compare different types")
```

Now that you're familiar with interfaces in F#, this code should be pretty self-explanatory. We implement IComparable and implement its one method: CompareTo(). Then, in a similar way to the Equals() override, we use pattern matching on types to recover the other LatLon instance. We take the latitudes and longitudes from the instances being compared, and pass them as tuples to the built-in compare function, which will do the real comparison work for us. Pleasingly, using compare means we don't have to worry about whether, for example, (50.07, -5.72) is less than or greater than (58.64, -3.07). Whatever the compare function does for us is going to be consistent.

In Listing 8-28 we prove that a list of LatLon instances from Listing 8-27 can be put into a Set, and that duplicates by geographical position are eliminated in the process.

Listing 8-28. Using class instances that implement IComparable

```
let demo() =

    let landsEnd = LatLon(50.07, -5.72)
    let johnOGroats = LatLon(58.64, -3.07)
    let landsEnd2 = LatLon(50.07, -5.72)

    let places = [ landsEnd; johnOGroats; landsEnd2 ]

    // 50.070000, -5.720000
    // 58.640000, -3.070000
    places
    |> Set.ofList
    |> Seq.iter (fun ll -> printfn "%f, %f" ll.Latitude ll.Longitude)
```

One final wrinkle: there are actually two versions of IComparable, a non-generic and a generic one. In Listing 8-27 we only implemented the non-generic one. This works, but there can be a benefit in also implementing the generic version. Some APIs will try to use both, starting with the generic version, which can improve performance. Listing 8-29 shows how to add the generic version of IComparable to the LatLon definition.

Listing 8-29. Adding a generic version of IComparable

```
open System

[<AllowNullLiteral>]
type LatLon(latitude : float, longitude : float) =

    let eq (that : LatLon) =
        if isNull that then
            false
        else
            latitude = that.Latitude
            && longitude = that.Longitude

    let comp (that : LatLon) =
        compare
            (latitude, longitude)
            (that.Latitude, that.Longitude)

    member __.Latitude = latitude
    member __.Longitude = longitude

    static member op_Equality(this : LatLon, that : LatLon) =
        this.Equals(that)

    override this.GetHashCode() =
        hash (this.Latitude, this.Longitude)

    override __.Equals(thatObj) =
        match thatObj with
        | :? LatLon as that ->
            eq that
        | _ ->
            false

    interface IEquatable<LatLon> with
        member __.Equals(that : LatLon) =
            eq that

    interface IComparable with
        member __.CompareTo(thatObj) =
```

```
        match thatObj with
        | :? LatLon as that ->
            comp that
        | _ ->
            raise <| ArgumentException("Can't compare different
            types")

    interface IComparable<LatLon> with
        member __.CompareTo(that) =
            comp that
```

As with equality, I've moved the implementation of comparison to a private function called comp, and delegated to that from both the IComparable and the new IComparable<LatLon> implementations.

Now you know why F# record types, with structural equality and comparison by default, are so valuable! If you even dip a toe into equality or comparison for classes, you pretty much have dive into the pool completely. Sometimes that's worth it, sometimes not.

Recommendations

Here are the ideas I'd like you to take away from this chapter:

- Use F# classes when the modeling possibilities offered by simpler structures, such as F# records and Discriminated Unions, aren't sufficient. Often this is because there is a requirement for asymmetric representation: the type is more than just a grouping of its construction values, or it needs to have moving parts.

- Also use classes when you need to participate in a class hierarchy, by inheriting from, or providing the ability to be inherited from. This is most common when interacting with C# codebases, but may also be perfectly legitimate in F#-only codebases in cases where class hierarchies are the easiest way to model the requirement.

- Be aware of the benefits and costs of going down the OO route. Don't just do it because you happen to have more experience in modeling things in an OO way. Explore the alternatives that F# offers first.

- Don't forget the power of object expressions to inherit from base types or implement interfaces without creating a new type.

- All the major OO modeling facilities offered by C# are also available in F#: classes, abstract classes, interfaces, read-only, and mutable properties – even nullability.

Summary

The chapter has two messages. The *explicit* message is "Here's how to do Object Orientation in F#. Here's how to write classes, use interfaces, override methods and so forth… ." The *implicit* message is "Object Orientation can be a slippery slope." Compare, for example, what we ended up with in Listing 8-29 with what would have been achieved, almost for free, using an F# record. (Accepting the dangers and limitations of comparing floating-point values, which apply to both the class and the record version.) Also, it's interesting to note that this chapter is the longest in the book, and was by far the hardest to write. It's hard to be concise when writing classes, or writing *about* classes!

Object Orientation has its own internal logic that, when followed, doesn't always lead to the simplest solution. Therefore, you need to be keenly aware of the costs (and, to be fair, benefits) of even starting down this path for any particular piece of design. The costs are, broadly speaking:

- The OO philosophy sometimes feels as though it involves taking something complicated and making it more complicated. (I'm indebted to Don Syme, "father of F#", for this phrase.)

- OO code can be harder to reason about than a good, functional implementation, especially once one opens the door to mutability.

- OO code tends to embrace the concept of nullability, which can complicate your code. That said, as we discovered in Chapter 3, the introduction of *nullable reference types* into C# may change the balance of power here.

At the same time, you shouldn't discount the benefits of an OO approach:

- .NET is fundamentally an OO platform. This isn't just built into the C# language – the lower level IL into which both C# and F# is compiled is also inherently object oriented. This fact can leak into your F# code, and frankly you shouldn't waste too much time fighting it.

- Many of the Nuget packages and other APIs you will be coding against will be written in terms of classes, interfaces, and so forth. Again, this is just a fact of life.

- The OO world has an immense depth of experience in building working, large-scale systems. A dyed-in-the wool F# developer like me would argue that these systems have often not been built in the most productive way. But there is no denying there have been many successes. It seems foolish to dismiss all this hard-won knowledge.

So that you can make informed design decisions, make sure you are familiar with the basics of F# classes, constructors, overrides, interfaces, and abstract classes. Don't forget how useful object expressions can be for making ad hoc extensions to a class without a proliferation of types. Above all, be extremely cautious about implementing deep hierarchies of classes. I've rarely seen this turn out well in F# codebases.

In the next chapter we'll return to F# fundamentals and look at how to get the best out of functions.

Exercises

```
┌─────────────────────────────────────────────────────────────┐
│                 EXERCISE 8-1 – A SIMPLE CLASS                 │
└─────────────────────────────────────────────────────────────┘
```

Make a class that takes three byte values called r, g, and b, and provides a byte property called Level, which contains a grayscale value calculated from the incoming red, green, and blue values.

The grayscale value should be calculated by taking the average of the r, g, and b values. You'll need to cast r, g, and b to integers to perform the calculation without overflow.

Note   This is a terrible way to calculate grayscale values, and probably a terrible way to model them! The focus of this and the next few exercises is on the mechanics of class definition.

EXERCISE 8-2 – SECONDARY CONSTRUCTORS

Add a secondary constructor for the GrayScale class from Exercise 8-1. It should take a System.Drawing.Color instance and construct a GrayScale instance from the color's R, G, and B properties.

EXERCISE 8-3 – OVERRIDES

Override the ToString() method of GrayScale so that it produces output like this, where the number is the Level value:

Greyscale(140)

EXERCISE 8-4 – EQUALITY

Implement equality for the GrayScale class by overriding GetHashCode() and Equals(), and implementing the generic version of IEquatable. The GrayScale class should not be nullable (don't add the [<AllowNullLiteral>] attribute).
Prove that GreyScale(Color.Orange) is equal to GreyScale(0xFFuy, 0xA5uy, 0x00uy).
Prove that GreyScale(Color.Orange) is not equal to GreyScale(Color.Blue).

What happens if you check equality for GreyScale(0xFFuy, 0xA5uy, 0x00uy) and GreyScale(0xFFuy, 0xA5uy, 0x01uy). Why is this?

Exercise Solutions

EXERCISE 8-1 – A SIMPLE CLASS

This can be done in three lines of code. Note the casting between `byte` and `int` and back again. This is done so that there is no overflow during the addition, but the `Level` property is still a byte.

```
type GreyScale(r : byte, g : byte, b : byte) =

    member __.Level =
        (int r + int g + int b) / 3 |> byte

let demo() =
    // 255
    GreyScale(255uy, 255uy, 255uy).Level |> printfn "%i"
```

EXERCISE 8-2 – SECONDARY CONSTRUCTORS

Add a secondary constructor using the new keyword, and pass the color values individually through to the main constructor.

```
open System.Drawing

type GreyScale(r : byte, g : byte, b : byte) =

    new (color : Color) =
        GreyScale(color.R, color.G, color.B)

    member __.Level =
        (int r + int g + int b) / 3 |> byte

let demo() =
    // 83
    GreyScale(Color.Brown).Level |> printfn "%i"
```

EXERCISE 8-3 – OVERRIDES

Add a straightforward override and use `sprintf` to produce the formatted output.

```
open System.Drawing

type GreyScale(r : byte, g : byte, b : byte) =

    new (color : Color) =
        GreyScale(color.R, color.G, color.B)

    member __.Level =
        (int r + int g + int b) / 3 |> byte

    override this.ToString() =
        sprintf "Greyscale(%i)" this.Level

let demo() =
    // Greyscale(140)
    GreyScale(Color.Orange) |> printfn "%A"
    // Greyscale(255)
    GreyScale(255uy, 255uy, 255uy) |> printfn "%A"
```

EXERCISE 8-4 – EQUALITY

Follow the pattern shown in Listing 8-24, but since you have not added the
[<AllowNullLiteral>] attribute, you shouldn't check for null in the eq function.

```
open System
open System.Drawing

type GreyScale(r : byte, g : byte, b : byte) =

    let level = (int r + int g + int b) / 3 |> byte

    let eq (that : GreyScale) =
        level = that.Level

    new (color : Color) =
        GreyScale(color.R, color.G, color.B)
```

```
        member __.Level =
            level

        override this.ToString() =
            sprintf "Greyscale(%i)" this.Level

        override this.GetHashCode() =
            hash level

        override __.Equals(thatObj) =
            match thatObj with
            | :? GreyScale as that ->
                eq that
            | _ ->
                false

        interface IEquatable<GreyScale> with
            member __.Equals(that : GreyScale) =
                eq that

    let demo() =
        let orange1 = GreyScale(Color.Orange)
        let blue = GreyScale(Color.Blue)
        let orange2 = GreyScale(0xFFuy, 0xA5uy, 0x00uy)
        let orange3 = GreyScale(0xFFuy, 0xA5uy, 0x01uy)
        // true
        printfn "%b" (orange1 = orange2)
        // false
        printfn "%b" (orange1 = blue)
        // true
        printfn "%b" (orange1 = orange3)
```

GreyScale(0xFFuy, 0xA5uy, 0x00uy) is equal to GreyScale(0xFFuy, 0xA5uy, 0x01uy) even though the input RGB levels are slightly different. This is because we lose some accuracy (we round down when doing integer division) in calculating Level to fit into a byte range (0..255), so certain different combinations of inputs will result in the same Level value.

CHAPTER 9

Programming with Functions

> *"Form follows function" – that has been misunderstood. Form and function should be one, joined in a spiritual union.*
>
> —Frank Lloyd Wright, Architect

Functions First

One of the things that makes F# a *functional-first* language is that its functions are "first-class values."[1] But what does that really mean, and how genuinely useful is it? In this chapter, you'll get the answers to these questions, and learn how you can use (and sometimes abuse) this feature to build simple, refactorable code. This is one of those topics where we move quite a way from the familiar ground of Object Oriented code. So buckle up and enjoy the ride!

Functions as Values

What does it mean to describe a function as a value? Consider a simple function that adds two numbers (Listing 9-1).

---

[1]Just to clarify for readers with English as an additional language: the word "class" in this paragraph doesn't refer to "classes" in a programming sense (i.e., as in Chapter 8). In this paragraph, by "first-class" we mean something that is built naturally into the language syntax, rather than something that needs extra ceremony to use.

© Kit Eason 2018
K. Eason, *Stylish F#*, https://doi.org/10.1007/978-1-4842-4000-7_9

Listing 9-1. Binding a function to another label

```
// int -> int -> int
let add a b = a + b

// int -> int -> int
let addUp = add

// 5
printfn "%i" (add 2 3)
// 5
printfn "%i" (addUp 2 3)
```

Listing 9-1 shows that we can not only define a function and use it: we can also bind it to another label (`let addUp = add`) and call that as if it were the original function. We can also pass it as an argument to some other function, and have that other function call the supplied function (Listing 9-2).

Listing 9-2. A function as a parameter for another function

```
let add a b = a + b

let applyAndPrint f a b =
    let r = f a b
    printfn "%i" r

// "5"
applyAndPrint add 2 3
```

In Listing 9-2, the function `applyAndPrint` has a parameter called `f`, whose signature is a function that takes two values and returns an integer. In its definition, `applyAndPrint` calls the provided function – whatever it is – and prints the result.

All this is achieved without any additional ceremony, for example having to make the function be a "delegate" or a "func." It's just a value that happens to be a function. The fact that is it is a function (and not a single integer value or a string or whatever) is deduced by the compiler entirely by the way it is used. In this case the key line is

`let r = f a b.`

Furthermore, the compiler knows the function must return an integer, because we use its result in a `printfn` statement that uses a `%i` format string.

Treating functions as values unlocks a rich store of possibilities for expressing yourself in code. But it comes with the need to understand a few distinctly non-Object-Oriented concepts, which I'll cover in the next few sections.

Currying and Partial Application

To get a bit more out of functions as values, we need to go into the twin concepts of *curried arguments* and *partial application*. You can think of curried arguments as being arguments expressed as separate values like this:

```
let add a b = a + b
```

...as opposed to the (for many people) more familiar style of *tupled arguments*, which are bracketed together like this:

```
let add (a, b) = a + b
```

Note I'm using the terms "curried **arguments**" and "tupled **arguments**" here even though, strictly speaking, these are function **parameters** (in the definition), not **arguments** (actual values at call-time). It just happens that "curried arguments" and "tupled arguments" are the more commonly used, if less, precise phrases.

Partial application is the act of binding a function while providing values for some, but not all, of the expected arguments (Listing 9-3).

Listing 9-3. Partial application

```
// int -> int -> int
let add a b = a + b

// int -> int
let addTwo = add 2

// 5
printfn "%i" (add 2 3)
// 5
printfn "%i" (addTwo 3)
```

In Listing 9-3 we bind a function called addTwo, which takes one argument and adds it to the constant 2. This is achieved by using (*applying*) add and providing one argument value: 2. The one "left-over" argument of add is now required by addTwo, and when we supply a value for it (last line of Listing 9-3) an actual calculation is done.

Incidentally, we can only use partial application because the add function's arguments are *curried*, not *tupled*. With tupled arguments the caller always has to provide the complete tuple.

Note   Another way to think of currying is that every function in F# takes only one parameter. If a function is bound with, say, two (non-tupled) parameters, it's really a function that takes one parameter, and returns a function that itself takes the other parameter.

You may well wonder why you'd ever want to curry and partially apply! The short answer is: code-reuse. Imagine you want a simple function that surrounds a string with two other strings. The surrounding strings might be brackets, quote marks, or even comment delimiters. Listing 9-4 shows how you can do this in a concise way using partial application.

Listing 9-4. Parenthesizing strings using partial application

```
let surround prefix suffix s =
    sprintf "%s%s%s" prefix s suffix

let roundParen = surround "(" ")"
let squareParen = surround "[" "]"
let xmlComment = surround "<!--" "-->"
let quote q = surround q q
let doubleQuote = quote "\""

let demo() =
    // ~~Markdown strikethrough~~
    printfn "%s" (surround "~~" "~~" "Markdown strikethrough")
    // (Round parentheses)
    printfn "%s" (roundParen "Round parentheses")
```

```
// [Square parentheses]
printfn "%s" (squareParen "Square parentheses")
// <!--XML comment-->
printfn "%s" (xmlComment "XML comment")
// "To be or not to be"
printfn "%s" (doubleQuote "To be or not to be")
```

In Listing 9-4 we start with a simple function called surround, which does the fundamental work of surrounding a string with two other strings. (Incidentally sprintf sometimes isn't the fastest way to do this, but I'm doing it that way here for simplicity.) The surround function has curried arguments, which means we can use partial application to specialize the function in various different ways: roundParen and squareParen parenthesize a string with round and square brackets respectively; and, just to prove that we can use longer surrounding strings, xmlComment surrounds the string with <!-- and -->. We also define a quote function, which uses the same string before and after the input string, again by calling surround. Then we specialize quote further, as doubleQuote, to surround the input string with double quotation marks.

Mixing Tupled and Curried Styles

There's nothing in the rule book that says you can't mix tupled and curried styles. Let's say you decide that it's invalid to allow the enclosing strings to be applied separately in the surround function. You could enforce that by tupling together the prefix and suffix parameters (Listing 9-5).

Listing 9-5. Mixed tupled and curried styles

```
let surround (prefix, suffix) s =
    sprintf "%s%s%s" prefix s suffix

let roundParen = surround ("(", ")")
let squareParen = surround ("[", "]")
let xmlComment = surround ("<!--", "-->")
let quote q = surround(q, q)
let doubleQuote = quote "\""
```

```
let demo() =
    // ~~Markdown strikethrough~~
    printfn "%s" (surround ("~~", "~~") "Markdown strikethrough")
    // (Round parentheses)
    printfn "%s" (roundParen "Round parentheses")
    // [Square parentheses]
    printfn "%s" (squareParen "Square parentheses")
    // <!--XML comment-->
    printfn "%s" (xmlComment "XML comment")
    // "To be or not to be"
    printfn "%s" (doubleQuote "To be or not to be")
```

Note how all the code in Listing 9-5 been amended so that `prefix` and `suffix` are provided as a single tuple. But there is still partial application going on, for instance, when we define specialized versions like `roundParen` and `quote`, where we provide the whole prefix/suffix tuple but no value for the `s` parameter.

Stylistically, mixing tupled and curried styles is relatively rare, though oddly enough we have encountered one example earlier in this book. It happened in Chapter 8, when we had to provide a tuple for the two indices of a two-dimensional array property in the property's setter, and yet the value to be set was curried. (The relevant lines are repeated in Listing 9-6).

Listing 9-6. Mixed tupled and curried styles in the wild

```
member __.Item
    with get(i, j) =
        _items.[i % leni, j % lenj]
    // (i, j) are tupled, value is curried
    and set (i, j) value =
        _items.[i % leni, j % lenj] <- value
```

It's also worth saying that many F# developers prefer the curried style even when they don't intend to use partial application, simply because it means there are fewer brackets to type and match up.

Function Signatures Revisited

We discussed function signatures a bit in Chapter 2, but I want to revisit the topic here because it's very important to start thinking in function signatures when designing code. Like me, you might initially have been a bit irritated to find that in F#, the type signature of a function like add is int -> int -> int. "Why," I thought, "can't they use a different symbol to separate the parameter list (int and another int) from what the function returns? (int). Why is it all just arrows?" The answer is because, when we use curried style, there truly is no distinction. Every time we provide an argument value for a parameter, one item gets knocked off that undifferentiated list of parameters, until we finally bind an actual value with a non-function type like int (Listing 9-7).

Listing 9-7. Function signatures and function application

```
// int -> int -> int
let add a b = a + b

// int -> int
let addTwo = add 2

// int
let result = addTwo 3
```

Note how the type signature of the add function differs if we tuple its parameters (Listing 9-8).

Listing 9-8. Function signature for tupled arguments

```
// int * int -> int
let add(a, b) = a + b

// int
let result = add(2, 3)
```

The asterisk in the construct int * int shows that these values are part of a tuple, and the function is expecting a whole tuple, not just two integers that might be provided separately.

It's worth getting familiar with F#'s way of expressing type signatures for two reasons: they let you verify that a function has the "shape" you expect; and they let you pin down that shape, if you want to, using *type hints*.

Type Hints for Functions

When a function takes another function as a parameter, the "outer" function obviously needs to apply the provided function appropriately. Think about the code in Listing 9-9, where we provide a function to another function.

Listing 9-9. A function as a parameter for another function

```
let add a b = a + b

let applyAndPrint f a b =
    let r = f a b
    printfn "%i" r

// "5"
applyAndPrint add 2 3
```

Type inference deduces that the signature of the function f is 'a -> 'b -> int; in other words, "function f takes a parameter of unknown type 'a and another parameter of unknown type 'b , and returns an integer." The actual add function that we send in fits this signature (where 'a and 'b also turn out to be integers). But sometimes you will want to think about things in a different way: choosing to specify the type of f up front, by giving a *type hint*. You write the type hint using the same notation as shown in the type signatures we've just been discussing, that is, a list of parameter types, separated by -> if the parameters are to be curried, or * if they are to be tupled together. Listing 9-10 shows this in action. First (in applyAndPrint1), we allow the incoming curried arguments to be unknown types 'a and 'b, expressed as (f : 'a -> 'b -> int). Secondly (in applyAndPrint2) we pin them down to be integers, expressed as (f : int -> int -> int). And finally (in applyAndPrint3) we require a tuple of two integers, expressed as (f : int * int -> int).

Listing 9-10. Using type hints to specify function types

```
// Takes curried arguments:
let add a b = a + b

// Takes tupled argument:
let addTupled(a, b) = a + b

// f must take curried arguments and return an int:
let applyAndPrint1 (f : 'a -> 'b -> int) a b =
    let r = f a b
    printfn "%i" r

// f must take curried integer arguments and return an int:
let applyAndPrint2 (f : int -> int -> int) a b =
    let r = f a b
    printfn "%i" r

// f must take tupled integer arguments and return an int:
let applyAndPrint3 (f : int * int -> int) a b =
    let r = f(a, b)
    printfn "%i" r

// Must use the curried version of add here:
applyAndPrint1 add 2 3
applyAndPrint2 add 2 3

// Must use the tupled version of add here:
applyAndPrint3 addTupled 2 3
```

This means that when writing a function (we'll call it newFunction) that takes another function (we'll call it paramFunction), you have two options:

- Work on the body of newFunction first, and let the compiler work out the type of paramFunction itself based on how it is used (as Listing 9-9).

- Specify the signature of the paramFunction in newFunction's parameter list using a type hint, so that the compiler can check that you call paramFunction correctly in newFunction's body (as Listing 9-10).

The final outcome can be just the same, because usually you can remove the type hint when everything is compiling successfully.

For me there is no hard and fast rule for which approach to take. I usually start by relying entirely on type inference at first, but if either the compiler or I get confused, I try adding a type hint in case that clarifies matters. I normally try removing the type hint at the end of the process, but I don't let it ruin my day if type inference can't work out the signature, which sometimes does happen in otherwise valid code. In those cases I leave the type hint in and move on. Even then, I often find later that my code elsewhere was imperfect, and when I sort that out I try again to remove type hints I left in earlier.

Functions That Return Functions

Not only can functions *take* functions; functions can *return* functions. Unlike with parameters, explicitly returning functions requires you to pay a tiny syntax overhead, the keyword fun followed by an argument list and a forward arrow ->. We can rejig the add function from Listing 9-1 so that it behaves in exactly the same way but works by explicitly returning a function (Listing 9-11).

Listing 9-11. Explicitly returning a function

```
// int -> int -> int
let add a =
    fun b -> a + b

// 5
printfn "%i" (add 2 3)
```

See how in Listing 9-11 we use fun b -> to specify that we want to create a function that takes one argument, which we call b. Since this is the last expression in the definition of add, it is this newly minted function that is returned. Notice also how the type signature of the new add is the same as it was in Listing 9-1. This bears out what I was saying earlier: that you can think of a function with two arguments as only really taking one argument and returning a function that itself requires the remaining argument.

Why on earth would you want to make a function definition more complicated by explicitly returning another function? The answer is: you can do useful work, and/or hide data, by placing it *inside* the outer function but *before* the returned function. In

Listing 9-12 we define a simple counter that takes a starting point, and each time it is invoked, returns the next integer.

Listing 9-12. A simple counter using explicit returning of a function

```
let counter start =
    let mutable current = start
    fun () ->
        let this = current
        current <- current + 1
        this

let demo() =

    let c1 = counter 0
    let c2 = counter 100

    // c1: 0
    // c2: 100
    // c1: 1
    // c2: 101
    // c1: 2
    // c2: 102
    // c1: 3
    // c2: 103
    // c1: 4
    // c2: 104
    for _ in 0..4 do
        printfn "c1: %i" (c1())
        printfn "c2: %i" (c2())
```

The counter function works by initializing a little bit of mutable state, then returning a function that returns the current value and increments the state. This is a nice way of using, but concealing, a mutable state. (As implemented here, though, I wouldn't want to warrant that it's thread safe.)

Another situation where you might like to create and use, but not expose, a bit of state, is random number generation. One way of generating random numbers is to create a new instance of the System.Random class, then call one of its methods to produce values. It's always a little annoying to have to worry about the scope of the System. Random instance. But you can get around this by binding a value that creates the System. Random, then returns a function that gets the next value from it (Listing 9-13).

Listing 9-13. Hiding a System.Random instance by returning a function

```
let randomByte =
    let r = System.Random()
    fun () ->
        r.Next(0, 255) |> byte

// A3-52-31-D2-90-E6-6F-45-1C-3F-F2-9B-7F-58-34-44-
let demo() =
    for _ in 0..15 do
        printf "%X-" (randomByte())
    printfn ""
```

In Listing 9-13, the function we return takes unit (expressed two round-brackets) and uses – but does not expose – a System.Random instance to return a random byte. Although we call randomByte() multiple times, only one System.Random() instance is created. In addition to the data-hiding aspect, this pattern is also useful where it takes significant time to initialize the state within the outer function.

Function Composition

Once we realize that functions are simply values, it's logical to ask if we can in some way add them together, as we can number values (by adding) or string values (by concatenating). The answer, you won't be surprised to learn, is "yes." Let's imagine you have the task of taking some text and replacing all the directional or *typographic* quote marks with non-directional or *neutral* ones. For example this text:

"Bob said 'Hello,'" said Alice.

... would be translated to this:

"Bob said 'Hello,'" said Alice.

The actual replacement is simply a matter of calling .NET's String.Replace method a couple of times in functions called fixSingleQuotes and fixDoubleQuotes (Listing 9-14). Then we bind a function called fixTypographicQuotes. which calls fixSingleQuotes and fixDoubleQuotes to do its work.

Listing 9-14. First cut of removing typographic quotes

```
module Typographic =
    let openSingle = "'
    let openDouble = '"'
    let closeSingle = "'
    let closeDouble = '"'

module Neutral =
    let single = '\"
    let double = '"'

/// Translate any typographic single quotes to neutral ones.
let fixSingleQuotes (s : string) =
    s
      .Replace(Typographic.openSingle, Neutral.single)
      .Replace(Typographic.closeSingle, Neutral.single)

/// Translate any typographic double quotes to neutral ones.
let fixDoubleQuotes (s : string) =
    s
      .Replace(Typographic.openDouble, Neutral.double)
      .Replace(Typographic.closeDouble, Neutral.double)

/// Translate any typographic quotes to neutral ones.
let fixTypographicQuotes (s : string) =
    s
    |> fixSingleQuotes
    |> fixDoubleQuotes
```

There's nothing inherently wrong with the way `fixTypographicQuotes` is defined in Listing 9-14. Indeed I would often be tempted to leave the code in that state. But there are several alternative ways of expressing the same logic, any of which you may encounter in the wild, and some of which you might even prefer.

Firstly, we note that `fixSingleQuotes` *returns* a string, and `fixDoubleQuotes` *takes* a string. Whenever some function takes the same type that another function returns, you can compose them together into a new function using the function composition operator `>>` (Listing 9-15).

Listing 9-15. Basic function composition

```
// Build a 'fixQuotes' function using composition:
let fixTypographicQuotes (s : string) =
    let fixQuotes = fixSingleQuotes >> fixDoubleQuotes
    s |> fixQuotes
```

In Listing 9-15 we define a function called `fixQuotes`, which is a combination of `fixSingleQuotes` and `fixDoubleQuotes`. When `fixQuotes` is called, `fixSingleQuotes` will be called first (using the input to `fixQuotes`), and its output will be passed to `fixDoubleQuotes`. Whatever `fixDoubleQuotes` returns will be returned as the result of `fixQuotes`. Having defined `fixQuotes`, we then call it by passing the input `s` into it.

We can eliminate still more code by not explicitly binding `fixQuotes`, instead doing the composition "on-the-fly" in brackets, and passing `s` into that (Listing 9-16).

Listing 9-16. Using a composed function without binding it to a name

```
// Remove the explicit binding of 'fix':
let fixTypographicQuotes (s : string) =
    s |> (fixSingleQuotes >> fixDoubleQuotes)
```

This does exactly the same thing as Listing 9-15, but without binding the composed function to an arguably unnecessary token.

Finally, we note that the explicit parameter `s` isn't really needed, because its sole purpose is to be passed into the composition of `fixSingleQuotes` and `fixDoubleQuotes`. If we simply delete it, we still end up with a function `fixTypographicQuotes` that takes a string and returns a string (Listing 9-17).

Listing 9-17. Eliminating an unnecessary parameter

```
// Remove the explicit parameter:
let fixTypographicQuotes =
    fixSingleQuotes >> fixDoubleQuotes
```

It takes a while before one starts automatically recognizing where functions can be composed with `>>`, rather than pipelined together with `|>`. But once you start "feeling the force," there is a temptation to go crazy with function composition. You may even find yourself bending other parts of your code just so that you can use composition.

This is often a good thing: functions that are easily composable are often well-designed functions. But also remember: *composition isn't a goal in itself.* The principles of *motivational transparency* and *semantic focus* trump everything else.

For example, if you use function composition extensively, the reader of your code will have fewer named bindings, like `fixQuotes`, to give them clues as to what is going on. And in the worst case, if the code has to be debugged, they won't have a bound value to look at because the composed functions have effectively been put into a black box. Sometimes code with a few explicitly bound intermediate values is simply more readable and more maintainable. Use function composition with restraint!

Recommendations

Here are some thoughts I'd like you to take away from this chapter:

- Remember the twin concepts of *currying* (defining parameters as separate, untupled items) and *partial application* (binding a function value by applying another function giving some, but not all its curried parameters).

- Consider defining the parameters of your function in curried style. It can reduce noise (brackets) and make your functions more flexible to use.

- Define curried parameters (more commonly known as curried arguments) in an order that is likely to make partial application by a consumer make the most sense.

- Use currying and partial application judiciously to clarify and simplify your code, and to eliminate code repetition.

- Functions can take other functions as arguments. Exploit this to create beautiful, decoupled code. Remember that you have a choice about whether to specify the signature of the incoming function using a type hint, or to allow type inference to infer its signature based on how it is used.

- Functions can explicitly return other functions. This can be a great way to get data-hiding without classes.

- Whenever a function's input is the same type as another function's output, they can be composed together using the >> operator. The fact that the functions you have written are composable is a good sign, but that doesn't mean you *have to* compose them with >>. You may be sacrificing readability and ease of debugging.

Summary

Coding gurus love to talk about "decoupled code." But in Object Oriented languages, functions are still coupled to classes in the form of methods, and parameters are still coupled to each other in the form of tuples. F# sets functions free by making them first class values, able to be declared independently, called, passed as arguments, returned as results, and composed together; all vastly increasing the expressiveness of the language. In part this is achieved by using the concept of curried arguments, which can be applied one at a time, with each supplied argument taking us one step closer to an actual computation.

One of the keys to writing stylish F# code is to make good, but not excessive use, of these powers. Above all, don't always use partial application and composition to reduce your code down to the most concise expression humanly possible. It won't be readable or maintainable.

In the next chapter we'll leave the rarefied world of F# functions and start our journey into performant F# code by looking at *asynchronous and parallel programming*.

Exercises

EXERCISE 9-1 – FUNCTIONS AS ARGUMENTS

Think back to the code from Listing 9-2, where we supplied an add function to applyAndPrint, which calls add and prints the results:

```
let add a b = a + b

let applyAndPrint f a b =
    let r = f a b
    printfn "%i" r

// "5"
applyAndPrint add 2 3
```

Define another function called `multiply` that multiplies its arguments. Can it be used by `applyAndPrint`?

What if you want to send in a function to subtract its second input from its first? Is it possible to do this without defining a named function called something like `subtract`?

EXERCISE 9-2 – FUNCTIONS RETURNING FUNCTIONS

In Listing 9-12, we defined a counter that returned a function to count up from a defined starting point:

```
let counter start =
    let mutable current = start
    fun () ->
let this = current
        current <- current + 1
        this

let demo() =

    let c1 = counter 0
    let c2 = counter 100

    for _ in 0..4 do
        printfn "c1: %i" (c1())
        printfn "c2: %i" (c2())
```

Define another function called `rangeCounter` that returns a function that generates numbers in a circular pattern between a specified range, for example, 3, 4, 5, 6, 3, 4, 5, 6, 3....

EXERCISE 9-3 – PARTIAL APPLICATION

The code below shows a function `featureScale` that "normalizes" a dataset, so that all the values fall into a specified range. The `scale` function calls `featureScale` to normalize a dataset into the range 0..1.

```
let featureScale a b xMin xMax x =
    a + ((x - xMin) * (b - a)) / (xMax - xMin)
```

```
let scale (data : seq<float>) =
    let minX = data |> Seq.min
    let maxX = data |> Seq.max
    // let zeroOneScale = ...
    data
    |> Seq.map (fun x -> featureScale 0. 1. minX maxX x)
    // |> Seq.map zeroOneScale

// seq [0.0; 0.5; 1.0]
let demo() =
    [100.; 150.; 200.]
    |> scale
```

How would you amend the code so that the mapping operation at the end of the scale function did not use a lambda function? That is, so that it reads something like this:

```
|> Seq.map zeroOneScale
```

You can assume that the provided dataset is non-empty.

EXERCISE 9-4 – FUNCTION COMPOSITION

You have a list of functions, each of which takes a float argument and returns another float, like this:

```
let pipeline =
    [ fun x -> x * 2.
      fun x -> x * x
      fun x -> x - 99.9 ]
```

The list is non-empty but otherwise can have any length.

How would you write a function `applyAll` that can take such a list of functions and apply them all, taking the result of the first function and feeding it into the second, taking the result of that and feeding it into the third function, and so forth, until a final result is produced? Your function should be callable like this:

```
let applyAll (p : (float -> float) list) =
    // Replace this:
    raise <| System.NotImplementedException()
```

```
let demo() =
    let x = 100. |> applyAll pipeline
    // 39900.1
    printfn "%f" x
```

Hints:

- Remember you can combine values in a non-empty list using `List.reduce`.

- Remember that there is an F# operator, which can combine (compose) two functions into one, providing that the output of the first is compatible with the input of the second.

Exercise Solutions

EXERCISE 9-1 – FUNCTIONS AS ARGUMENTS

It's straightforward to define a `multiply` function and pass it into `applyAndPrint`:

```
let add a b = a + b
let multiply a b = a * b

let applyAndPrint f a b =
    let r = f a b
    printfn "%i" r

// "5"
applyAndPrint add 2 3
// "6"
applyAndPrint multiply 2 3
```

To define a subtract function without naming it, you can use the `fun` keyword in the call to `applyAndPrint`:

```
applyAndPrint (fun x y -> x - y) 2 3
```

Or you could just pass an operator straight in:

```
applyAndPrint (-) 2 3
```

EXERCISE 9-2 – FUNCTIONS RETURNING FUNCTIONS

You can achieve this using a similar pattern to Listing 9-12 but with a little if/then logic to calculate the next value and wrap it round when it passes the upper bound.

```
let rangeCounter first last =
    let mutable current = first
    fun () ->
        let this = current
        let next = current + 1
        current <-
            if next <= last then
                next
            else
                first
        this

// r1: 3 r2: 6
// r1: 4 r2: 7
// r1: 5 r2: 8
// r1: 6 r2: 9
// r1: 3 r2: 10
// r1: 4 r2: 11
// ...
// r1: 3 r2: 8
let demo() =
    let r1 = rangeCounter 3 6
    let r2 = rangeCounter 6 11

    for _ in 0..20 do
        printfn "r1: %i r2: %i" (r1()) (r2())
```

EXERCISE 9-3 – PARTIAL APPLICATION

You need to bind a value called something like `zeroOneScale`, which is a partial application of `featureScale` providing values for the a, b, xMin, and xMax parameters. The resulting function only has one parameter, x, and so can be used directly in a `Seq.map` operation.

```
let featureScale a b xMin xMax x =
    a + ((x - xMin) * (b - a)) / (xMax - xMin)

let scale (data : seq<float>) =
    let minX = data |> Seq.min
    let maxX = data |> Seq.max
    let zeroOneScale = featureScale 0. 1. minX maxX
    data
    |> Seq.map zeroOneScale

// seq [0.0; 0.5; 1.0]
let demo() =
    [100.; 150.; 200.]
    |> scale
```

EXERCISE 9-4 – FUNCTION COMPOSITION

This can be achieved using `List.reduce` (or `Seq.reduce`) and the `>>` (function composition) operator.

```
let pipeline =
    [ fun x -> x * 2.
      fun x -> x * x
      fun x -> x - 99.9 ]

let applyAll (p : (float -> float) list) =
    p |> List.reduce (>>)

let demo() =
    let x = 100. |> applyAll pipeline
    // 39900.1
    printfn "%f" x
```

Since `List.reduce` is a partial function and raises an exception if the list is empty, the function pipeline list must contain at least one function.

If you want, you can omit the explicit parameter for `applyAll`, as the reduce operation will return a composed function, which itself expects a parameter.

```
let applyAll =
    List.reduce (>>)
```

CHAPTER 10

Asynchronous and Parallel Programming

I know how hard it is to watch it go.
And all the effort that it took to get there in the first place.
And all the effort not to let the effort show.

—Everything but the Girl, Band

Ordering Pizza

In *asynchronous programming*, we embrace the fact that certain operations are best represented by running them separately from the main flow of logic. Instead of stopping everything while we wait for a result, we expect those separate computations to notify us when they have completed, at which point we'll deal with their results. It's a bit like one of those restaurants where you order, say, a pizza, and they give you a pager that flashes when your order is ready. You're free to grab a table and chat with your friends. When the pager goes off, you collect your pizza and carry on with the main business of your visit – eating!

F# offers an elegant model for asynchronous computation, but it has to be said that working asynchronously inevitably complicates the business logic of your code. The trick is to keep the impacts to the minimum. Fortunately, by adopting a small set of coding patterns, you can keep your code elegant and readable, while still getting the benefits of asynchronous working.

251

© Kit Eason 2018
K. Eason, *Stylish F#*, https://doi.org/10.1007/978-1-4842-4000-7_10

A World Without Async

Because the benefits and impacts of asynchronous working tend to manifest across the whole structure of your program, I'm going to break with the practice of most of this book and offer a complete, potentially useful program as the example for this whole chapter. The example is a "bulk file downloader," a console program that can find all the file download links in a web page and download all the files. It'll also be able to filter what it downloads. For example, you could download just the files whose names end in ".gz". As a starting point, I'll offer a *synchronous* version of the program. Then I'll go through all the steps necessary to make it work asynchronously. This reflects my normal coding practice: I tend to write a synchronous version initially to get all the business logic clear, then I translate relevant portions into an asynchronous world.

To avoid including a huge listing, I've broken up the program into parts that I'll discuss separately. If you want to follow along, create an F# console program and simply add the code from each successive listing into `Program.fs`.

We'll start with a module that can print colored messages to the console, which will be useful to show when downloads start, complete, fail, and so forth (Listing 10-1). The `report` function also shows the managed thread ID for the current thread, which will help us explore the behavior of our program as we transition it to an asynchronous approach.

Notice also how I use partial application, as introduced in the previous chapter, to provide functions called `red`, `yellow,` and so forth to issue messages in those colors.

Listing 10-1. Printing colored console messages

```
module Log =

    open System
    open System.Threading

    /// Print a colored log message.
    let report (color : ConsoleColor) (message : string) =
        Console.ForegroundColor <- color
        printfn "%s (thread ID: %i)"
            message Thread.CurrentThread.ManagedThreadId
        Console.ResetColor()

    let red = report ConsoleColor.Red
```

```
let green = report ConsoleColor.Green
let yellow = report ConsoleColor.Yellow
let cyan = report ConsoleColor.Cyan
```

Next, we have a module to model the fact that a download can succeed or fail. I haven't used the `Option` type here because I want to be able to report back the name of a file that has failed. Hence both the `OK` and `Failed` cases of the Discriminated Union (DU) have a `filename` payload (Listing 10-2).

Listing 10-2. A Discriminated Union to model success and failure

```
module Outcome =

    type Outcome =
        | OK of filename:string
        | Failed of filename:string

    let isOk = function
        | OK _ -> true
        | Failed _ -> false

    let fileName = function
        | OK fn
        | Failed fn -> fn
```

The `Outcome` module also offers convenience functions for deciding whether a given `Outcome` instance is a success or not, and for recovering a filename from an `Outcome` instance. In these functions, I use the `function` keyword, which allows me to pattern match from a DU instance to a case without providing an explicit DU instance parameter. For example, the `isOk` function could also have been expressed as in Listing 10-3.

Listing 10-3. The isOk function in more verbose form

```
let isOk outcome =
    match outcome with
    | OK _ -> true
    | Failed _ -> false
```

Now let's write some functions that get the file's download links from the target web page (Listing 10-4). The `absoluteUri` function deals with the fact that some web pages provide download links relative to their own addresses (e.g., `downloads/myfile.txt`) while others provide absolute addresses (e.g., `https://mysite.org/downloads/myfile.txt`). The code here is pretty simplistic and may not work in all cases, but I wanted to keep it simple, as URL processing is not the main topic of this chapter.

The `getLinks` function takes a URI and a regular expression pattern, and parses the web page to get all the download links that match the pattern. Note that this function uses `HtmlDocument.Load`, which is provided by the `FSharp.Data` Nuget package. You'll need to use Nuget or Paket to add this package to your console project.

Listing 10-4. Functions for getting download links from a web page

```
module Download =

    open System
    open System.IO
    open System.Net
    open System.Text.RegularExpressions
    // From Nuget package "FSharp.Data"
    open FSharp.Data

    let private absoluteUri (pageUri : Uri) (filePath : string) =
        if filePath.StartsWith("http:")
           || filePath.StartsWith("https:") then
            Uri(filePath)
        else
            let sep = '/'
            filePath.TrimStart(sep)
            |> (sprintf "%O%c%s" pageUri sep)
            |> Uri

    /// Get the URLs of all links in a specified page matching a
    /// specified regex pattern.
    let private getLinks (pageUri : Uri) (filePattern : string) =
        Log.cyan "Getting names..."
        let re = Regex(filePattern)
```

```
    let html = HtmlDocument.Load(pageUri.AbsoluteUri)

    let links =
        html.Descendants ["a"]
        |> Seq.choose (fun node ->
            node.TryGetAttribute("href")
            |> Option.map (fun att -> att.Value()))
        |> Seq.filter (re.IsMatch)
        |> Seq.map (absoluteUri pageUri)
        |> Seq.distinct
        |> Array.ofSeq

    links
```

Next up we have a function that attempts to download a file from a given URI to a given local path (Listing 10-5). If you are following along, the code for this listing, and for Listing 10-6, should be included in the Download module we started in Listing 10-4. The tryDownload function uses WebClient.DownloadFile to do its work. It reports success by returning Outcome.OK, or failure (if there is an exception) by returning Outcome.Failed.

Listing 10-5. The tryDownload function

```
/// Download a file to the specified local path.
let private tryDownload (localPath : string) (fileUri : Uri) =
    let fileName = fileUri.Segments |> Array.last
    Log.yellow (sprintf "%s - starting download" fileName)
    let filePath = Path.Combine(localPath, fileName)

    use client = new WebClient()
    try
        client.DownloadFile(fileUri, filePath)
        Log.green (sprintf "%s - download complete" fileName)
        Outcome.OK fileName
    with
    | e ->
        Log.red (sprintf "%s - error: %s" fileName e.Message)
        Outcome.Failed fileName
```

Also within the Download module, we have one public function, GetFiles (Listing 10-6). GetFiles uses getLinks to list the required download links, and calls tryDownload for each of the resulting paths. The results are divided into successes and failures using Array.partition, and finally these are mapped into a tuple of arrays of names for the failures and successes respectively.

Listing 10-6. The GetFiles function

```
/// Download all the files linked to in the specified webpage, whose
/// link path matches the specified regular expression, to the specified
/// local path. Return a tuple of succeeded and failed file names.
let GetFiles
        (pageUri : Uri) (filePattern : string) (localPath : string) =
    let links = getLinks pageUri filePattern

    let downloaded, failed =
        links
        |> Array.map (tryDownload localPath)
        |> Array.partition Outcome.isOk

    downloaded |> Array.map Outcome.fileName,
    failed |> Array.map Outcome.fileName
```

Finally, in Listing 10-7, we have a main function for the console program. It calls Download.GetFiles to do its work. We also use a System.Diagnostics.Stopwatch to time the whole operation, and we list out all the failed files at the end of processing.

Note   You'll need to create a directory called "c:\temp\downloads," or amend the code to use a directory that exists.

Listing 10-7. The console program's main function

```
open System
open System.Diagnostics

[<EntryPoint>]
let main argv =
```

```
// Some minor planets data:
let uri = Uri @"https://minorplanetcenter.net/data"
let pattern = @"neam.*\.json\.gz$"

let localPath = @"c:\temp\downloads"

let sw = Stopwatch()
sw.Start()

let downloaded, failed =
    Download.GetFiles uri pattern localPath

failed
|> Array.iter (fun fn ->
    Log.report ConsoleColor.Red (sprintf "Failed: %s" fn))

Log.cyan
    (sprintf "%i files downloaded in %0.1fs, %i failed. Press a key"
        downloaded.Length sw.Elapsed.TotalSeconds failed.Length)

Console.ReadKey() |> ignore

0
```

In case you want to try out the program on different web pages, here is a table of web pages where you will find some files to download, and some corresponding regular expression patterns (Table 10-1).

Table 10-1. *Some Download URLs and Name Patterns*

Url	Pattern	Comments
https://minorplanetcenter.net/data	neam.*\.json\.gz$	Minor planets
http://compling.hss.ntu.edu.sg/omw	\.zip$	Computational Linguistics
http://storage.googleapis.com/books/ ngrams/books/datasetsv2.html	eng\-1M\-2gram.*\. zip$	Google n-grams Very large. Don't download this over a metered connection!

Running the Synchronous Downloader

Here's the output I got when I ran our synchronous program for the minor planets data (Listing 10-8).

Listing 10-8. Behavior of the synchronous downloader

```
Getting names... (thread ID: 1)
neam00_extended.json.gz - starting download (thread ID: 1)
neam00_extended.json.gz - download complete (thread ID: 1)
neam01_extended.json.gz - starting download (thread ID: 1)
neam01_extended.json.gz - download complete (thread ID: 1)
...
neam15_extended.json.gz - starting download (thread ID: 1)
neam15_extended.json.gz - download complete (thread ID: 1)
16 files downloaded in 52.7s, 0 failed. Press a key (thread ID: 1)
```

The files are downloaded one at a time, everything happens on the same thread (ID: 1), and the whole process takes about a minute.

Figure 10-1 shows what's happening on my WiFi connection during the run period.

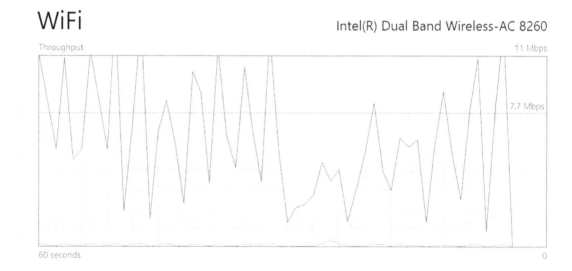

Figure 10-1. *WiFi usage during a run of the synchronous mass downloader*

While the WiFi connection is kept fairly busy, it certainly isn't maxed out. But the main concern with the behavior of this synchronous version is the fact that it hogs an entire thread throughout the time it is running. It does this even though much of the time is spent waiting for server responses as blocks of data are sent over the network. In .NET a thread is considered quite an expensive resource, one which – on a busy machine – could be doing other work during these waits. This other work could be for other unrelated programs on the same machine, or simply downloading other files for this same bulk download run.

Converting Code to Asynchronous

To remedy the situation, we need to go through all our code to identify operations where our code is "ordering pizza": in other words, starting an operation that will take a significant amount of time, and which doesn't require our main thread's attention to complete. Typically, this will be input/output operations, where the real work happens in disc controllers, network interfaces, networks, and remote servers. The first place where our code orders pizza is in the getLinks function (back in Listing 10-4), where we load an HTML document that comes from a remote server:

```
let html = HtmlDocument.Load(pageUri.AbsoluteUri)
```

If you look at the Intellisense for HtmlDocument, you might notice that there's also an AsyncLoad function. What if you simply use this in your html binding? (Listing 10-9).

Listing 10-9. The return type of HtmlDocument.AsyncLoad

```
let private getLinks (pageUri : Uri) (filePattern : string) =
    Log.cyan "Getting names..."
    let re = Regex(filePattern)

    // val html : Async<HtmlDocument>
    let html = HtmlDocument.AsyncLoad(pageUri.AbsoluteUri)
```

The code following the let html = binding won't compile now, because html is no longer an HtmlDocument instance, it's an Async<HtmlDocument>. Instead of giving you a pizza, the person at the counter has given you a pager: effectively the promise of a pizza and a means of knowing when it's ready. So, just like when you enter a restaurant that uses a pager system, you need to adjust your expectations and behave a little differently: that is, don't eat the pager!

259

The way to achieve this change of worldview in F# is with an *async computation expression*, which is very easy to use. Firstly, move the whole body of the getLinks function into curly brackets, and place the word async before these. Instead of let to bind the html value, use let!. Finally, instead of simply "mentioning" the links value at the end of the function to return it, explicitly return it using the return keyword (Listing 10-10).

Listing 10-10. Placing a function body into an async computation expression

```
/// Get the URLs of all links in a specified page matching a
/// specified regex pattern.
let private getLinks (pageUri : Uri) (filePattern : string) =
    async {
        Log.cyan "Getting names..."
        let re = Regex(filePattern)

        let! html = HtmlDocument.AsyncLoad(pageUri.AbsoluteUri)

        let links =
            html.Descendants ["a"]
            |> Seq.choose (fun node ->
                node.TryGetAttribute("href")
                |> Option.map (fun att -> att.Value()))
            |> Seq.filter (re.IsMatch)
            |> Seq.map (absoluteUri pageUri)
            |> Seq.distinct
            |> Array.ofSeq

        return links
    }
```

The let! and return keywords are only valid in the context of computation expressions such as async {}. Here, let! effectively means "Please get me a pizza and page me when it's ready. I will come back to this exact point when you page me. In the meantime, I'll feel free to talk to my friends." Using return is analogous to linking a particular pizza order with a pager, and handing over the pager instead of the pizza.

The next place where we "order pizza" is in the tryDownload function, where we use WebClient.DownloadFile:

client.DownloadFile(fileUri, filePath)

Again this is an I/O operation that is going to take time, in this case an eternity in CPU terms because we might be downloading large files. There are two asynchronous methods in the WebClient API to choose from: DownloadFileAsync and DownloadFileTaskAsync. The one we want is DownloadFileTaskAsync. The other one requires us to provide an event handler to notify us of completion, almost as if we had to give the pizza restaurant our own pager. This seems a bit too much trouble to be worth it, even for pizza.

To use DownloadFileTaskAsync in the context of an F# async computation expression, we need to do two things. First, we need to translate it from a C# Task into an F# Async, which you can easily do using Async.AwaitTask. (I'll follow up on the differences between Task and Async in a moment.) Second, since this is an imperative operation that doesn't of itself return anything, we need to use the do! keyword instead of let! to specify that it should be run asynchronously without returning a value. And finally, we need to use the return keyword to return the Outcome.OK or Outcome.Failed results (Listing 10-11).

Listing 10-11. Using Async.AwaitTask and do! to perform an async imperative operation

```
/// Download a file to the specified local path.
let private tryDownload (localPath : string) (fileUri : Uri) =
    async {
        let fileName = fileUri.Segments |> Array.last
        Log.yellow (sprintf "%s - starting download" fileName)
        let filePath = Path.Combine(localPath, fileName)

        use client = new WebClient()
        try
            do!
                client.DownloadFileTaskAsync(fileUri, filePath)
                |> Async.AwaitTask
```

```
        Log.green (sprintf "%s - download complete" fileName)
        return (Outcome.OK fileName)
    with
    | e ->
        Log.red (sprintf "%s - error: %s" fileName e.Message)
        return (Outcome.Failed fileName)
}
```

By now you should be able to see a pattern emerging in what we need to do to make a function asynchronous:

- Place the body in an `async {}`.

- Identify any time-consuming external operations where the API you are using offers an `Async` version.

- Use `let!` or `do!` to bind or imperatively execute them. Where necessary, use `Async.AwaitTask` to translate from C# `Task` to F# `Async`.

- Return (the promise of) results using the `return` keyword.

Incidentally, from F# 4.5 there is also a `match!` keyword, which you can use to call async functions, and pattern match on the results, in a single operation.

Next we need to apply a similar recipe to the next level up: the `GetFiles` function that calls `getLinks` and `tryDownload` to do its work. We can start off in exactly the same way, placing the whole function body in `async{}` and using `let!` to bind `getLinks` (Listing 10-12).

Listing 10-12. Starting to make GetFiles asynchronous

```
let AsyncGetFiles
    (pageUri : Uri) (filePattern : string) (localPath : string) =
    async {
        let! links = getLinks pageUri filePattern
        ...
```

Since `GetFiles` is effectively the public API of the `Download` module, I've also renamed it `AsyncGetFiles` to cue callers that this is an asynchronous function.

The next few lines of `GetFiles` require a little more thought. The current code looks like what is in Listing 10-13.

Listing 10-13. Synchronous download code

```
let downloaded, failed =
    links
    |> Array.map (tryDownload localPath)
    |> Array.partition Outcome.isOk
```

This is no longer good enough because `tryDownLoad` is now not a function that will immediately do its work: instead it's a promise of work not yet even started. We could make the code compile by forcing the computation to execute and awaiting its result in (Listing 10-14), but then we've gained almost nothing, because the download operations are still performed one at a time, even though they run on different threads.

Listing 10-14. An anti-pattern for multiple, similar async computations

```
let downloaded, failed =
    links
    |> Array.map (fun link ->
        tryDownload localPath link
        |> Async.RunSynchronously)
    |> Array.partition Outcome.isOk
```

```
Getting names... (thread ID: 1)
neam00_extended.json.gz - starting download (thread ID: 9)
neam00_extended.json.gz - download complete (thread ID: 15)
neam01_extended.json.gz - starting download (thread ID: 7)
neam01_extended.json.gz - download complete (thread ID: 15)
neam02_extended.json.gz - starting download (thread ID: 15)
...
neam15_extended.json.gz - starting download (thread ID: 15)
neam15_extended.json.gz - download complete (thread ID: 7)
16 files downloaded in 56.1s, 0 failed. Press a key (thread ID: 1)
```

This is like ordering multiple pizzas, taking the pager for each pizza, but then standing at the counter in everyone else's way until each pager flashes.

Instead what we want to do is gather all the ready-to-go computations and run them simultaneously (or at least allow .NET to run them as simultaneously as resources allow). This can be achieved by sending the results of `Seq.map (tryDownload...)` into the function `Async.Parallel`, and using a `let!` binding to bind the results (Listing 10-15).

Listing 10-15. Using Async.Parallel

```
let AsyncGetFiles (pageUri : Uri) (filePattern : string)
(localPath : string) =
    async {
        let! links = getLinks pageUri filePattern

        let! downloadResults =
            links
            |> Seq.map (tryDownload localPath)
            |> Async.Parallel

        let downloaded, failed =
            downloadResults
            |> Array.partition Outcome.isOk

        return
            downloaded |> Array.map Outcome.fileName,
            failed |> Array.map Outcome.fileName
    }
```

We'll refine this logic later, but this is good enough for now. Finally, we need to amend the program's `main` function slightly, so that it calls `AsyncGetFiles` and waits for its results (Listing 10-16).

Listing 10-16. Calling AsyncGetFiles

```
open System
open System.Diagnostics

[<EntryPoint>]
let main argv =
    // Some minor planets data:
    let uri = Uri @"https://minorplanetcenter.net/data"
    let pattern = @"neam.*\.json\.gz$"
```

```
let localPath = @"c:\temp\downloads"

let sw = Stopwatch()
sw.Start()

let downloaded, failed =
    Download.AsyncGetFiles uri pattern localPath
    |> Async.RunSynchronously

failed
|> Array.iter (fun fn ->
    Log.report ConsoleColor.Red (sprintf "Failed: %s" fn))

Log.cyan
    (sprintf "%i files downloaded in %0.1fs, %i failed. Press a key"
        downloaded.Length sw.Elapsed.TotalSeconds failed.Length)

Console.ReadKey() |> ignore

0
```

Locking Shared Resources

There's one more task to do, and that is to control access to a shared, mutable resource that all the download tasks will use concurrently. And what is that resource? It's the console, with its colored messages! Each of the simultaneous computations might output to the console at any time, so if you don't control access to it you'll get jumbled-up messages and colors. The fix is relatively easy: use the lock keyword (Listing 10-17).

Listing 10-17. Make a function thread safe using a lock expression

```
let report =
    let lockObj = obj()
    fun (color : ConsoleColor) (message : string) ->
        lock lockObj (fun _ ->
            Console.ForegroundColor <- color
            printfn "%s (thread ID: %i)"
                message Thread.CurrentThread.ManagedThreadId
            Console.ResetColor())
```

The new version of `report` is a nice example of the technique we introduced in the previous chapter: using a binding that creates some state but keeps it private, then returns a function that uses that state. In this case the state in question is simply an arbitrary object that is used by the `lock` expression to ensure exclusive access.

Needless to say, locking is a very complex subject. But in this context, Listing 10-17 shows a simple and effective way to achieve exclusive access for an operation that won't take long to run.

Testing Asynchronous Downloads

It is time to check whether our shiny new asynchronous download performs better. Here are the results of running against the minor planets data (Listing 10-18, compare with Listing 10-8).

Listing 10-18. Log messages from an asynchronous run

```
Getting names... (thread ID: 1)
neam01_extended.json.gz - starting download (thread ID: 7)
neam00_extended.json.gz - starting download (thread ID: 4)
neam02_extended.json.gz - starting download (thread ID: 3)
...
neam15_extended.json.gz - starting download (thread ID: 7)
neam03_extended.json.gz - download complete (thread ID: 23)
neam00_extended.json.gz - download complete (thread ID: 22)
neam02_extended.json.gz - download complete (thread ID: 21)
neam01_extended.json.gz - download complete (thread ID: 21)
...
neam12_extended.json.gz - download complete (thread ID: 18)
16 files downloaded in 14.1s, 0 failed. Press a key (thread ID: 1)
```

The differences between this and Listing 10-8 are striking:

- The downloads run on several threads, and the thread that logs the completion of a download is usually different from the thread that started it. This is the magic of `let!` and `do!`.

- *All* the downloads are started before *any* of them complete. Compare that with the way started/completed messages simply alternate in the synchronous version.

- Most importantly of all, the whole operation takes 14 seconds instead of a minute.

The usage of my WiFi connection is equally striking (Figure 10-2).

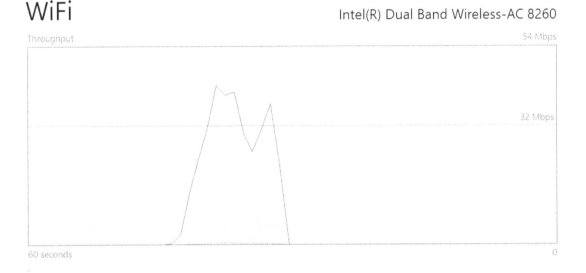

Figure 10-2. *WiFi throughput downloading files asynchronously*

In Figure 10-1, throughput on the interface was very spiky and peaked at about 11Mbps. In the asynchronous version, we get up to over 40Mbps, and the throughput is pretty consistent over the brief time the run lasts. Given this is going over WiFi, through my home's highly questionable, main wiring, then through England's almost equally, questionable fiber infrastructure, this is really pretty good.

Batching

One thing I've learned in several decades of coding is never to trust one's first successful run! Let's try the same code against some of the Google n-grams dataset. (You'll find the URL and regular expression pattern for this in Table 10-1).

> **Note**   This is a large dataset. Don't do this on a metered connection, or while your household is trying to watch Netflix!

This is how things looked after a few minutes of running (Listing 10-19 and Figure 10-3).

Listing 10-19. Downloading a large number of files

```
Getting names... (thread ID: 1)
googlebooks-eng-1M-2gram-20090715-14.csv.zip - starting download
(thread ID: 17)
googlebooks-eng-1M-2gram-20090715-0.csv.zip - starting download (thread ID: 3)
...approximately 100 similar lines...
googlebooks-eng-1M-2gram-20090715-98.csv.zip - starting download
(thread ID: 13)
```

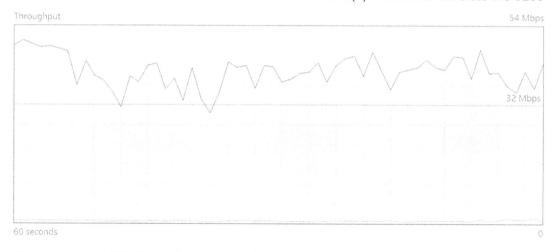

Figure 10-3. *WiFi throughput while downloading a large number of files*

Something is certainly going on, as evidenced by the WiFi throughput. But even after about 10 minutes, no download had been completed. This pattern might not be ideal for a couple of reasons:

- Although Google's servers will probably be just fine, some other services might throttle if you ask for too much at once. Database servers might even run out of connection resources if not configured to service a tsunami of requests like this.[1]

- We might want to start work on some downloaded files as soon as possible. For instance, we might want to start uncompressing them or getting data out of them as soon as they are downloaded. In the pizza analogy, we don't want all the cooks to spend their time kneading dough and chopping toppings for a large order, when they could be spending at least some time putting batches of assembled pizzas into ovens.

So how do we deal with this? One possibility is to explicitly batch our computations into groups of a specified size, then send each batch through individually using `Async.Parallel` just across the batch (Listing 10-20).

Listing 10-20. Using Seq.chunkBySize to create computation batches

```
let AsyncGetFilesBatched
    (pageUri : Uri) (filePattern : string) (localPath : string)
    (batchSize : int) =
    async {
        let! links = getLinks pageUri filePattern

        let downloaded, failed =
            links
            |> Seq.map (tryDownload localPath)
            |> Seq.chunkBySize batchSize
            |> Seq.collect (fun batch ->
                batch
                |> Async.Parallel
                |> Async.RunSynchronously)
```

---

[1] I had precisely this problem in my "day job," during the period I was writing this chapter.

```
            |> Array.ofSeq
            |> Array.partition Outcome.isOk

        return
            downloaded |> Array.map Outcome.fileName,
            failed |> Array.map Outcome.fileName
    }
```

In Listing 10-20 we use `Seq.chunkBySize`, which groups a sequence into batches of specified size (the last batch might be smaller). Then for each such batch we do an `Async.Parallel |> Async.RunSynchronously` to run just that batch in parallel. If you are following along, don't forget to alter the main function code to call the new `AsyncGetFilesBatched`:

```
Download.AsyncGetFilesBatched uri pattern localPath 4
```

The behavior for this version is shown in Listing 10-21 and Figure 10-4, using a batch size of 4.

Listing 10-21. Behavior of explicitly batched download

```
Getting names... (thread ID: 1)
googlebooks-eng-1M-2gram-20090715-11.csv.zip - starting download (thread ID: 14)
googlebooks-eng-1M-2gram-20090715-1.csv.zip - starting download (thread ID: 4)
googlebooks-eng-1M-2gram-20090715-10.csv.zip - starting download (thread ID: 5)
googlebooks-eng-1M-2gram-20090715-0.csv.zip - starting download (thread ID: 3)
googlebooks-eng-1M-2gram-20090715-1.csv.zip - download complete (thread ID: 16)
googlebooks-eng-1M-2gram-20090715-0.csv.zip - download complete (thread ID: 16)
googlebooks-eng-1M-2gram-20090715-10.csv.zip - download complete (thread ID: 4)
googlebooks-eng-1M-2gram-20090715-11.csv.zip - download complete (thread ID: 15)
googlebooks-eng-1M-2gram-20090715-13.csv.zip - starting download (thread ID: 15)
googlebooks-eng-1M-2gram-20090715-12.csv.zip - starting download (thread ID: 3)
googlebooks-eng-1M-2gram-20090715-14.csv.zip - starting download (thread ID: 4)
googlebooks-eng-1M-2gram-20090715-15.csv.zip - starting download (thread ID: 14)
```

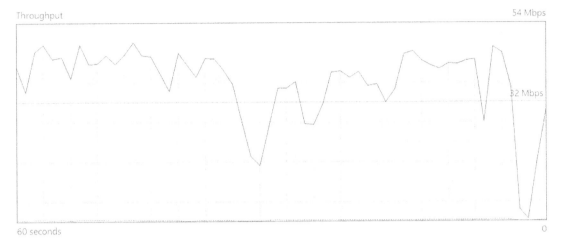

Figure 10-4. *WiFi throughput during explicitly batched download*

On the plus side, we do start seeing downloads complete much earlier in the process, meaning that we could get started with further processing of those files. But notice the pattern of the log messages. The first file of the second batch doesn't start downloading until the last file of the first batch has finished downloading. Hence the four-deep bands of "started" and "completed" messages in the log. This is reflected in the network throughput: it dips toward the end of each batch as the last part of the last file dribbles through.

What we need is *throttling*: the ability to start a limited number of computations simultaneously, and to start a new one each time a previous one completes.

Throttling

It would certainly be possible to write one's own throttled, parallel computation logic. But this is such a common pattern, it's worth looking to see if someone has solved it in a general way. As it turns out, the F# extensions library FSharpx contains exactly the functionality we need. (At the time of writing, this functionality had not been moved into the core F# libraries, but we live in hope that this will eventually happen.)

Use Nuget or Paket to add the package "FSharpx.Async" to your project. Then add an AsyncGetFilesThrottled function that uses Async.ParallelWithThrottle (Listing 10-22).

Listing 10-22. Asynchronous, parallel, throttled downloads

```
// From nuget package "FSharpx.Async"
open FSharpx.Control

let AsyncGetFilesThrottled
    (pageUri : Uri) (filePattern : string) (localPath : string)
    (throttle : int) =
    async {
        let! links = getLinks pageUri filePattern

        let! downloadResults =
            links
            |> Seq.map (tryDownload localPath)
            |> Async.ParallelWithThrottle throttle

        let downloaded, failed =
            downloadResults
            |> Array.partition Outcome.isOk

        return
            downloaded |> Array.map Outcome.fileName,
            failed |> Array.map Outcome.fileName
    }
```

Async.ParallelWithThrottle is like Async.Parallel but takes one additional parameter to specify the throttle size: the largest number of computations that will be started simultaneously. If you are following along, change the main function code to call AsyncGetFilesThrottled:

Download.AsyncGetFilesThrottled uri pattern localPath 4

This behaves really nicely, as you can see from its log messages and WiFi throughput (Listing 10-23 and Figure 10-5).

Listing 10-23. Behavior of a parallel, throttled download

```
Getting names... (thread ID: 1)
googlebooks-eng-1M-2gram-20090715-11.csv.zip - starting download (thread ID: 7)
googlebooks-eng-1M-2gram-20090715-1.csv.zip - starting download (thread ID: 14)
googlebooks-eng-1M-2gram-20090715-10.csv.zip - starting download (thread ID: 12)
googlebooks-eng-1M-2gram-20090715-0.csv.zip - starting download (thread ID: 3)
googlebooks-eng-1M-2gram-20090715-10.csv.zip - download complete (thread ID: 14)
googlebooks-eng-1M-2gram-20090715-12.csv.zip - starting download (thread ID: 12)
googlebooks-eng-1M-2gram-20090715-0.csv.zip - download complete (thread ID: 14)
googlebooks-eng-1M-2gram-20090715-13.csv.zip - starting download (thread ID: 3)
googlebooks-eng-1M-2gram-20090715-11.csv.zip - download complete (thread ID: 7)
```

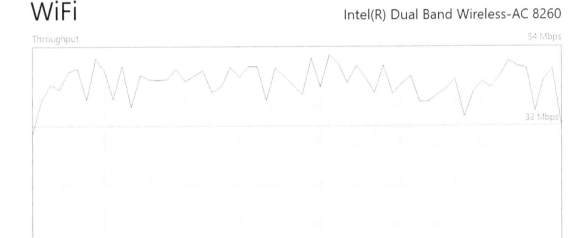

Figure 10-5. *WiFi throughput during parallel, throttled download*

Initially a batch of 4 downloads is started, then as soon as one completes, another one is started on whatever thread happens to be available. This keeps the network connection nice and busy but without having a great number of downloads all fighting for limited bandwidth.

C# Task versus F# Async

Now that you've seen the benefits of asynchronous programming, it's time to revisit something we glossed over earlier: the difference between an F# Async and a C# Task. They each represent their language's conception of an asynchronous computation that will return some type when completed. However, there is an important difference. C# uses a "hot task" model: when something creates a Task instance, the underlying computation is already running. F# uses a "cold task" model: the caller is responsible for starting the computation. This has some advantages in terms of composability. For example, in Listing 10-20 we had the opportunity to group tasks into batches of a fixed size using Seq.chunkBySize before finally launching them using Async.Parallel and Async.RunSynchronously.

Both Async and Task are, of course, valid models: the problems arise when we have to stand astride both worlds. For example, in Listing 10-10 we were able to use the result of HtmlDocument.AsyncLoad directly in a let! binding thus:

```
let! html = HtmlDocument.AsyncLoad(pageUri.AbsoluteUri)
```

...because HtmlDocument is an F#-first API and returns an Async - which is what let! expects. By contrast, in Listing 10-11 we used WebClient.DownloadFileTaskAsync, which returns a C# Task. To make it compatible with do!, which expects an F# Async, we had to pipe it into Async.AwaitTask.

```
do!
    client.DownloadFileTaskAsync(fileUri, filePath)
    |> Async.AwaitTask
```

Although we happened to be using do! in this case, the same would have applied for a let! binding.

The Async versus Task dichotomy has a number of practical and stylistic implications that you should always be aware of when coding in F#.

- As we've already said, when an API returns a C# Task, you'll have to convert it into an F# Async using Async.AwaitTask if you want to use it in an async computation expression with let! and do!.

- If you're writing a general-purpose API that exposes asynchronous functions, you should by default return a C# `Task` rather than an F# `Async`. This follows the general guidance that APIs for use in languages other than F# should not expose F#-specific types. You can work in terms of F# `Async` internally, and at the last moment convert into C# `Task` using `Async.StartAsTask`.

- API functions that return a C# `Task` should be named with a *suffix* of `Async` – for example, `WebClient.DownloadFileTaskAsync`.

- It's OK, though, for APIs aimed primarily at F# consumers, such as `FSharpx.HtmlDocument`, to expose asynchronous functions that return F# `Async` instances.

- F#-centric APIs that return an F# `Async` should be named with a *prefix* of `Async` – for example, `HtmlDocument.AsyncLoad`.

Incidentally, if you want to provide overloads to allow cancellation tokens to be sent in, you can use code as in Listing 10-24.

Listing 10-24. Overloads for exposing C# Task functions

```
type NiceCSharp =
  static member AsyncSomeWork(…) =
    Async.StartAsTask(someWork(…))
  static member AsyncSomeWork(cancellationToken) =
    Async.StartAsTask(someWork(…), cancellationToken = cancellationToken)
```

(The code in Listing 10-24 is courtesy of Tomas Petricek via stackoverflow.com.)

Finally, I should point out that, at the time of writing, there is an F# language proposal to offer a `task  {}` computation expression, that is, one that works in terms of C# `Task` rather than F# `Async`. This may simplify some coding in this area, but perhaps at the cost of some of the composability that F# `Async` offers.

Recommendations

Here are some basic steps that are worth taking away from this chapter:

- Get your business logic working correctly in a synchronous way.

- Identify places where you are "ordering pizza," in other words. making a request, usually via an API, which will take some time and doesn't require the involvement of the current thread. Any good API should offer an asynchronous implementation of the call you are making.

- Assuming the function from where you are ordering pizza is reasonably well factored, simply enclose its body with `async {}`. Change the ordering-pizza calls from `let` to `let!`, or if they are imperative, use `do!` If you are using F# 4.5 or later you can also use `match!`.

- If the function from where you are ordering pizza is not well factored, you may need to break it down to make it easier to enclose the appropriate code in `async {}` blocks.

- If an asynchronous API call returns a C# `Task` rather than an F# `Async`, you'll also have to convert the `Task` to an `Async` using `Async.StartAsTask`.

- Return (the promise of) data from the `async{}` expression using the `return` keyword.

- Do the same thing to any higher-level functions that call the functions you just changed. Keep on going until you reach the top of the hierarchy, where you actually use the data or expose an API. I've heard this process referred to as implementing async "all the way down."

- If exposing an API for use by other languages, translate the F# `Async` to a C# `Task` using `Async.StartAsTask`. This avoids exposing F# types where they may not be natively understood.

- To actually get results, use `Async.RunSynchronously`. But do this as little as possible – generally at the top of your "async-all-the-way-down" chain. You may not have to do it at all if you want external code that calls your functions to decide when to wait for results.

- To run similar, independent requests in parallel, use `Async.Parallel`, or `Async.ParallelWithThrottle` from the FSharpx.Async package. (Eventually this may move into core F# libraries.)

- Finally, all this is moot if your computation is limited by the local CPU power available ("CPU bound"). In those cases, you might as well use `Array.Parallel.map` or one of its siblings from the `Array.Parallel` module. We'll revisit this topic in Chapter 12.

Summary

In this chapter you learned how to deal with situations where your application is "ordering pizza" – in other words, setting off a computation that will take some time, and for which it isn't necessary for the current thread to stay involved. You found out how to deal with these cases by enclosing them in an `async {}` block and using `let!`, `match!` and `do!` to set off the time-consuming computation, and to have control to return to the same point (but likely on a different thread) once a result is obtained.

Asynchronous and parallel programming is a huge topic. In a wide-ranging book like this. we can really only scratch the surface. If you want to learn more, I would suggest studying a superb blog post on medium.com, entitled "F# Async Guide," by Lev Gorodinski (of Jet.com). Then you may also wish to look at the Nuget package "Hopac," which is a concurrent programming library for F# in the style of Concurrent ML.[2] You will find implementations there of most of the concurrent programming patterns you are likely to need in mainstream programming. Having said that, the techniques described in this chapter should serve you well in most situations.

In the next chapter, we'll look at *railway oriented programming*, a coding philosophy that encourages you to think about errors as hard as you think about successes, so that both the "happy" and "sad" paths in your code are equally well expressed.

---

[2]This is ML the programming language, not ML as in "Machine Learning."

Exercises

This section contains exercises to help you get used to translating code into an asynchronous world.

EXERCISE 10-1 – MAKING SOME CODE ASYNCHRONOUS

In the following code the `Server` module contains a simulated server endpoint that returns a random string, taking half a second to do so. In the `Consumer` module, we call the server multiple times to build up an array of strings, which we then sort to produce a final result.

```
open System

module Random =

    let private random = System.Random()

    let string() =
        let len = random.Next(0, 10)
        Array.init len (fun _ -> random.Next(0, 255) |> char)
        |> String

module Server =

    let AsyncGetString (id : int) =
        // id is unused
        async {
            do! Async.Sleep(500)
            return Random.string()
        }

module Consumer =

    let GetData (count : int) =
        let strings =
            Array.init count (fun i ->
                Server.AsyncGetString i
                |> Async.RunSynchronously)
        strings
        |> Array.sort
```

```
let demo() =

    let sw = System.Diagnostics.Stopwatch()
    sw.Start()

    Consumer.GetData 10
    |> Array.iter (printfn "%s")
    printfn "That took %ims" sw.ElapsedMilliseconds
```

If you run the demo() function, you'll notice that this operation takes over 5 seconds to get 10 results.

Change the Consumer.GetData() function so that it is asynchronous, and so that it runs all its calls to Server.AsyncGetString() in parallel.

You don't need to throttle the parallel computation. Consumer.GetData() should be an F# style async function, that is, it should return Async<String[]>.

Hint: You'll also need to change the demo() function so that the result of Consumer.GetData is passed into Async.RunSynchronously.

EXERCISE 10-2 – RETURNING TASKS

How would your solution to Exercise 10-1 change if Consumer.GetData() needed to return a C# style Task?

Exercise Solutions

EXERCISE 10-1 – MAKING SOME CODE ASYNCHRONOUS

Rename Consumer.GetData() to AsyncGetData() to reflect its new return type. Enclose its body in an async {} block. Change the binding of strings from let to let!. Remove the call to Async.RunSynchronously and instead pass the results of the Array.init (which will now be an array of Async<string> instances) into Async.Parallel. Finally, return the result of sorting the array explicitly using the return keyword.

```
let AsyncGetData (count : int) =
    async {
        let! strings =
            Array.init count (fun i -> Server.AsyncGetString i)
            |> Async.Parallel

        return
            strings
            |> Array.sort
    }
```

In the demo() function, pass the result of Consumer.AsyncGetData into Async.RunSynchronously to actually run the computation.

```
let demo() =

    let sw = System.Diagnostics.Stopwatch()
    sw.Start()

    Consumer.AsyncGetData 10
    |> Async.RunSynchronously
    |> Array.iter (printfn "%s")

    printfn "That took %ims" sw.ElapsedMilliseconds
```

Run demo() to verify that the computation takes roughly half a second.

EXERCISE 10-2 – RETURNING TASKS

Rename `Consumer.AsyncGetData()` to `GetDataAsync()` to reflect its new return type. After the end of its `async {}` block, add `|> Async.StartAsTask` to start the computation running and return a C# `Task`.

```
let GetDataAsync (count : int) =
    async {
        let! strings =
            Array.init count (fun i -> Server.AsyncGetString i)
            |> Async.Parallel

        return
            strings
            |> Array.sort
    } |> Async.StartAsTask
```

In the `demo()` function, add an `Async.AwaitTask` call to await the result of the task.

```
let demo() =

    let sw = System.Diagnostics.Stopwatch()
    sw.Start()

    Consumer.GetDataAsync 10
    |> Async.AwaitTask
    |> Async.RunSynchronously
    |> Array.iter (printfn "%s")

    printfn "That took %ims" sw.ElapsedMilliseconds
```

CHAPTER 11

Railway Oriented Programming

On two occasions I have been asked, "Pray, Mr. Babbage, if you put into the machine wrong figures, will the right answers come out?" I am not able rightly to apprehend the kind of confusion of ideas that could provoke such a question.

—Charles Babbage, Computer Pioneer

Going Off the Rails

Railway Oriented Programming (ROP) is an analogy invented by F#'s premier educator, Scott Wlaschin. It describes a programming philosophy in which we embrace errors as a core part of program flow, rather than exiling them to the separate domain of *exception handling*. Scott didn't invent the technique, but he did invent the analogy, which has helped many F# developers understand this initially daunting but powerful technique. Although I've titled this chapter according to Scott's analogy, I'm going to use a slightly different way to describe what is going on. Rest assured, I am still talking about ROP. I just thought it might be interesting to look at it using an alternative mental image. You may want to treat this chapter as a companion piece to Scott's own description of ROP, which you can find (among a cornucopia of other invaluable material) at `https://fsharpforfunandprofit.com`.

© Kit Eason 2018
K. Eason, *Stylish F#*, https://doi.org/10.1007/978-1-4842-4000-7_11

On the Factory Floor

You've decided to get into the widget business! You are going to build your very own highly automated widget factory. You'll make them so cheaply the entire widget industry will be disrupted. Investors and admirers will flock to your door!

One small problem – how do you lay this factory out? Widget making is a complex process: machining the raw material into shape, polishing certain parts, coating other parts, bolting on sub-assemblies, and so on. You want to keep your factory compact and easy to manage, otherwise you'll just be another widget wannabe. Your initial layout design is like this (Figure 11-1).

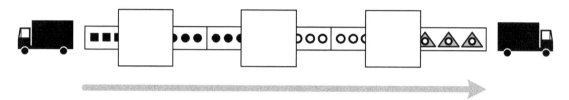

Figure 11-1. *Naïve layout for a widget factory*

Each box represents a machine tool performing one of the manufacturing processes. Leading *into* each box is a conveyor for taking items into the machine, and leading *out* of each box is another conveyor that takes items on to the next process. The conveyor coming out of a machine will not be the same as the one going in, because work items that come out will be a different shape from what goes in. Luckily numerous styles of conveyors are available, so you just pick (or even build) the conveyor style to suit each stage. Laying out the machines is pretty straightforward: you place them in a line, in the order the processes must be performed. This way the conveyors with matching styles naturally link up. You can hardly go wrong.

You show your production line design to an experienced manufacturing engineer. But she isn't impressed.

"What about quality control?," she asks. "Is the whole production line going to stop every time a single step goes wrong for one widget?"

Shamefaced you return, literally, to the drawing board. Diversion is your answer! Within each process there will be a quality control step. If the widget being processed fails that step, it is shot out on a different conveyor and into a rejects hopper (Figure 11-2).

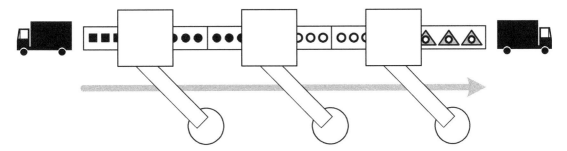

Figure 11-2. *Simple handling for rejects*

You show the engineer your new layout.

"That's better," she says, "But still not great. Someone will have to keep an eye on all those rejects hoppers, and they're scattered all the way along the line." She grabs the pencil. "Maybe you want something more like this?" (Figure 11-3).

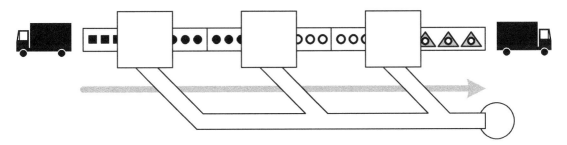

Figure 11-3. *Combining rejects*

This solves the multiple-rejects-hoppers problem, but it's messy in other ways. It's going to be fiddly linking up both sets of conveyors, especially with the rejects conveyors sticking out of the side like that. It feels repetitive somehow.

"No worries," says the engineer. "I know some folks who build special adapter housings for machine tools. The housing has two conveyors going in. The main one takes good parts into the machine tool inside. The other one takes rejects in and just passes them straight on out again. If there is a new reject from the current machine, it gets put onto the rejects conveyer along with any existing rejects. Once you've put each of your machine tools in one of those housings, you can join the housings together as simply as your original concept." She draws another diagram (Figure 11-4).

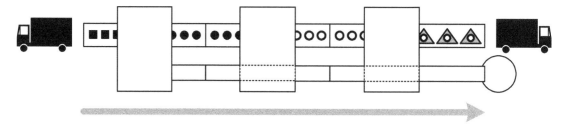

Figure 11-4. *Adapter housings for easier process linkage*

This is getting exciting, but you need to check your understanding.

"So internally the housing looks something like this, right? The machine tool needs to put rejects from its own process on the rejects conveyer, and good parts on the main out-conveyer. And it can pass through incoming rejects untouched?" (Figure 11-5).

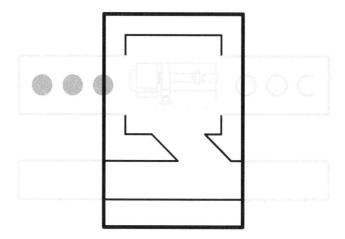

Figure 11-5. *Adapter housing detail*

"Spot on," replies the engineer. "And you're going to need a couple of other housings. I'm guessing some of your processes never fail, so better include a housing which just passes rejects through." (Figure 11-6).

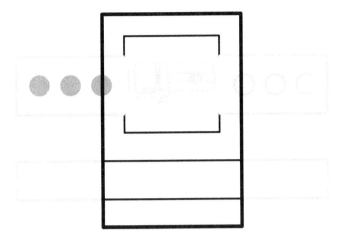

Figure 11-6. *Adapter housing detail for processes that never fail*

"And you'll also need to pay a bit of attention to what happens at the end of the line. Do you really want to just toss all the rejects into the trash? I think you might want to count them by kind of failure, report them, or something like that. If so you'll need the reject adapter housing." (Figure 11-7).

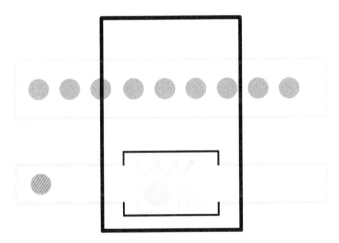

Figure 11-7. *Reject adapter housing detail*

"You can put in any machine you like to handle incoming rejects. It might pass them on in some form, it might report them, or it might just destroy them. Good inputs just pass straight through the adapter untouched."

"What about the *first* machine on the line?," you ask. "Won't that need a special type of adapter?"

"Nope," replies the engineer. "If it's a typical machine that takes a good input and produces a good output or a failure, it can just sit at the front of the line, because its good/bad outputs will fit into the second machine's adapted inputs."

This makes so much sense, and you're keen to get on with the details.

"Can you hook me up with the folks who make these magic housings?," you ask.

"Sure!," replies the engineer. "There's just the small matter of my fee."

"Will you accept stock options?," you ask...

Adapting Functions for Failure

In the widget manufacturing example, your initial stab at rejects handling (Figure 11-2) is like the concept of raising and handling exceptions in .NET languages like C# and F#. When something goes wrong, you "jump out" of the natural sequence of processing (you raise an exception), and what happens to that exception is no concern of the local section of code. The exception will be handled elsewhere or (all too often) simply ignored (Listing 11-1).

Listing 11-1. Raising an exception. Where she stops, nobody knows!

```
open System

let checkString (s : string) =
    if isNull(s) then
        raise <| ArgumentNullException("Must not be null")
    elif String.IsNullOrEmpty(s) then
        raise <| ArgumentException("Must not be empty")
    elif String.IsNullOrWhiteSpace(s) then
        raise <| ArgumentException("Must not be white space")
    else
        s
```

This makes the type signature of the function a lie: the function can *really* either return its official result type, or an exception. This is, arguably, a violation of the principle of *semantic focus.* You can't tell from the *outside* (by its signature) what kinds of things a function will do under all circumstances; and you can't tell from the *inside* (looking at the body of the function) whether the function's callers have any strategy at all for handling errors. The aim of ROP is to get away from this by making failures part of the signature of a function, and by providing a bypass mechanism so that, as in Figure 11-4, functions can be joined together in such a way that failures whizz past any later functions in the production line.

Writing a Bypass Adapter

Although the "adapters" you'll need do exist in F# 4.1 onward, it's worth trying to write a couple of them from scratch, as this makes it much easier to understand how the whole concept works. Let's start with the adapter from Figure 11-5. It needs to take a function (the equivalent to the machine tool hidden within the adapter housing) and an input (the equivalent of an incoming, partially made widget). If the input is currently *valid*, it needs to be processed using the supplied function. If the input is already a *failure*, it needs to be passed through untouched.

Since a function can only have one type, this means we need to bundle together good values and failures in the same type. And by now you probably realize that bundling different things together usually means a Discriminated Union. Let's call it Outcome (Listing 11-2).

Listing 11-2. An Outcome Discriminated Union

```
type Outcome<'TSuccess, 'TFailure> =
    | Success of 'TSuccess
    | Failure of 'TFailure
```

In Listing 11-2 there's a Success case and a Failure case. We keep the payload types of the DU generic using 'TSuccess and 'TFailure, because we don't want to commit to a specific payload type for either the success or the failure path.

Now we need to write the adapter itself. Let's start with a spot of pseudocode.

- Take a function and an input (which might already be a success or a failure).

- If the input is valid so far, pass it to the supplied function.

- If the input is already an error, pass it through untouched.

It only takes a few lines of F# to achieve this (Listing 11-3).

Listing 11-3. The basic adapter in code

```
type Outcome<'TSuccess, 'TFailure> =
    | Success of 'TSuccess
    | Failure of 'TFailure

let adapt func input =
    match input with
    | Success x -> func x
    | Failure f -> Failure f
```

Writing a Pass-Through Adapter

Now we need the second kind of adapter the manufacturing engineer suggested (Figure 11-6): a "pass-through" adapter, which is used to wrap processes that can't themselves fail, and which allows failure inputs to whizz by (Listing 11-4).

Listing 11-4. The pass-through adapter in code

```
let passThrough func input =
    match input with
    | Success x -> func x |> Success
    | Failure f -> Failure f
```

Listing 11-4 is almost laughably similar to Listing 11-3; I have highlighted the only difference. Whereas the func of Listing 11-3 is itself capable of returning Success or Failure, the func of Listing 11-4 is (by definition) one which can't fail. Therefore, to let it participate in the pipeline, its result has to be wrapped in a Success case. So, we simply say func x |> Success.

Building the Production Line

Now we'll need an example process to try out this new concept. Let's take a requirement to accept a password, validate it in various ways, then save it if it is valid. The validations will be:

- The password string can't be null, empty, or just whitespace.

- It must contain mixed case alphabetic characters.

- It must contain at least one of these characters: - _ ! ?

- Any leading/trailing whitespace must be trimmed.

The password should be saved to a database if valid; if not there needs to be an error message.

Listing 11-5 shows the code to perform each of these steps individually. (We haven't joined them into a pipeline yet.)

Listing 11-5. Some password validation code

```
open System

let notEmpty (s : string) =
    if isNull(s) then
        Failure "Must not be null"
    elif String.IsNullOrEmpty(s) then
        Failure "Must not be empty"
    elif String.IsNullOrWhiteSpace(s) then
        Failure "Must not be white space"
    else
        Success s

let mixedCase (s : string) =
    let hasUpper =
        s |> Seq.exists (Char.IsUpper)
    let hasLower =
        s |> Seq.exists (Char.IsLower)
    if hasUpper && hasLower then
        Success s
    else
        Failure "Must contain mixed case"

let containsAny (cs : string) (s : string) =
    if s.IndexOfAny(cs.ToCharArray()) > -1 then
        Success s
    else
        Failure (sprintf "Must contain at least one of %A" cs)
```

```
let tidy (s : string) =
    s.Trim()

let save (s : string) =
    let dbSave s : unit =
        printfn "Saving password '%s'" s
        // Uncomment this to simulate an exception:
        // raise <| Exception "Dummy exception"
    let log m =
        printfn "Logging error: %s" m
    try
        dbSave s
        |> Success
    with
    | e ->
        log e.Message
        Failure "Sorry, there was an internal error saving your
        password"
```

The exact details of the code in Listing 11-5 are less important than the general
pattern of these functions: if validation succeeds, they return a value wrapped in a
Success case. If validation fails, they return a message wrapped in a Failure case. The
save() function is slightly more complicated: it handles any exceptions that come back
from writing to the (imaginary) database, and returns a message wrapped in a Failure
case if an exception occurred. It just happens that the result of a successful database save
operation is just unit, but unit can still be returned wrapped in a Success like any other
type. The tidy() function is an example of a "can't fail" process (assuming the string
isn't null, which is tackled in an earlier step).

Now we need to make sure these functions are all called in the right order – the
equivalent of rolling the machines onto the factory floor, putting them inside their
adapters, and bolting them all together into a production line. Listing 11-6 shows a first
cut of this stage. (It assumes that the Outcome DU, the adapt and passThrough functions,
and the password validation functions from previous listings are available.)

Listing 11-6. Lining the machines up on the factory floor

```
// password:string -> Outcome<unit, string>
let validateAndSave password =

    let mixedCase' = adapt mixedCase
    let containsAny' = adapt (containsAny "-_!?")
    let tidy' = passThrough tidy
    let save' = adapt save

    password
    |> notEmpty
    |> mixedCase'
    |> containsAny'
    |> tidy'
    |> save'
```

In Listing 11-6 we take each of the validation functions (apart from the first) and partially apply adapt or passThrough by providing the validation function as an argument. This is the precise equivalent, in our analogy, to putting the machine tool inside its adapter. In each case I've just added a single quote (') to the name of the adapted version, just so you can tell which functions have been adapted. Items such as mixedCase' are now functions that require their input value to be wrapped in Outcome, and which will just pass on Failure cases untouched.

Why didn't we have to adapt the first function (notEmpty)? Well, exactly as the manufacturing engineer said, the very first machine tool doesn't need an adapter, because it already takes non-wrapped input and returns an Outcome case, and so it can be plugged into the second (adapted) machine without change.

At this point we can do a sanity check by looking at the signature of the validateAndSave function. We see that the signature is password:string -> Outcome<unit, string>. This makes sense because we want to accept a string password, and get back either an Outcome.Success with a payload of unit (because the database save operation returns unit) or an Outcome.Failure with a payload of string, which will be the validation or saving error message.

Now we need to try this all out. Listing 11-7 exercises our code for various invalid passwords and one valid one.

Listing 11-7. Exercising the validateAndSave function

```
let demo() =

    // Failure "Must not be null"
    null |> validateAndSave |> printfn "%A"

    // Failure "Must not be empty"
    "" |> validateAndSave |> printfn "%A"

    // Failure "Must not be white space"
    " " |> validateAndSave |> printfn "%A"

    // Failure "Must contain mixed case"
    "the quick brown fox" |> validateAndSave |> printfn "%A"

    // Failure "Must contain at least one of "-_!?""
    "The quick brown fox" |> validateAndSave |> printfn "%A"

    // Success ()
    "The quick brown fox!" |> validateAndSave |> printfn "%A"
```

Listing 11-7 shows that our function works – invalid passwords are rejected with a user-friendly message, and valid ones are "saved." If you want to see what happens when there is an exception during the save process (maybe we lost the database connection?), simply uncomment the line in the save function (in Listing 11-5) that raises an exception. In that case, the specific error details will be logged, and a more general error message will be returned that would be safe to show to the user (Listing 11-8).

Listing 11-8. Results of an exception during saving

```
Saving password 'The quick brown fox!'
Logging error: Dummy exception
Failure "Sorry, there was an internal error saving your password"
```

Listing 11-6 is a little wordy! If you were paying attention in Chapter 9, you might recognize this as a prime candidate for *function composition* using the >> operator. Listing 11-9 shows the magic that happens when you do this!

Listing 11-9. Composing adapted functions

```
// string -> Outcome<unit, string>
let validateAndSave =

    notEmpty
    >> adapt mixedCase
    >> adapt (containsAny "-_!?")
    >> passThrough tidy
    >> adapt save
```

We've moved the "adapting" of the various functions into the body of the pipeline, and joined the adapted functions with the >> operator. We get rid of the password parameter because a string input is expected anyway by notEmpty, and this requirement of a parameter "bubbles out" to the validateAndSave function. The type signature of validateAndSave is unchanged (although the password string is now unlabeled), and if we run it again using the demo() function from Listing 11-7, it works exactly the same. Amazing!

Making It Official

I said at the outset that F# (from 4.1) has its own ROP types. So how do we use these rather than our handcrafted Outcome type? The DU we named Outcome is officially called Result, and the DU cases are Ok and Error. So each of the password validation and processing functions needs some tiny naming changes (for example, Listing 11-10).

Listing 11-10. Using the official Result DU

```
let notEmpty (s : string) =
    if isNull(s) then
        Error "Must not be null"
    elif String.IsNullOrEmpty(s) then
        Error "Must not be empty"
    elif String.IsNullOrWhiteSpace(s) then
        Error "Must not be white space"
    else
        Ok s
```

Likewise, the official name for what I called `adapt` is `bind`, and the official name for `passThrough` is `map`. So the `validateAndSave` function needs to open the `Result` namespace and call `map` and `bind` (Listing 11-11).

Listing 11-11. Using bind and map

```
open Result

// string -> Result<unit, string>
let validateAndSave =

    notEmpty
    >> bind mixedCase
    >> bind (containsAny "-_!?")
    >> map tidy
    >> bind save
```

Incidentally, you may notice a close resemblance between `Result.bind`/`Result.map` and `Option.bind`/`Option.map`, which we discussed way back in Chapter 3. These two names, *map* and *bind*, are pretty standard in functional programming and theory. You eventually get used to them.

Love Your Errors

Remember when the engineer said you were going to need an adapter for the rejects? Well it's time to tackle that. At the moment we have cheated a little, by making all the functions return `Error` cases that have strings as payloads. It's as if we assume that on the production line, rejects at every stage would fit on the same rejects conveyor – which might well not the be case if the rejects from different stages were different shapes. Luckily in F# world, we can force all the kinds of rejects into the same wrapper by (say it aloud with me) *creating another Discriminated Union*!

This DU will have to list all the kinds of things that can go wrong, together with payloads for any further information that might need to be passed along (Listing 11-12).

Listing 11-12. An error-types Discriminated Union

```
open System

type ValidationError =
    | MustNotBeNull
    | MustNotBeEmpty
    | MustNotBeWhiteSpace
    | MustContainMixedCase
    | MustContainOne of chars:string
    | ErrorSaving of exn:Exception

let notEmpty (s : string) =
    if isNull(s) then
        Error MustNotBeNull
    elif String.IsNullOrEmpty(s) then
        Error MustNotBeEmpty
    elif String.IsNullOrWhiteSpace(s) then
        Error MustNotBeWhiteSpace
    else
        Ok s

let mixedCase (s : string) =
    let hasUpper =
        s |> Seq.exists (Char.IsUpper)
    let hasLower =
        s |> Seq.exists (Char.IsLower)
    if hasUpper && hasLower then
        Ok s
    else
        Error MustContainMixedCase

let containsAny (cs : string) (s : string) =
    if s.IndexOfAny(cs.ToCharArray()) > -1 then
        Ok s
    else
        Error (MustContainOne cs)
```

```
let tidy (s : string) =
    s.Trim()

let save (s : string) =
    let dbSave s : unit =
        printfn "Saving password '%s'" s
        // Uncomment this to simulate an exception:
        raise <| Exception "Dummy exception"
    try
        dbSave s
        |> Ok
    with
    | e ->
        Error (ErrorSaving e)
```

Listing 11-12 starts with the new DU. Most of the cases have no payload because they just need to convey the fact that a certain kind of thing went wrong. The `MustContainOne` has a payload that lets you say what characters were expected. The `ErrorSaving` case has a slot to carry the exception that was raised, which a later step may choose to inspect if it needs to. See how we also had to change most of the validation functions so that their `Error` results wrap a `ValidationError` case – for example, `Error MustNotBeNull`. Here, to be clear, we have a DU wrapped up in another DU. Another small change in Listing 11-12 is that I've removed the log function from the `save()` function, for reasons that will become clear in a moment.

Now we need the rejects adapter the engineer suggested. The adapter function lives with `map` and `bind` in the `Result` namespace, and it is called `mapError`. The best way to think about `mapError` is by comparing the physical diagrams from Figures 11-6 and 11-7. Here they are again side by side (Figure 11-8).

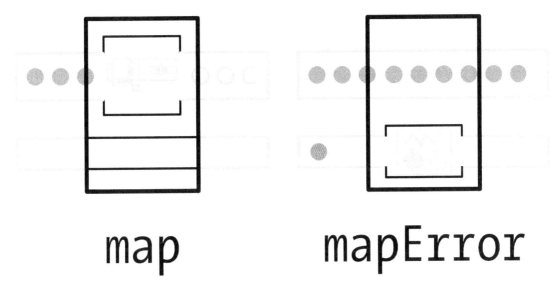

Figure 11-8. *Comparing map and mapError*

The map function takes an input and if it is good, processes it using a supplied function (which cannot fail), and returns a good output. It passes through preexisting bad inputs untouched. mapError is like a vertical flip of the same thing. It takes an input, and if it is *good* passes it through untouched. If it the input is *bad*, it processes it using a supplied function, which itself returns a bad result.

We can use mapError to branch our logic depending on what kind of error occurred, maybe just translating it into a readable message, maybe logging exceptions (but hiding them from the end user), and so forth (Listing 11-13).

Listing 11-13. Using mapError

```
open Result

// string -> Result<unit, ValidationError>
let validateAndSave =

    notEmpty
    >> bind mixedCase
    >> bind (containsAny "-_!?")
    >> map tidy
    >> bind save

let savePassword =
```

```
let log m =
    printfn "Logging error: %s" m

validateAndSave
>> mapError (fun err ->
    match err with
    | MustNotBeNull
    | MustNotBeEmpty
    | MustNotBeWhiteSpace ->
        sprintf "Password must be entered"
    | MustContainMixedCase ->
        sprintf "Password must contain upper and lower case
        characters"
    | MustContainOne cs ->
        sprintf "Password must contain one of %A" cs
    | ErrorSaving e ->
        log e.Message
        sprintf "Sorry there was an internal error saving the
        password")
```

See in Listing 11-13 how the signature of validateAndSave has changed to string ->
Result<unit, ValidationError>, because we made all the validation functions return
ValidationError cases when there was a problem. Then in the savePassword function,
we composed validateAndSave with Result.mapError. We gave mapError a lambda
function that matches on the ValidationError cases to generate suitable messages, and
in one case to log an exception.

This approach has the interesting consequence that it forces you to enumerate every
kind of thing that could go wrong with your process, all in a single DU. This certainly
takes some getting used to, but it is potentially a very useful discipline. It helps you avoid
wishful thinking or an inconsistent approach to errors.

Recommendations

If you've been enthused about Railway Oriented Programming, here's how I recommend
you get started:

- Identify processes that involve several steps, each of which might fail
  in predictable ways.

- Write a DU that enumerates the kinds of errors that can occur. (You can obviously add cases to this as you go along.) Some cases might just identify the kind of error; others might have a payload with more information, such as an exception instance, or more details about the input that triggered the failure.

- Write a function for each step in your process. Each should take a non-wrapped input (or inputs), and return either a good output in the form of a `Result.Ok` that wraps the step's successful output, or a `Result.Error` that wraps a case from your error-types DU.

- Compose the steps into a single pipeline. To do this, wrap each function but the first using `Result.bind` (or `Result.map` for operations that need to fit into the pipeline but which can't fail). Compose the wrapped functions with the function composition operator `>>`.

- Use `Result.mapError` at the end of the pipeline to process failure cases, for example, by attaching error messages or writing to a log.

Summary

I hope you now understand enough about ROP to make an informed decision about whether to use it. You're also equipped to dive in and maintain existing codebases that use ROP or some variation of it.

I'd worry, though, if I succeeded too well, and left you an uncritical enthusiast for the technique. The truth is that ROP is rather controversial in the F# community, with both passionate advocates and passionate critics. The official F# coding conventions have quite a lot to say on the subject. They conclude:

> *Types such as Result<'Success, 'Error> are appropriate for basic operations where they aren't nested, and F# optional types are perfect for representing when something could either return something or nothing. They are not a replacement for exceptions, though, and should not be used in an attempt to replace exceptions. Rather, they should be applied judiciously to address specific aspects of exception and error management policy in targeted ways.*

> —F# Style Guide, Microsoft and contributors

In my opinion, ROP works rather nicely in the same sorts of places where function composition works nicely: constrained pipelines of operations, where the pipeline has limited scope, such as our password validation example. Using it at an architectural level works less well in my experience, tending to blur *motivational transparency*, at least for ordinary mortals.

In the next chapter we'll look at *performance* – how to measure the speed of F# functions and how to make them faster.

Exercises

EXERCISE 11-1 – REPRODUCING MAPERROR

You might remember that we started by writing our own versions of map and bind in the form of adapt and passThrough functions:

```
type Outcome<'TSuccess, 'TFailure> =
    | Success of 'TSuccess
    | Failure of 'TFailure

let adapt func input =
    match input with
    | Success x -> func x
    | Failure f -> Failure f

let passThrough func input =
    match input with
    | Success x -> func x |> Success
    | Failure f -> Failure f
```

Can you implement a passThroughRejects function, with the same behavior as the built-in mapError function?

Hint: Look carefully at Figure 11-8 and the surrounding text.

EXERCISE 11-2 – WRITING A ROP PIPELINE

You are working on a project to handle some incoming messages, each containing a filename and some data. The filename is a string representation of a DateTimeOffset when the data was captured. The data is an array of floating-point values. The process should attempt to parse the filename as a DateTimeOffset (some might fail due to spurious messages), and should also reject any messages where the data array contains any NaN ("not-a-number") values. Any rejects need to be logged.

The listing below contains a partial implementation of the requirement. Your task is to fill in the code marked with TODO, removing the exceptions that have been placed there. Each TODO should only take a line or two of code to complete.

```
open System

type Message =
    { FileName : string
      Content : float[] }

type Reading =
    { TimeStamp : DateTimeOffset
      Data : float[] }

let example =
    [|
        { FileName = "2019-02-23T02:00:00-05:00"
          Content = [|1.0; 2.0; 3.0; 4.0|] }
        { FileName = "2019-02-23T02:00:10-05:00"
          Content = [|5.0; 6.0; 7.0; 8.0|] }
        { FileName = "error"
          Content = [||] }
        { FileName = "2019-02-23T02:00:20-05:00"
          Content = [|1.0; 2.0; 3.0; Double.NaN|] }
    |]

let log s = printfn "Logging: %s" s

type MessageError =
    | InvalidFileName of fileName:string
    | DataContainsNaN of fileName:string * index:int
```

```
let getReading message =
    match DateTimeOffset.TryParse(message.FileName) with
    | true, dt ->
        let reading = { TimeStamp = dt; Data = message.Content }
        // TODO Return an OK result containing a tuple of the
        // message file name and the reading:
        raise <| NotImplementedException()
    | false, _ ->
        // TODO Return an Error result containing an
        // InvalidFileName error, which itself contains
        // the message file name:
        raise <| NotImplementedException()

let validateData(fileName, reading) =
    let nanIndex =
        reading.Data
        |> Array.tryFindIndex (Double.IsNaN)
    match nanIndex with
    | Some i ->
        // TODO Return an Error result containing an
        // DataContainsNaN error, which itself contains
        // the file name and error index:
        raise <| NotImplementedException()
    | None ->
        // TODO Return an Ok result containing the reading:
        raise <| NotImplementedException()

let logError (e : MessageError) =
    // TODO match on the MessageError cases
    // and call log with suitable information
    // for each case.
    raise <| NotImplementedException()

// When all the TODOs are done, uncomment this code
// and see if it works!

//open Result

//let processMessage =
```

```
//    getReading
//    >> bind validateData
//    >> mapError logError

//let processData data =
//    data
//    |> Array.map processMessage
//    |> Array.choose (fun result ->
//        match result with
//        | Ok reading -> reading |> Some
//        | Error _ -> None)

//let demo() =
//    example
//    |> processData
//    |> Array.iter (printfn "%A")
```

Exercise Solutions

EXERCISE 11-1 – REPRODUCING MAPERROR

The function you want is a kind of mirror image of passThrough. I've repeated passThrough here for comparison:

```
let passThrough func input =
    match input with
    | Success x -> func x |> Success
    | Failure f -> Failure f

let passThroughRejects func input =
    match input with
    | Success x -> Success x
    | Failure f -> func f |> Failure
```

EXERCISE 11-2 – WRITING A ROP PIPELINE

Here is a possible solution. Added lines are marked with DONE.

```
open System

type Message =
    { FileName : string
      Content : float[] }

type Reading =
    { TimeStamp : DateTimeOffset
      Data : float[] }

let example =
    [|
        { FileName = "2019-02-23T02:00:00-05:00"
          Content = [|1.0; 2.0; 3.0; 4.0|] }
        { FileName = "2019-02-23T02:00:10-05:00"
          Content = [|5.0; 6.0; 7.0; 8.0|] }
        { FileName = "error"
          Content = [||] }
        { FileName = "2019-02-23T02:00:20-05:00"
          Content = [|1.0; 2.0; 3.0; Double.NaN|] }
    |]

let log s = printfn "Logging: %s" s

type MessageError =
    | InvalidFileName of fileName:string
    | DataContainsNaN of fileName:string * index:int

let getReading message =
    match DateTimeOffset.TryParse(message.FileName) with
    | true, dt ->
        let reading = { TimeStamp = dt; Data = message.Content }
        // DONE
        Ok(message.FileName, reading)
    | false, _ ->
        // DONE
        Error (InvalidFileName message.FileName)
```

```fsharp
let validateData(fileName, reading) =
    let nanIndex =
        reading.Data
        |> Array.tryFindIndex (Double.IsNaN)
    match nanIndex with
    | Some i ->
        // DONE
        Error (DataContainsNaN(fileName, i))
    | None ->
        // DONE
        Ok reading

let logError (e : MessageError) =
    // DONE
    match e with
    | InvalidFileName fn ->
        log (sprintf "Invalid file name: %s" fn)
    | DataContainsNaN (fn, i) ->
        log (sprintf "Data contains NaN at position: %i in file:
        %s" i fn)

open Result

let processMessage =
    getReading
    >> bind validateData
    >> mapError logError

let processData data =
    data
    |> Array.map processMessage
    |> Array.choose (fun result ->
        match result with
        | Ok reading -> reading |> Some
        | Error _ -> None)

let demo() =
    example
    |> processData
    |> Array.iter (printfn "%A")
```

CHAPTER 12

Performance

Since the engine has a mode of acting peculiar to itself, it will in every particular case be necessary to arrange the series of calculations conformably to the means which the machine possesses; for such or such a process which might be very easy for a [human] calculator may be long and complicated for the engine, and vice versâ.

—L. F. Menabrea, describing Charles Babbage's Analytical Engine, 1842

(Translated by Ada Lovelace)

Design Is Compromise

In programming, there is always a tension between *abstraction* and *efficiency*. Code that has a higher level of abstraction is less likely to define the minimum number of operations needed to achieve the correct result *in a specific situation*. Conversely, code that is written at a lower level will often be faster, but will be less widely applicable, leading to more repetition and sometimes worse maintainability. As a language that encourages you to work at a relatively high level of abstraction, F# can sometimes leave you at the wrong end of this trade-off. This chapter aims to give you the tools to recognize common performance bottlenecks in F# code; and the skills needed to resolve these to a reasonable degree, without fatally compromising the readability of your code.

Getting from correct code to correct, *efficient* code is one of the coding tasks that I find the most satisfying. I hope that by the end of this chapter, you'll feel the same way.

© Kit Eason 2018
K. Eason, *Stylish F#*, https://doi.org/10.1007/978-1-4842-4000-7_12

Some Case Studies

.NET performance, and code performance generally, is a huge topic. Rather than get lost in a sea of performance-related issues, I'm going to focus on a few case studies that represent mistakes I commonly see being made (often by me). Incidentally, you might notice that I haven't included asynchronous code in these case studies: this topic was covered in Chapter 10. For each case study, I'm going to present some correctly functioning but inefficient code. Then I'll help you identify why it's inefficient, and show you the steps you can go through to make it relatively fast, but still correct and maintainable.

But before we can embark on the case studies, we need a framework for measuring and comparing performance. Enter "BenchmarkDotNet."

BenchmarkDotNet

Through most of this book I've avoided using third-party libraries, as I wanted to focus on the language itself. But in the case of performance, we need something that can provide a fair measure of execution speed, which includes running our code a number of times, and performing back-to-back comparisons of different versions. BenchmarkDotNet does exactly this and works nicely with F#.

You can either use the source code provided with this book, or create your own project using the following steps:

- Create a command-line F# project. I used the "Console App (.NET Core)" template.

- Use Nuget or Paket to add the package "BenchmarkDotNet."

- Add a file called `Dummy.fs` and populate it with the code from Listing 12-1.

- Replace the code in `Program.fs` with the code from Listing 12-2.

- Ensure that `Dummy.fs` appears before `Program.fs` in the compilation order.

Listing 12-1. Dummy functions to benchmark (Dummy.fs)

```
module Dummy

let slowFunction() =
    System.Threading.Thread.Sleep(100)
    99

let fastFunction() =
    System.Threading.Thread.Sleep(10)
    99
```

The code in (Listing 12-1), Dummy.fs, is the test subject – the actual code whose performance we want to check. Initially this will be a dummy, but later we'll add real code to test.

Listing 12-2. Executing the benchmarks (Program.fs)

```
open System
open BenchmarkDotNet.Running
open BenchmarkDotNet.Attributes

module Harness =

    [<MemoryDiagnoser>]
    type Harness() =

        [<Benchmark>]
        member __.Old() =
            Dummy.slowFunction()

        [<Benchmark>]
        member __.New() =
            Dummy.fastFunction()

[<EntryPoint>]
let main _ =

    BenchmarkRunner.Run<Harness.Harness>()
    |> printfn "%A"

    Console.ReadKey() |> ignore
    0
```

The code in Listing 12-2, `Program.fs`, is the "boiler plate" we need to get BenchmarkDotNet to call our code repeatedly to measure its performance.

Once you have all the source in place, set your build configuration to `Release` and run the project. You should get a large volume of diagnostic output, and toward the end a table of timings as in Listing 12-3.

Listing 12-3. Dummy benchmark output

```
Method |       Mean |      Error |   StdDev |    Median | Allocated |
------- |----------:|----------:|---------:|----------:|----------:|
    Old | 107.15 ms | 2.1261 ms | 2.088 ms | 107.04 ms |       0 B |
    New |  13.67 ms | 0.5215 ms | 1.538 ms |  14.38 ms |       0 B |
```

The "Method" column contains the names of the methods in the `Harness` class that we used to call our actual test-subject functions. As we are going to be back-to-back testing original versus performance-enhanced versions, I've called these "Old" and "New." The "Mean" column shows the average time needed to execute the functions we are testing. Not surprisingly, the "Old" function (`slowFunction()`) takes more time than the "New" function (`fastFunction()`). The difference in means is roughly 10:1, reflecting the fact that the slow dummy function sleeps for 10 times as long. (It's not exactly 10:1 because of other overheads that are the same for each version.)

The "Error," "StdDev" and "Median" columns give other relevant statistical measures of run times. For the purposes of this chapter we'll focus mainly on the "Mean" column. If the function being tested causes garbage collections, there will be additional columns in the table showing how many Generation 0, 1, and 2 collections occurred.

Case Study: Inappropriate Collection Types

Now that we have some nice benchmarking infrastructure in place, it's time to look at common performance antipatterns, and their remedies. We'll start with what happens if you use an inappropriate collection type, or access it inappropriately.

Imagine you have a need to create a "sample" function. It takes a collection of values and returns only every n'th value, for some provided value of n which we'll call `interval`. For example, if you gave it the collection `['a';'b';'c';'d']` and an interval of 3, it would return `['a';'d']`. The requirement doesn't say anything about what type of collection contains the input, so you decide to be idiomatic and use F# lists as both the input and the return values. Listing 12-4 shows your first cut of this logic.

Listing 12-4. First cut of a sample function

```
let sample interval data =
    [
        let max = (List.length data) - 1
        for i in 0..interval..max ->
            data.[i]
    ]
```

We want to generate an F# list, so we use a list comprehension (the whole body of the function is in [ ]). We use a for loop with a skip value of interval as the sampling mechanism. Items are returned from the input list using the -> operator (a shortcut for yield in for-loops) together with indexed access to the list, that is, data.[i]. Seems reasonable – but does it perform?

To find out we'll need to integrate it with the project we put together in Listings 12-1 and 12-2. Add another file called InappropriateCollectionType.fs and ensure that it is first in the compilation order. Populate it with the code from Listing 12-5.

Listing 12-5. Integrating a function with benchmarking

```
module InappropriateCollectionType

module Old =

    let sample interval data =
        [
            let max = (List.length data) - 1
            for i in 0..interval..max ->
                data.[i]
        ]
```

```
module New =

    let sample interval data =
        [
            let max = (List.length data) - 1
            for i in 0..interval..max ->
                data.[i]
        ]
```

In Listing 12-5 we declare modules Old and New to hold baseline and (in the future) improved versions of our function-under-test. At this stage the Old and New implementations of sample are the same.

To make the test harness call these functions, and to give them something to work on, change the Harness module within Program.fs to look like Listing 12-6.

Listing 12-6. Modifying the test harness

```
module Harness =

    [<MemoryDiagnoser>]
    type Harness() =

        let r = Random()
        let list = List.init 1_000_000 (fun _ -> r.NextDouble())

        [<Benchmark>]
        member __.Old() =
            list
            |> InappropriateCollectionType.Old.sample 1000
            |> ignore

        [<Benchmark>]
        member __.New() =
            list
            |> InappropriateCollectionType.New.sample 1000
            |> ignore
```

In Listing 12-6 we create some test data, called list, for the test functions to work on, and we link up the Old and New benchmark functions to the Old and New implementations in the InappropriateCollectionType module.

> **Note**   BenchmarkDotNet offers ways to ensure that time-consuming initializations occur only once globally, or once per iteration. Search online for "benchmarkdotnet setup and cleanup" for details. I haven't done this here for simplicity. This won't greatly affect the measurements, but it will have some impact on the time the overall benchmarking process takes to run.

With the code from Listings 12-5 and 12-6 in place, you can run the project and check the results. Your timings should look something like Listing 12-7, though obviously the absolute values will depend on the speed of your machine, what .NET and compiler version you are using, and so forth.

Listing 12-7. Baseline timings

```
Method |    Mean |    Error |   StdDev | Allocated |
------- |--------:|---------:|---------:|----------:|
    Old | 1.631 s | 0.0090 s | 0.0084 s | 31.51 KB |
    New | 1.627 s | 0.0067 s | 0.0063 s | 31.51 KB |
```

The key points are that the Old and New methods take similar times (to be expected as they are currently calling the same function), and that the amount of time per iteration, at over one and a half seconds, is significant. We have a baseline from which we can optimize!

Avoiding Indexed Access to Lists

One red flag in this code is that fact that it does indexed access into an F# list: data.[i]. Indexed access into *arrays* is fine: the runtime can calculate an offset from the beginning of the array using the index, and retrieve the element directly from the calculated memory location. (The situation might be a little more complex for multidimensional arrays.) But indexed access to an *F# list* is a really bad idea. The runtime will have to start at the head of the list, and repeatedly get the next item until it has reached the n'th item. This is an inherent property of linked lists such as F# lists.

Indexed access to an F# list element is a so-called $O(n)$ operation, that is, the time it takes on average is directly proportional to the length of the list. By contrast, indexed access to an array element is an $O(1)$ operation: the time it takes on average is

315

independent of the size of the array. Also, it takes no longer to retrieve the last element of an array than the first (ignoring any effects of the low-level caching that might go on in the processor).

So can we still use an F# list (which, rightly or wrongly was our original design decision), while avoiding indexed access? My first thought on this was Listing 12-8, which I wrote almost as a "straw man," not expecting it to be particularly effective.

Listing 12-8. First attempt at optimization

```
let sample interval data =
    data
    |> List.indexed
    |> List.filter (fun (i, _) ->
        i % interval = 0)
    |> List.map snd
```

In Listing 12-8, we use `List.indexed` to make a copy of the original list, but containing tuples of an index and the original value, for example `[(0, 1.23); (1, 0.98); ...]`. Then we use `List.filter` to pick out the values whose indexes are a multiple of the required interval. Finally, we use `List.map snd` to recover just the element values as we no longer need the index values.

I had low expectations of this approach, as it involves making a whole additional list (the one with the indexes tupled in); filtering it (with some incidental pattern matching) – which will create another list; and mapping to recover the filtered values - which will create a third list. Also, a bit more vaguely, this version is very functional, and we've been conditioned over the years to expect that functional code is inherently less efficient than imperative code.

To check my expectations, add the code from Listing 12-8 into the New module in `InappropriateCollectionType.fs` replacing the existing `sample` implementation, and run the project. Were you surprised? Listing 12-9 shows the results I got. (I've omitted some of the statistical columns to save space.)

Listing 12-9. Results of first optimization attempt

Method	Mean	Gen 0	Gen 1	Gen 2	Allocated
Old	1,624.9 ms	-	-	-	31.51 KB
New	177.7 ms	11333.3333	5666.6667	1000.0000	62563.95 KB

The good – and perhaps surprising – news is that this is very nearly an order of magnitude faster: 178ms versus 1625ms. The takeaway here is that indexed access to F# lists is a disaster for performance. But the fix has come at a cost: there is a great deal of garbage collection going on, and in all three generations. This aspect should not be a surprise: as we just said, the code in Listing 12-8 creates no less than three lists to do its work, only one of which is needed in the final result.

Using Arrays Instead of Lists

Time for another optimization. What if we revoke our initial design decision to use F# lists for the input and output, and work with arrays instead? An array is an inherently more efficient data structure for many operations, because it is a contiguous block of memory. There is no overhead, as there is with lists, for pointers from the n'th to the n+1'th element. Changing the code to use arrays simply means changing all the references to the List module to use the Array module instead (Listing 12-10).

Listing 12-10. Directly replacing Lists with Arrays

```
let sample interval data =
    data
    |> Array.indexed
    |> Array.filter (fun (i, _) ->
        i % interval = 0)
    |> Array.map snd
```

You'll also have to add a line to the test harness (in Program.fs) to make and use an array version of the test data (Listing 12-11).

Listing 12-11. Providing an array in the test harness

```
type Harness() =

    let r = Random()
    let list = List.init 1_000_000 (fun _ -> r.NextDouble())
    let array = list |> Array.ofList
    ...
```

```
[<Benchmark>]
member __.New() =
    array
    |> InappropriateCollectionType.New.sample 1000
    |> ignore
```

This improves on the elapsed time of the list-based version by about 30%, but still does a considerable amount of garbage collection (Listing 12-12).

Listing 12-12. Results of using Arrays instead of Lists

```
Method |        Mean |     Gen 0 |     Gen 1 |     Gen 2 |  Allocated |
------- |------------:|----------:|----------:|----------:|-----------:|
   Old | 1,622.1 ms |         - |         - |         - |   31.51 KB |
   New |    120.6 ms | 6200.0000 | 3400.0000 | 1000.0000 | 39201.9 KB |
```

Again, perhaps this isn't too surprising: array creation might be a bit more efficient than list creation, but we are still creating three arrays, and using two of them only for a brief moment.

Use Sequences Instead of Arrays

There's tension between the fact that we'd quite like to keep the code idiomatic (a pipeline of collection functions), and the fact that the current version creates some big transient objects. Is there any way to reconcile that? Whenever we want a collection to exist-but-not-exist, we should think about F# sequences. What happens if we replace all the Array module references with Seq references? (Listing 12-13)

Listing 12-13. Using Sequences instead of Arrays

```
let sample interval data =
    data
    |> Seq.indexed
    |> Seq.filter (fun (i, _) ->
        i % interval = 0)
    |> Seq.map snd
```

To make this a fair test we ought to make sure the sequence is actually retrieved, so add an `Array.ofSeq` to the calling code. We can also revert back to the original list as input, as lists can be used as sequences (Listing 12-14).

Listing 12-14. Retrieving the sequence

```
[<Benchmark>]
member __.New() =
    list
    |> InappropriateCollectionType.New.sample 1000
    |> Array.ofSeq
    |> ignore
```

This makes a very satisfactory difference (Listing 12-15).

Listing 12-15. Results of using Sequences instead of Lists

Method	Mean	Gen 0	Allocated
Old	1,714.18 ms	-	31.51 KB
New	36.77 ms	15214.2857	31274.59 KB

We reduced the average elapsed time by 70% compared with the previous iteration, and although there is still a lot of garbage collection going on, it is all in Generation 0. Compared with the original baseline, our code is now nearly 50 times faster.

Avoiding Collection Functions

We've spent quite a long time tweaking a collection-function-based implementation of `sample`. The current implementation has the advantage that it is highly idiomatic and has a reasonable degree of *motivational transparency*. But is it really the best we can do?

If we go back to Listing 12-4, we observe that the main problem was that we were using indexed access to an F# list. Now that we have relaxed the requirement to have lists as inputs and outputs, what happens if we restate the same code in array terms? (Listing 12-16)

Listing 12-16. Array comprehension instead of list comprehension

```
let sample interval data =
    [|
        let max = (Array.length data) - 1
        for i in 0..interval..max ->
            data.[i]
    |]
```

In Listing 12-16, I've highlighted all the differences from Listing 12-4: all we have to do is use array clamps ([|...|]) instead of list brackets ([...]) to enclose the comprehension, and `Array.length` instead of `List.length` to measure the length of the data. You'll also need to undo the changes to `Program.fs` we made in Listing 12-14, as we're back to accepting and returning an array rather than a sequence.

With those simple changes, we've fixed the main issue with the baseline version: indexed access into a linked list structure. How does it perform? (Listing 12-17)

Listing 12-17. Results of using array comprehension instead of list comprehension

Method	Mean	Gen 0	Allocated
Old	1,663,428.72 us	-	31.51 KB
New	28.61 us	11.8103	24.29 KB

Note that in Listing 12-17, the measurements are now shown in microseconds (us) rather than milliseconds (ms), because the New measurement is too small to measure in milliseconds. This is impressive: we've now improved execution time from the baseline by an astonishing factor of 60,000, more than four orders of magnitude. And we've done so using only functional constructs: an array comprehension and a yielding-for-loop. I've sometimes encountered people who consider this style non-functional, but I disagree. There is no mutation, no declare-then-populate patterns, and it's very concise.

Avoiding Loops Having Skips

I've heard it said that loops with skips (for i in 1..10..1000 ...) compile to less efficient IL than loops with an implicit skip size of 1 (for i in 1..100 ...). I've no idea if this is still true (we're not going to get into the whole business of inspecting IL in this book), but it's relatively easy to check whether this makes a difference in practice. Listing 12-18 shows an implementation that avoids a skipping for-loop. We calculate an array index by multiplying the loop counter by the interval. The hard part is defining the upper bound of the loop.

Listing 12-18. Avoiding a skipping for loop

```
let sample interval data =
    [|
        let max =
            ( (data |> Array.length |> float) / (float interval)
             |> ceil
             |> int ) - 1

        for i in 0..max ->
            data.[i * interval]
    |]
```

This makes no significant difference to performance (Listing 12-19). Either it's no longer true that skipping loops are substantially less efficient, or the overhead of multiplying up the array index has overwhelmed any gains from avoiding a skipping loop.

Listing 12-19. Results of avoiding a skipping loop

Method	Mean	Gen 0	Allocated
Old	1,704,387.26 us	-	31.51 KB
New	29.30 us	11.8103	24.27 KB

Apart from the fact that it makes no difference to performance, there are several reasons why I'd be reluctant to go this far in real code:

- It lowers the *motivational transparency* of the code, by making it a little bit less obvious what the author was intending to do.

- It's a true micro-optimization, with effects that could easily change between architectures or compiler versions. By working at this level, we deny ourselves any potential improvements in the way the compiler and runtime work with respect to skipping loops.

- The code is much riskier, with a complicated calculation for defining the upper bound of the loop. (It took me no less than *six* attempts to get it right!) In going down this route, we are laying ourselves open to off-by-one errors and other silly bugs: exactly the kind of thing that idiomatic F# code excels at avoiding.

Inappropriate Collection Types – Summary

Figure 12-1 shows a chart of the effects of our various changes.

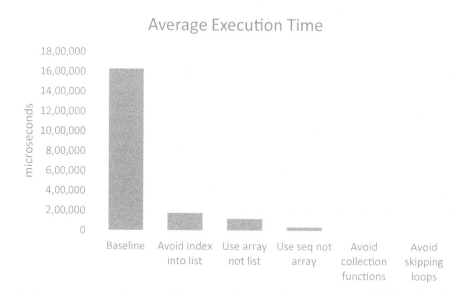

Figure 12-1. *Impact of various improvements to collection usage*

The improvements are dominated by the simple change of not using indexing into an F# list. Figure 12-2 shows the same measurements on a logarithmic scale, which makes it easier to compare the last few items.

Figure 12-2. *Impact of various improvements to collection usage on a log scale*

The takeaways from this section are as follows:

- Don't do indexed access into F# lists – that is, `myList.[i]`. Either use a different collection type, or find another way of processing the list.

- Be familiar with the performance characteristics of the collection data structures and functions that you are using. At the time of writing, these functions are somewhat patchily documented regarding their time complexity ($O(n)$, $O(1)$, etc.), so you may have to do a little online searching or experimentation to pin this down. Don't default to using F# lists just because they might be considered more idiomatic. Unless you are playing to the strengths of lists (which boils down to use of the `head::tail` construct), arrays are often the better choice.

- Pipelines of collection functions (`.filter`, `.map,` and so forth) can have decent performance, provided you choose the right collection type in the first place.

- Sequences (and functions in the Seq module) can sometimes be a way of expressing your logic in terms of pipelines of collection functions, without the overhead of creating and destroying short-lived collection instances.

- Comprehensions (for example, placing code in array clamps and using yield or a for...-> loop) can have stellar performance. Don't be fooled into thinking such code is in some way "not functional" just because the for keyword is involved.

- Beware of low-level micro-optimizations: are you denying yourself the benefits of potential future compiler or platform improvements? Have you introduced unnecessary risk into the code?

Case Study: Short-Term Objects

An oft-quoted dictum in .NET programming is that you shouldn't unnecessarily create and destroy large numbers of reference types, because of the overhead of allocating them and later garbage collecting them. How true is this in practice, and how can we avoid it?

Imagine you are tasked with taking in a large number of 3-dimensional points (x, y, z positions), and identifying those which are within a given radius of some other fixed point. (For example, you might be trying to identify all the stars that fall within a certain radius of the sun.) We'll assume that the API of the function must take a radius value, a tuple of three floats for the "fixed" point, and an array of tuples of three points for the candidate positions (Listing 12-20).

Listing 12-20. The required API for a point-searching function

```
let withinRadius
    (radius : float)
    (here : float*float*float)
    (coords : (float*float*float)[]) : (float*float*float)[] =
    ...
```

As a further given, you have access to a class that can do 3D distance calculations (Listing 12-21).

Listing 12-21. A 3D point class that can do distance calculations

```
type Point3d(x : float, y : float, z : float) =
    member __.X = x
    member __.Y = y
    member __.Z = z
    member val Description = "" with get, set
    member this.DistanceFrom(that : Point3d) =
        (that.X - this.X) ** 2. +
        (that.Y - this.Y) ** 2. +
        (that.Z - this.Z) ** 2.
        |> sqrt
    override this.ToString() =
        sprintf "X: %f, Y: %f, Z: %f" this.X this.Y this.Z
```

The type from Listing 12-21 can do the required distance calculation, but you might notice it contains other things – a mutable `Description` field and a `ToString` override – which we don't particularly need for the requirement. This is pretty typical in an object-oriented scenario: the functionality you need is coupled with a certain amount of other stuff you don't need.

To start exploring this requirement, add another file called `ShortTermObjects.fs` to your project, and populate it with the code from Listings 12-21 and 12-22.

Listing 12-22. First cut of the withinRadius function

```
module ShortTermObjects

type Point3d(x : float, y : float, z : float) =
    // Code as Listing 12-21

type Float3 = (float * float * float)

module Old =

    let withinRadius (radius : float) (here : Float3) (coords : Float3[]) =
        let here = Point3d(here)
        coords
        |> Array.map Point3d
        |> Array.filter (fun there ->
```

```
                    there.DistanceFrom(here) <= radius)
        |> Array.map (fun p3d -> p3d.X, p3d.Y, p3d.Z)

module New =

    let withinRadius (radius : float) (here : Float3) (coords : Float3[]) =
        let here = Point3d(here)
        coords
        |> Array.map Point3d
        |> Array.filter (fun there ->
            there.DistanceFrom(here) <= radius)
        |> Array.map (fun p3d -> p3d.X, p3d.Y, p3d.Z)
```

As in the previous section, the Old and New implementations are the same initially. Note also that we use a type alias (type Float3 = (float * float * float)) to avoid repeating the tuple of three floats throughout the code.

We do the required selection by mapping the incoming array of tuples into Point3d instances, and filtering the result using the DistanceFrom instance method. Finally, we map back to an X, Y, Z tuple, as the requirement states we have to return tuples not Point3d instances.

To integrate with the benchmarking, you'll also need to alter Program.fs so that the Harness module looks like Listing 12-23.

Listing 12-23. Integrating the 3D distance calculation with benchmarking

```
module Harness =

    [<MemoryDiagnoser>]
    type Harness() =

        let r = Random(1)
        let coords =
            Array.init 1_000_000 (fun _ ->
                r.NextDouble(), r.NextDouble(), r.NextDouble())
        let here = (0., 0., 0.)

        [<Benchmark>]
        member __.Old() =
            coords
```

```
        |> ShortTermObjects.Old.withinRadius 0.1 here
        |> ignore

    [<Benchmark>]
    member __.New() =
        coords
        |> ShortTermObjects.New.withinRadius 0.1 here
        |> ignore
```

When I ran this code, I didn't have particularly high hopes: this was going to create a million instances of Point3d just so that we could use the DistanceFrom method for each instance. Listing 12-24 shows the results. (Old and New are roughly the same here, as the same function is being used in this first version.)

Listing 12-24. Results of a baseline run

Method	Mean	Gen 0	Gen 1	Gen 2	Allocated
Old	268.9 ms	8500.0000	4500.0000	1000.0000	53.56 MB
New	282.8 ms	8500.0000	4500.0000	1000.0000	53.56 MB

The statistics in Listing 12-24 aren't as bad as I'd feared – the average execution time works out at about 0.27 milliseconds per input position. Not terrible, though of course that depends entirely on your objectives. Over 50Mb of memory is being allocated during processing, which might have an effect on the wider system, and there are garbage collection "survivors" into Generations 1 and 2. The .NET garbage collector is pretty good at collecting so-called "Generation 0" items, but for every extra generation that an object survives, it will have been marked and copied, and all pointers to it will have been updated This is costly! So, can we improve on our baseline?

Sequences Instead of Arrays

We learned earlier that sequences can sometimes be a better choice than arrays (or other concrete collections) for pipeline operations that create reference types. It's simple enough to apply this to the current example (Listing 12-25).

Listing 12-25. Using sequences instead of arrays

```
let withinRadius (radius : float) (here : Float3) (coords : Float3[]) =
    let here = Point3d(here)
    coords
    |> Seq.map Point3d
    |> Seq.filter (fun there ->
        there.DistanceFrom(here) <= radius)
    |> Seq.map (fun p3d -> p3d.X, p3d.Y, p3d.Z)
    |> Seq.toArray
```

This runs a little faster and allocates a bit less memory than the baseline example, and no objects survive into Generation 1 - but the overall improvement is nothing to write home about (Listing 12-26).

Listing 12-26. Results of using sequences instead of arrays

Method	Mean	Gen 0	Gen 1	Allocated
Old	259.1 ms	8000.0000	4000.0000	53.55 MB
New	213.7 ms	22666.6667	-	45.82 MB

Avoiding Object Creation

Maybe it's time to question the whole approach of creating Point3d instances just so we can use one of Point3d's methods. Even if you didn't have access to Point3d's source code, you'd probably be able to code the calculation for a 3D distance yourself, based on the widely known formula $\sqrt{((x1-x2)^2 + (y1-y2)^2 + (z1-z2)^2)}$.

Listing 12-27 shows what happens when we do this.

Listing 12-27. Avoiding object creation

```
let withinRadius (radius : float) (here : Float3) (coords : Float3[]) =

    let distance (p1 : float*float*float) (p2: float*float*float) =
        let x1, y1, z1 = p1
        let x2, y2, z2 = p2
        (x1 - x2) ** 2. +
```

```
        (y1 - y2) ** 2. +
        (z1 - z2) ** 2.
        |> sqrt

    coords
    |> Array.filter (fun there ->
        distance here there <= radius)
```

This shaves about 35% off the execution time, and is vastly lighter on memory allocation. There is no recorded garbage collection (Listing 12-28).

Listing 12-28. Results of avoiding object creation

Method	Mean	Gen 0	Gen 1	Allocated
Old	238.7 ms	8000.0000	4000.0000	54838.86 KB
New	151.0 ms	-	-	126.33 KB

Reducing Tuples

You might be wondering what happens if we simplify the signature of the distance function, so that it takes six separate floating-point values instead of two tuples of three floating-point values. This enables us to decompose here into x, y, and z only once, though we still have to decompose each candidate point, now using pattern matching in the filter lambda (Listing 12-29).

Listing 12-29. Reducing tuples

```
let withinRadius (radius : float) (here : Float3) (coords : Float3[]) =

    let distance x1 y1 z1 x2 y2 z2 =
        (x1 - x2) ** 2. +
        (y1 - y2) ** 2. +
        (z1 - z2) ** 2.
        |> sqrt

    let x1, y1, z1 = here
```

```
      coords
      |> Array.filter (fun (x2, y2, z2) ->
            distance x1 y1 z1 x2 y2 z2 <= radius)
```

This makes no useful difference as compared with the results in Listing 12-28. (Listing 12-30)

Listing 12-30. Result of reducing tuples

```
Method |     Mean |     Gen 0 |      Gen 1 |    Allocated |
------- |---------:|----------:|-----------:|-------------:|
   Old | 242.9 ms | 8000.0000 | 4000.0000 | 54838.86 KB |
   New | 156.2 ms |        -  |         - |    126.33 KB |
```

Using Struct Tuples

F# 4.1 introduced the concept of "struct tuples" – tuples that are value types rather than reference types. Would using struct tuples improve the performance of our `withinDistance` function? Listing 12-31 shows the new code. At the time this book was written, you couldn't declare a type alias of a struct tuple, so the parameters of the function are a little more verbose. See also how we have to use the `struct` keyword everywhere we instantiate or pattern match on a struct tuple.

Listing 12-31. Using struct tuples

```
let withinRadius
    (radius : float)
    (here : struct(float*float*float))
    (coords : struct(float*float*float)[]) =

    let distance p1 p2 =
        let struct(x1, y1, z1) = p1
        let struct(x2, y2, z2) = p2
        (x1 - x2) ** 2. +
        (y1 - y2) ** 2. +
        (z1 - z2) ** 2.
        |> sqrt
```

```
    coords
    |> Array.filter (fun there ->
        distance here there <= radius)
```

For this change, we'll also have to amend `Program.fs`, as the signature of the function being tested has changed slightly (Listing 12-32). (This would be a practical disadvantage of this optimization if the original source of the data couldn't be changed to produce struct tuples: you'd have to map all your tuples to struct tuples before calling `withinDistance`.)

Listing 12-32. Providing struct tuples

```
module Harness =

    [<MemoryDiagnoser>]
    type Harness() =

        let r = Random(1)
        let coords =
            Array.init 1_000_000 (fun _ ->
                r.NextDouble(), r.NextDouble(), r.NextDouble())
        let here = (0., 0., 0.)
        let coordsStruct =
            coords
            |> Array.map (fun (x, y, z) -> struct(x, y, z))
        let hereStruct = struct(0., 0., 0.)

        [<Benchmark>]
        member __.Old() =
            coords
            |> ShortTermObjects.Old.withinRadius 0.1 here
            |> ignore

        [<Benchmark>]
        member __.New() =
            coordsStruct
            |> ShortTermObjects.New.withinRadius 0.1 hereStruct
            |> ignore
```

Unfortunately, the move to struct tuples doesn't make much difference for this benchmark (Listing 12-33).

Listing 12-33. Results of moving to struct tuples

```
Method |     Mean |     Gen 0 |     Gen 1 |    Gen 2 |    Allocated |
------- |---------:|----------:|----------:|---------:|------------:|
   Old | 287.7 ms | 8000.0000 | 3500.0000 | 500.0000 | 54838.87 KB |
   New | 153.1 ms |        - |        - |       - |   134.64 KB |
```

Operator Choice

We seem to be scraping the bottom of the barrel in relation to memory management. Does anything else stand out as being capable of improvement? What is the code doing most?

One thing it is doing a lot is squaring, in the lines that look like this: (x1 - x2) ** 2. + ... This seems pretty innocent, but there is a tiny clue to a potential problem – the fact that we are squaring by raising to a floating-point exponent, 2.0. Maybe the ** operator is more general than it needs to be. What if we use the pown function, which raises to an integer exponent? It's a simple change (Listing 12-33).

Listing 12-34. Using pown instead of the ** operator

```
let withinRadius (radius : float) (here : Float3) (coords : Float3[]) =

    let distance x1 y1 z1 x2 y2 z2 =
        pown (x1 - x2) 2 +
        pown (y1 - y2) 2 +
        pown (z1 - z2) 2
        |> sqrt

    let x1, y1, z1 = here

    coords
    |> Array.filter (fun (x2, y2, z2) ->
        distance x1 y1 z1 x2 y2 z2 <= radius)
```

You'll also have to undo the changes to Program.fs that we made in Listing 12-32, as we are no longer bothering with struct tuples. The results of using pown are very satisfying! (Listing 12-35)

Listing 12-35. Results of using pown instead of the ** operator

Method	Mean	Gen 0	Gen 1	Gen 2	Allocated
Old	281.60 ms	8500.0000	4500.0000	1000.0000	54841.41 KB
New	16.08 ms	-	-	-	126.32 KB

This is 10 times faster than anything we've achieved before. Looking at the compiler source, perhaps this isn't too surprising. There are several steps involved in getting to the final operation of multiplying x by itself, of which Listing 12-36 is just the last.

Listing 12-36. Part of the compiler logic behind the ** operator

```
let inline ComputePowerGenericInlined one mul x n =
    let rec loop n =
        match n with
        | 0 -> one
        | 1 -> x
        | 2 -> mul x x
        | 3 -> mul (mul x x) x
        | 4 -> let v = mul x x in mul v v
        | _ ->
            let v = loop (n/2) in
            let v = mul v v in
            if n%2 = 0 then v else mul v x in
    loop n
```

Are we satisfied yet? Well even pown x 2 is a little more general than we need, as we know that we really just want to do x*x. What if we make one last change to do exactly that? (Listing 12-37)

Listing 12-37. Avoiding using pown for squaring

```
let withinRadius (radius : float) (here : Float3) (coords : Float3[]) =

    let distance x1 y1 z1 x2 y2 z2 =
        let dx = x1 - x2
        let dy = y1 - y2
        let dz = z1 - z2
```

```
        dx * dx +
        dy * dy +
        dz * dz
        |> sqrt

    let x1, y1, z1 = here

    coords
    |> Array.filter (fun (x2, y2, z2) ->
        distance x1 y1 z1 x2 y2 z2 <= radius)
```

This makes a further factor-of-three difference! (Listing 12-38)

Listing 12-38. Results of avoiding using pown

```
Method |        Mean |     Gen 0 |     Gen 1 |      Gen 2 |   Allocated |
------- |------------:|----------:|----------:|-----------:|------------:|
   Old | 270.396 ms | 8500.0000 | 4500.0000 | 1000.0000 | 54841.41 KB |
   New |   5.555 ms |         - |         - |          - |   126.32 KB |
```

We've now achieved a gain of 98% over the original implementation. It's probably time to stop scraping the barrel...

Short-Term Objects – Summary

Figure 12-3 shows a chart of the effects of our various changes.

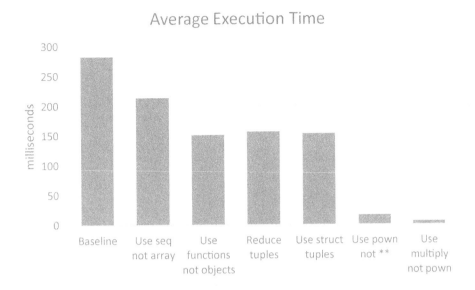

Figure 12-3. *Impact of various improvements to object usage on a log scale*

The results are dominated by one kind of change: not the way we use objects or collections, but our choice of operator to do the distance calculation.

The takeaways from this section are as follows:

- If many reference objects are placed into collections, the collections and their functions can have a bearing on performance over and above the cost of the objects themselves. For example, when dealing with long lists of reference type instances, pipelines of sequence functions can be better than pipelines of array functions.

- Think about *why* you are creating objects. Could the methods you are calling be factored out into stand-alone functions, meaning that the whole object-instantiation/collection issue goes away (unless those functions themselves allocate memory)? Refactoring into independent functions has additional benefits in terms of conciseness, decoupling, and testability.

- Concerns about allocation of tuples, and the possible gains from using struct tuples, can be important; but quick wins are not guaranteed.

- Though discussions of performance in .NET languages often focus on memory management, this is far from being the whole story. Consider algorithms and operators as well.

- Only use ** for raising to non-integer exponents. Use pown when raising to integer exponents, and also consider simple self-multiplication when the exponent is known in advance (e.g., squaring, cubing…).

Case Study: Naive String Building

As developers, we often find ourselves building up strings, for example, for formatting values in UIs or data exports, or sending messages to other servers. It's easy to get wrong on .NET – but fortunately not too hard to get right either.

For this section we'll imagine we've been tasked with formatting a two-dimensional array of floating-point values as a single CSV (comma-separated values) string, with line-ends between each row of data. For simplicity we'll assume that F#'s default floating-point formatting (with the "%f" format specifier) is sufficient. We'll further assume that the array, while not trivial, fits in memory; and that its CSV also fits in memory, so we don't need a fancy streaming approach.

Add a new file called NaiveStringBuilding.fs to the benchmarking project and copy into it the code from Listing 12-39.

Listing 12-39. First cut of a CSV builder

```
module NaiveStringBuilding

open System

module Old =

    let private buildLine (data : float[]) =
        let mutable result = ""
        for x in data do
            result <- sprintf "%s%f," result x
        result.TrimEnd(',')
```

```
    let buildCsv (data : float[,]) =
        let mutable result = ""
        for r in 0..(data |> Array2D.length1) - 1 do
            let row = data.[r, *]
            let rowString = row |> buildLine
            result <- sprintf "%s%s%s" result rowString Environment.NewLine
        result

module New =

// Code as in Old module above.
```

Also change the Harness module in Program.fs to look like Listing 12-40.

Listing 12-40. Integrating CSV generation with benchmarking

```
module Harness =

    [<MemoryDiagnoser>]
    type Harness() =

        let data =
            Array2D.init 500 500 (fun x y ->
                x * y |> float)

        [<Benchmark>]
        member __.Old() =
            data
            |> NaiveStringBuilding.Old.buildCsv
            |> ignore

        [<Benchmark>]
        member __.New() =
            data
            |> NaiveStringBuilding.New.buildCsv
            |> ignore
```

In Listing 12-40 we generate a 500 x 500 element array: not exactly "big data," but it's still a quarter of a million elements, so will give our CSV builder a decent workout. (You can reduce the number of elements if the benchmarks run too slowly for you.) How does the naive, mutation-based solution shape up? (Listing 12-41)

Listing 12-41. Results of naive CSV string building

```
Method |   Mean  |     Gen 0     |    Gen 1     |    Gen 2     | Allocated |
------- |--------:|-------------:|------------:|------------:|----------:|
   Old  | 2.307 s | 1048000.0000 | 241000.0000 | 236000.0000 |   3.08 GB |
   New  | 2.288 s | 1052000.0000 | 245000.0000 | 240000.0000 |   3.08 GB |
```

This… is not good. Building the CSV for our relatively modest 500 x 500 array takes nearly two and a half seconds, and allocates an astonishing 3GB of memory. There is garbage collection going on in all three generations. Imagine you'd put this code on a web server for, say, generating client downloads for scientific or banking customers. You would not be popular! The reason things are so bad is the level at which we are mutating things. Every time we do a `result <- sprintf...` we are discarding the string object that was previously referred to by the label `result` (making it available for garbage collection in due course) and creating another string object. This means allocating and almost immediately freeing vast amounts of memory.

StringBuilder to the Rescue

The problems of string mutation aren't unique to F#. There is a nice solution in .NET called `System.Text.StringBuilder`, which is designed to tackle exactly this kind of situation. Listing 12-42 shows how you can use it. The code doesn't have to change much: the mutable `result` is replaced by a `StringBuilder` instance, and the actual mutation of `result` in `buildLine` is replaced by calling the string builder's `Append()` method. (Confusingly, calling `Append` both does an in-place append *and* returns the `StringBuilder` instance, which is why we have to pipe its result into ignore.) In the `buildCsv` function we use `StringBuilder.AppendLine()` to get the line breaks. Finally, we call the string builder's `ToString()` method to get the built-up string.

Listing 12-42. Using StringBuilder for string concatenation

```
open System.Text

let private buildLine (data : float[]) =
    let sb = StringBuilder()
    for x in data do
        sb.Append(sprintf "%f," x) |> ignore
    sb.ToString().TrimEnd(',')
```

```
let buildCsv (data : float[,]) =
    let sb = StringBuilder()
    for r in 0..(data |> Array2D.length1) - 1 do
        let row = data.[r, *]
        let rowString = row |> buildLine
        sb.AppendLine(rowString) |> ignore
    sb.ToString()
```

The results are impressive: a 13-fold speed up and a 32-two-fold improvement in memory allocation (Listing 12-43).

Listing 12-43. Result of using StringBuilder for string concatenation

Method	Mean	Gen 0	Gen 1	Gen 2	Allocated
Old	2,227.5 ms	1039000.0000	234000.0000	228000.0000	3151.65 MB
New	166.5 ms	17333.3333	2666.6667	1000.0000	95.63 MB

Using String.Join

If we now focus on the buildLine function, we notice a few things about it that should make us a little unhappy:

- It's too much code for what must surely be a commonly required operation: joining a set of strings together with some separator at the joins.

- At the end of the string building process, we have to go back and trim off the final separator.

It turns out that .NET offers a built-in function for doing pretty much all we want. String.Join takes a separator and an array of strings to join, so all we need do before calling it is map the floats into strings in the required format (Listing 12-44).

Listing 12-44. Using String.Join

```
open System.Text

let private buildLine (data : float[]) =
    let cols = data |> Array.map (sprintf "%f")
    String.Join(',', cols)
```

```
let buildCsv (data : float[,]) =
    let sb = StringBuilder()
    for r in 0..(data |> Array2D.length1) - 1 do
        let row = data.[r, *]
        let rowString = row |> buildLine
        sb.AppendLine(rowString) |> ignore
    sb.ToString()
```

This gives a further incremental improvement in performance (Listing 12-45).

Listing 12-45. Result of using String.Join

```
Method |       Mean |         Gen 0 |        Gen 1 |         Gen 2 | Allocated |
------ |-----------:|--------------:|-------------:|--------------:|----------:|
   Old | 2,853.5 ms | 1036000.0000 | 229000.0000 | 224000.0000 | 3151.6 MB |
   New |   135.7 ms |    9500.0000 |   2500.0000 |    750.0000 |  50.85 MB |
```

Using Array.Parallel.map

If we look again at Listing 12-44, we notice that we have an array mapping operation. With such operations you can often speed things up by using `Array.Parallel.map` instead (Listing 12-46). `Array.Parallel.map` has the same type signature and observable behavior as `Array.map`, except that the computations it specifies are done in parallel, spread across your available cores. Obviously, we don't want to do this until we are convinced that the operation we are doing is itself reasonably efficient, but here it seems justified.

Listing 12-46. Using Array.Parallel.map

```
open System.Text

let private buildLine (data : float[]) =
    let cols = data |> Array.Parallel.map (sprintf "%f")
    String.Join(',', cols)

let buildCsv (data : float[,]) =
    let sb = StringBuilder()
    for r in 0..(data |> Array2D.length1) - 1 do
        let row = data.[r, *]
```

```
        let rowString = row |> buildLine
        sb.AppendLine(rowString) |> ignore
    sb.ToString()
```

This brings us a considerable speed improvement, a great cost-benefit given the simplicity of the code change (Listing 12-47).

Listing 12-47. Result of using Array.Parallel.map

Method	Mean	Gen 0	Gen 1	Gen 2	Allocated
Old	2,745.12 ms	1038000.0000	229000.0000	226000.0000	3151.66 MB
New	91.21 ms	10833.3333	2166.6667	833.3333	30.95 MB

A couple of things to be aware of when using `Array.Parallel.map`. First, its impact will obviously be very dependent on the number of available cores. It's not uncommon for cheaper cloud instances (for example, on Microsoft Azure) to have fewer cores than a typical developer machine, so the in-production speedup may be disappointing. You may have to experiment with running your benchmarks on a cloud instance to clarify this. And second, try not to nest `Array.Parallel` operations. You will rapidly bump into the law of diminishing returns.

If you are really concentrating, you may be wondering if another couple of optimizations in the `buildLine` function might squeeze out a little more performance:

- Using `Seq.map` instead of `Array.map`.

- Using `String.Format` instead of F#'s `sprintf`. to format the floating-point values into strings.

I tried both of these and they actually resulted in slightly worse performance in this particular case.

Overall, we've a achieved approximately a 25-fold improvement in performance, and two orders of magnitude less memory allocation.

Naive String Building – Summary

Figure 12-4 shows a chart of the effects of our various changes.

Figure 12-4. *Impact of various improvements to string building*

The takeaways from this section are as follows:

- Mutating string instances really means discarding and replacing the entire instance with another one. This is a disaster for performance.

- The .NET `StringBuilder` class is optimized for exactly this requirement and can offer a huge speed and memory efficiency boost.

- When joining strings together with a separator, `String.Join` gives good performance with minimal code.

- Using `Array.Parallel.map` gives a great low-code-impact speed boost. Bear in mind the number of cores on the machine where the code will be running live. Nest `Array.Parallel.map` operations at your peril.

Other Common Performance Issues

I should mention a few other common performance issues. We don't have room for case studies for these, but a brief description should be enough to help you avoid them.

Searching Large Collections

If you find yourself repeatedly searching through large collections using `Array.find`, `Array.tryFind`, `Array.contains,` and so forth, consider making the collection an F# Map, a .NET Dictionary, or some other collection optimized for lookup. In some cases, it may be useful to make a separate dictionary whose keys are the items you want to look up by, and whose values are indexes into the original array.

Comparison Operators and DateTimes

If you need to do large numbers of less-than, greater-than, or equality comparisons with `DateTime` or `DateTimeOffset` instances, consider using `DateTime.CompareTo` or `DateTimeOffset.CompareTo`. At the time of writing, this works about five times faster (in a brief informal test) than =, >, >=, < and <=.

Concatenating Lists

The @ operator concatenates two F# lists. This is a relatively expensive operation, so you may want to avoid doing it in performance critical code. Building up lists using the cons operator (`::`) is OK (assuming that a list is otherwise suitable for what you are doing), because that's what linked lists are optimized for.

For Loop with Unexpected List Creation

What's the practical difference between these two lines of code? (Listing 12-48)

Listing 12-48. A right way and a wrong way to write a simple indexed for loop

```
for i in 0..9999 do...

for i in [0..9999] do...
```

The first is a simple for-loop and is correct. The second instantiates a list instance with 10,000 elements and iterates over the list. The body of the loops could be the same and the second would perform much more slowly, and would use more memory.

F# 4.5 and Span Support

Be aware that F# 4.5 introduces support for the new .NET type Span<T>. To quote *MSDN Magazine:*

> *System.Span<T> is a new value type at the heart of .NET. It enables the representation of contiguous regions of arbitrary memory, regardless of whether that memory is associated with a managed object, is provided by native code via interop, or is on the stack. And it does so while still providing safe access with performance characteristics like that of arrays.*

Usage of Span is too low-level an undertaking to into detail here, but if you are really struggling for performance and you think working directly with a range of memory might help, you can do so using F# 4.5's support for Span.

The Importance of Tests

I've done all this benchmarking without having shown any tests to prove that the functions being tested still work correctly. This is simply to keep down the amount of code included in the book. In reality, it would be important to have passing tests before you started the optimization process – and to keep running them for each optimization pass. Broadly your workflow should be like Figure 12-5.

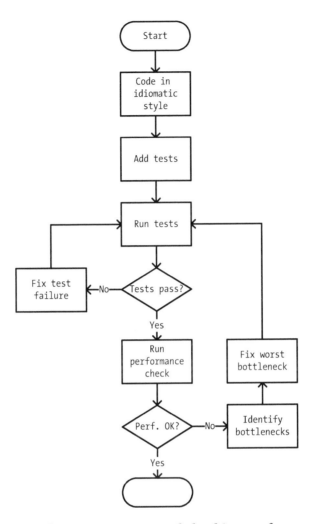

Figure 12-5. *Workflow for running tests and checking performance*

You might shortcut the process a bit by doing several performance optimization passes before rerunning tests. But the important thing is that nothing gets included in your product that doesn't *both* pass functional tests *and* have acceptable performance.

This is especially true when replacing pipelines of collection functions with more hand-crafted logic. The lower the level of abstraction you are working at, the more potential there is for silly off-by-one errors and so forth: just the kinds of things that one avoids if one sticks to using collection functions.

Recommendations

Here are some lessons that are worth taking away from this chapter:

- When performance is important, have a method for measuring it in a simple and repeatable way. BenchmarkDotNet is a good choice.

- Be keenly aware of the performance characteristics of any collection types and functions you are using. Indexed access into F# lists, and list concatenation with @, are traps that are particularly easy to fall into.

- Instantiating and later destroying reference values (i.e., classes) have a cost. Be mindful of whether those objects need to exist – could a function do the work instead?

- When instances are in a collection, the type of collection used can also affect memory behavior. Using sequence functions instead of concrete collection functions for intermediate steps in a pipeline can sometimes help (e.g., `Seq.map` instead of `Array.map`).

- Although discussion of .NET performance often focuses on the memory footprint and life cycles of objects, other considerations, such as the choice of operators, can sometimes have a greater impact. Remember the impact of using **, versus `pown` or simple multiplication.

- Naive string building is a common source of performance problems. `StringBuilder` and `String.Join` can help.

- `Array.Parallel.map` can have a big impact on performance when multiple cores are available. Add it as a last step when you are sure the mapping function itself is efficient.

- When dealing with `DateTimes` and `DateTimeOffsets`, `CompareTo` is currently faster than comparison operators such `<`, `>`, and `=`.

- Don't use for `x in [y..z]` unless you really did intend to create a collection of values to iterate over. Omit the brackets.

- You can get great improvements in performance without moving away from a functional, immutable style. Beware of micro-optimizations that make your code less reliable, less maintainable, and less likely to benefit from future compiler or platform enhancements.

Summary

Optimizing F# code can be a pleasure rather than a chore, provided you set up good benchmarks, and code with a degree of *mechanical sympathy*. Code a baseline version that works, bearing in mind the principles of *motivational transparency* and *semantic focus*. While you should avoid obvious howlers (like indexed access into F# lists), you shouldn't worry overly much about performance during this step. Ensure tests and benchmarks are in place for this baseline version. *Then* tackle bottlenecks. You can often achieve improvements of several orders of magnitude without compromising the clarity and maintainability of your code.

Finally, I want to say a big thanks to the authors and maintainers of BenchmarkDotNet. It's an awesome library, and we've only skimmed the surface of its capabilities here.

In the next chapter we'll move our focus back from the computer to the human, and discuss how to use *code layout and naming* to maximize the readability, and hence the revisability of our code.

Exercises

EXERCISE 12-1 – CONCATENATING COLLECTIONS

You come across the following code, which adds some new transactions to an existing collection of transactions. It seems to be a bottleneck in your system.

```
type Transaction = { Id : int } // Would contain more fields in reality

let addTransactions
    (oldTransactions : Transaction list)
    (newTransactions : Transaction list) =
    oldTransactions @ newTransactions
```

Assuming that the old and new transaction collections don't have to be F# lists, how could you speed up the system with minimal code changes?

EXERCISE 12-2 – SPEEDING UP FILTERING

A colleague suggests that you could speed up the following code (from Listing 12-37), by mapping to the distance in parallel, then filtering. (At the time of writing there is no `Array.Parallel.filter` function, which is why you'd have to map first.)

```
let withinRadius (radius : float) (here : Float3) (coords : Float3[]) =

    let distance x1 y1 z1 x2 y2 z2 =
        let dx = x1 - x2
        let dy = y1 - y2
        let dz = z1 - z2
        dx * dx +
        dy * dy +
        dz * dz
        |> sqrt

    let x1, y1, z1 = here

    coords
    // Original code:
    //|> Array.filter (fun (x2, y2, z2) ->
    //    distance x1 y1 z1 x2 y2 z2 <= radius)
    |> Array.Parallel.map (fun (x2, y2, z2) ->
        distance x1 y1 z1 x2 y2 z2)
    |> Array.filter (fun d -> d <= radius)
```

Would you expect this to improve performance? Why/why not?

EXERCISE 12-3 – CHANGING THE APPROACH TO CSV GENERATION

How could you change the code below (originally from Listing 12-46) so that the entire 2D array is mapped into string representations of the numbers in one step, and only then converted into CSV lines?

```
open System.Text

let private buildLine (data : float[]) =
```

```
        let cols = data |> Array.Parallel.map (sprintf "%f")
        String.Join(',', cols)

   let buildCsv (data : float[,]) =
        let sb = StringBuilder()
        for r in 0..(data |> Array2D.length1) - 1 do
            let row = data.[r, *]
            let rowString = row |> buildLine
            sb.AppendLine(rowString) |> ignore
        sb.ToString()
```

What impact does doing this have on performance?

Hints:

- You can get rid of the buildLine function in your new version.

- Remember there is an Array2D module.

- You won't be able to work in parallel.

Exercise Solutions

EXERCISE 12-1 – CONCATENATING LISTS

Concatenating lists with @ tends to be slow. Given that we are not required to use lists, it's simple to replace them with arrays and to use Array.append to perform the joining.

```
type Transaction = { Id : int } // Would contain more fields in reality

let addTransactions
    (oldTransactions : Transaction[])
    (newTransactions : Transaction[]) =
    Array.append oldTransactions newTransactions
```

EXERCISE 12-2 – SPEEDING UP FILTERING

Generally speaking, the suggested change would be slower. This is because the `Array.Parallel.map` operation creates a whole new array, which we then filter.

EXERCISE 12-3 – CHANGING THE APPROACH TO CSV GENERATION

This can be achieved by doing an `Array2D.map` to generate the string representation of every array value, then iterating over the result row-wise, doing a `String.Join` and an `AppendLine` in a single line of code.

```
open System.Text

let buildCsv (data : float[,]) =
    let dataStrings =
        data |> Array2D.map (sprintf "%f")
    let sb = StringBuilder()
    for cols in 0..(dataStrings |> Array2D.length1) - 1 do
        sb.AppendLine(String.Join(',', cols)) |> ignore
    sb.ToString()
```

The performance results are considerably worse than the prior (Listing 12-46) version.

Method	Mean	Gen 0	Gen 1	Gen 2	Allocated
12-46	91.21 ms	10833.3333	2166.6667	833.3333	30.95 MB
New	308.4 ms	8000.0000	3000.0000	1000.0000	54.47 MB

This is at least partly because we are no longer doing an `Array.Parallel.map` to generate the string representations. There is no `Array2D.Parallel.map`.

CHAPTER 13

Layout and Naming

I think for a lot of amateurs, their alignment is always out.

—Karrie Webb, Professional Golfer

Where Are My Braces?

Newcomers to F# are often disorientated by how *different* everything seems. Indentation is semantically significant – most code isn't enclosed in curly brackets. There's an increased emphasis on functions "floating free" without being in classes. And there are strange-seeming practices such as currying and partial application. These factors combine to undermine the comfortable naming and layout habits we might rely on in, say C#. To make things worse, at the time of writing there is no widely adopted "auto layout" tool.[1] All this means that it can hard to be sure that one is coding in a team-friendly, maintainable style. In this chapter I'll demonstrate some practices and conventions that should help you get over this feeling.

There is a very comprehensive guide to layout and naming within the F# Style Guide (`https://docs.microsoft.com/en-us/dotnet/fsharp/style-guide/`), which I'd urge you to read as soon as you've come to grips with the basics of F# syntax. Rather than reiterate the style guide's recommendations in this chapter, I'm going to take a case-study approach. We'll start with some code that embodies some... let's say "infelicities" I commonly see being perpetrated in F# code. We'll progressively tidy and refactor the example until it is code to be proud of. Please don't treat my suggestions as rules (I have a personal horror of "coding standards"),

---

[1]There is a project called Fantomas (`https://github.com/fsprojects/fantomas`), which seeks to address this. As you read this book, it would be worth checking the current status of that project and its relationship with the Ionide tooling project.

but as useful suggestions born of experience. It's more important that you finish this chapter *wanting* to organize your code well, than it is to memorize this or that convention.

It's Okay Pluto, I'm Not a Planet Either

Our example will be some code to process data from the International Astronomical Union's Minor Planet Center. In case astronomy isn't your forte, a *minor planet* is essentially anything natural orbiting the Sun, which isn't a proper planet or a comet. The Minor Planet Center provides a data file of all the known minor planets, which you can download from here: `https://www.minorplanetcenter.net/iau/MPCORB/MPCORB.DAT`. The format is documented here: `https://minorplanetcenter.net/iau/info/MPOrbitFormat.html`.

The aim of our code is to let consumers easily query the data file, to produce information such as a list of the brightest minor planets, or those with the most eccentric orbits.

Note   This chapter has made use of data and/or services provided by the International Astronomical Union's Minor Planet Center.

To help understand the code, let's take a quick look at the file format. Listing 13-1 shows an abridged version of the start of the file.

Listing 13-1. The start of the MPCORB.DAT file

```
MINOR PLANET CENTER ORBIT DATABASE (MPCORB)

This file contains published orbital elements for all numbered and
unnumbered multi-opposition minor planets for which it is possible to make
reasonable

(about 30 more lines of explanation)
```

```
Des'n     H     G     Epoch    M          Peri.      Node       Incl.
e         n            a       Reference      #Obs  #Opp  Arc            rms
Perts              Computer

---------------------------------------------------------------------------

00001     3.34  0.12  K183N    352.23052  73.11528   80.30992   10.59351
0.0755347  0.21413094  2.7670463  0 MPO448910  6714  114   1801-2018  0.60 M-v
30h MPCLINUX    0000       (1) Ceres                  20180430

00002     4.13  0.11  K183N    334.32318  310.00631  173.08380  34.83687
0.2305056  0.21346869  2.7727662  0 MPO435694  7950  108   1821-2018  0.58 M-v
28h MPCLINUX    0000       (2) Pallas                 20180210
```

The MPCORB.DAT file begins with some explanatory text, then some heading information followed by a set of dashes, and finally lines of data in fixed-length columns. (I've wrapped and separated the data lines in Listing 13-1 to make it clearer where the break is.)

Let's also look at the documentation file (Listing 13-2).

Listing 13-2. Extract from the file format documentation

```
The column headed 'F77' indicates the Fortran 77/90/95/2003/2008 format
specifier that should be used to read the specified value.

   Columns    F77    Use

    1 -    7  a7     Number or provisional designation
                         (in packed form)
    9 -   13  f5.2   Absolute magnitude, H
   15 -   19  f5.2   Slope parameter, G

(several more columns)

  124 - 126  i3      Number of oppositions

     For multiple-opposition orbits:
     128 - 131  i4      Year of first observation
     132        a1      '-'
     133 - 136  i4      Year of last observation
```

```
For single-opposition orbits:
128 - 131  i4     Arc length (days)
133 - 136  a4     'days'
```

(several more columns)

So essentially the logic of the code to read the file will need to be:

- Skip all the lines up to and including the line that looks like -------...

- For each subsequent line...

- Take characters 1–7 and use them as a string for the designation.

- Take characters 9–13 and interpret them as a floating-point value for the absolute magnitude.

- ...and so forth for each data item.

One complication will be the data between columns 128 and 136, which is interpreted differently depending on the value of the preceding "Number of oppositions" item. An *opposition* is simply the passage of the body through the opposite side of the sky from the Sun, when viewed from Earth. It's significant because during opposition, the body is as its most visible.

Some Infelicitous Code

With those requirements in mind, Listing 13-3 shows messy but working code. Have a read – how typical is this of F# you have written or have had to maintain?

Listing 13-3. Initial state of the minor planets reading code

```
module MinorPlanets =

    open System

    let charArray (s : string) =
        s.ToCharArray()
```

```
let toDouble (s : string) =
    match Double.TryParse(s) with
    | true, x -> Some x
    | false, x -> None

let toChar (s : string) =
    if String.IsNullOrWhiteSpace(s) then None
    else
        Some(s.[0])

let toInt (s : string) =
    match Int32.TryParse(s) with
    | true, x -> Some x
    | false, x -> None

let columnAsString startInd endInd (line : string) =
    line.Substring(startInd-1,endInd-startInd+1).Trim()

let columnAsCharArray startInd endInd (line : string) =
    charArray(columnAsString startInd endInd line)

let columnAsInt startInd endInd (line : string) =
    toInt(columnAsString startInd endInd line)

let columnAsDouble startInd endInd (line : string) =
    toDouble(columnAsString startInd endInd line)

let columnAsChar startInd endInd (line : string) =
    toChar(columnAsString startInd endInd line)

type ObservationRange =
| SingleOpposition of int
| MultiOpposition of int * int

let rangeFromLine (oppositions : int option) (line : string) =
    match oppositions with
    | None -> None
    | Some o when o = 1 ->
        line |> columnAsInt 128 131
        |> Option.map SingleOpposition
```

```
    | Some o ->
        match (line |> columnAsInt 128 131),
              (line |> columnAsInt 133 136) with
        | Some(firstObservedYear), Some(lastObservedYear) ->
            MultiOpposition(firstObservedYear,
                lastObservedYear) |> Some
        | _ -> None

type MinorPlanet = {
    Designation : string; AbsMag : float option
    SlopeParam : float option; Epoch : string
    MeanAnom : float option; Perihelion : float option
    Node : float option; Inclination : float option
    OrbEcc : float option; MeanDaily : float option
    SemiMajor : float option; Uncertainty : char option
    Reference : string; Observations : int option
    Oppositions : int option; Range : ObservationRange option
    RmsResidual : double option; PerturbersCoarse : string
    PerturbersPrecise : string; ComputerName : string
    Flags : char[]; ReadableDesignation : string
    LastOpposition : string }

let private create (line : string) =

    let oppositions = line |> columnAsString 124 126 |> toInt
    let range = line |> rangeFromLine oppositions

    { Designation = columnAsString 1 7 line
      AbsMag = columnAsDouble 9 13 line
      SlopeParam = columnAsDouble 15 19 line
      Epoch = columnAsString 21 25 line
      MeanAnom = columnAsDouble 27 35 line
      Perihelion = columnAsDouble 38 46 line
      Node = columnAsDouble 49 57 line
      Inclination = columnAsDouble 60 68 line
      OrbEcc = columnAsDouble 71 79 line
      MeanDaily = columnAsDouble 81 91 line
      SemiMajor = columnAsDouble 93 103 line
```

```
        Uncertainty = columnAsChar 106 106 line
        Reference = columnAsString 108 116 line
        Observations = columnAsInt 118 122 line
        Oppositions = oppositions
        Range = range
        RmsResidual = columnAsDouble 138 141 line
        PerturbersCoarse = columnAsString 143 145 line
        PerturbersPrecise = columnAsString 147 149 line
        ComputerName = columnAsString 151 160 line
        Flags = columnAsCharArray 162 165 line
        ReadableDesignation = columnAsString 167 194 line
        LastOpposition = columnAsString 195 202 line
    }

let createFromData (data : seq<string>) =
    data
    |> Seq.skipWhile (fun line ->
                              line.StartsWith("----------")
                              |> not) |> Seq.skip 1
    |> Seq.filter (fun line ->
                        line.Length > 0)
    |> Seq.map (fun line -> create line)
```

It's important to say that this code, messy though it is, actually works! Listing 13-4 gives a demo function you can use to try it out. As we make our way through the various issues, we won't be changing any of the functionality at all: this chapter is entirely about organization and presentation.

Listing 13-4. Trying out the code

```
open System.IO

let demo() =

    // Brightest 10 minor planets (absolute magnitude)

    // Edit the path to reflect where you stored the file:
    @"C:\Data\MinorPlanets\MPCORB.DAT"
    |> File.ReadLines
```

```
        |> MinorPlanets.createFromData
        |> Seq.filter (fun mp ->
            mp.AbsMag |> Option.isSome)
        |> Seq.sortBy (fun mp ->
            mp.AbsMag.Value)
        |> Seq.truncate 10
        |> Seq.iter (fun mp ->
            printfn "Name: %s Abs. magnitude: %0.2f"
                mp.ReadableDesignation
                (mp.AbsMag |> Option.defaultValue nan))

> demo();;
Name: (136199) Eris Abs. magnitude: -1.10
Name: (134340) Pluto Abs. magnitude: -0.76
Name: (136472) Makemake Abs. magnitude: -0.20
Name: (136108) Haumea Abs. magnitude: 0.20
Name: (90377) Sedna Abs. magnitude: 1.50
Name: (225088) 2007 OR10 Abs. magnitude: 1.80
Name: (90482) Orcus Abs. magnitude: 2.20
Name: (50000) Quaoar Abs. magnitude: 2.40
Name: 2013 FY27 Abs. magnitude: 3.00
Name: (4) Vesta Abs. magnitude: 3.20
```

Note by the way that in astronomy, a lower magnitude number means a greater brightness.

Convenience Functions

So where do we start? It might help to organize the code into smaller modules, thus improving the *semantic focus* that's available to the reader. One grouping is obvious: functions such as charArray and toDouble are general-purpose convenience functions that don't have any direct relationship with the astronomy domain. We can move these into a module called Convert (Listing 13-5).

Listing 13-5. A Convert module

```
module Convert =
    open System

    let charArray (s : string) =
        s.ToCharArray()

    let tryDouble (s : string) =
        match Double.TryParse(s) with
        | true, x -> Some x
        | false, _ -> None

    let tryChar (s : string) =
        if String.IsNullOrWhiteSpace(s) then None
        else
            Some(s.[0])

    let tryInt (s : string) =
        match Int32.TryParse(s) with
        | true, x -> Some x
        | false, _ -> None
```

Putting just these functions in a module helps us focus what else might be wrong with them. Some of them return option types, so I renamed them using the "try" idiom – for example, `tryDouble`. Also, the match expressions contained a bound but unused value x in the `false` branch. I replaced these with underscores. Always try to remove unused bindings in your code: explicitly ignoring them using underscore shows that you didn't just overlook them, adding *motivational transparency*.

If you are following along, now would be a good time to rerun the edited code and make sure it still works.

Column Extraction Functions

Another obvious set of candidates for moving into a module is functions such as `columnAsString` and `columnAsCharArray`, which are all about picking out a substring from a data line and converting it into some type. Moving them into a `Column` module means we can get rid of the repetitive use of the `column` prefix in their names. We also use the "try" idiom here when an option type is returned. (Many of the columns have missing values in the dataset – some minor planets are in the process of discovery so not all the parameters will be known. For robustness I've assumed that almost anything might be missing.) (Listing 13-6)

Listing 13-6. A Column module

```
module Column =

    let asString startInd endInd (line : string) =
        line.Substring(startInd-1,endInd-startInd+1).Trim()

    let asCharArray startInd endInd (line : string) =
        Convert.charArray(asString startInd endInd line)

    let tryAsInt startInd endInd (line : string) =
        Convert.tryInt(asString startInd endInd line)

    let tryAsDouble startInd endInd (line : string) =
        Convert.tryDouble(asString startInd endInd line)

    let tryAsChar startInd endInd (line : string) =
        Convert.tryChar(asString startInd endInd line)
```

Again, now the functions are in a module, we can focus on what could be improved within them. Listing 13-7 shows an arguably more idiomatic version.

Listing 13-7. Alternative layout for dot notation, and using function composition

```
module Column =

    let asString startInd endInd (line : string) =
        let len = endInd - startInd + 1
        line
            .Substring(startInd-1, len)
            .Trim()

    let asCharArray startInd endInd =
        (asString startInd endInd) >> Convert.charArray

    let tryAsInt startInd endInd =
        (asString startInd endInd) >> Convert.tryInt
```

```
let tryAsDouble startInd endInd =
    (asString startInd endInd) >> Convert.tryDouble

let tryAsChar startInd endInd =
    (asString startInd endInd) >> Convert.tryChar
```

The things that have changed in Listing 13-7 are:

- In `asString`, I removed the length calculation that was being done on-the-fly in the `Substring` call. Instead I've put it into a separate binding (`let len = ...`). This reduces the number of things the reader has to think about at any one time.

- Also in the `asString` function, I changed the layout to an indented style where each method call (`.Substring()` and `.Trim()`) is on its own line. I quite like this style because, again, it lets the reader think about one thing at a time. It's mimicking of the F# pipeline style where you put each `|> someFunction` on a separate line.

- In the other functions (`asCharArray` etc.), I've used function composition. For example, in `asCharArray`, we explicitly compose the `asString` and `Convert.charArray` to produce the desired mapping from a data line to a value. This means we can remove the explicit `line` parameter, because the partial application of `asString` still leaves the requirement of a `line` input. You might want to reflect on whether this is truly an improvement: it's one of those cases where it depends on the skill levels of the maintainers.

The Observation Range Type

The next category of code that deserves to go into a separate module is the code relating to the "observation range" data. Just to recap, one of the data items needs to be different depending on the number of oppositions of the minor planet that have been observed. When only one opposition has been seen, we need to show how many days the body was observed for. When more than one opposition has been seen, we give the calendar years of the first and last observation. Listing 13-8 shows the relevant section from the documentation.

Listing 13-8. Observation range of a minor planet

```
124 - 126  i3      Number of oppositions

   For multiple-opposition orbits:
   128 - 131  i4      Year of first observation
   132        a1      '-'
   133 - 136  i4      Year of last observation

   For single-opposition orbits:
   128 - 131  i4      Arc length (days)
   133 - 136  a4      'days'
```

The existing code rightly models this as a Discriminated Union. But the DU and its constructing function need to be pulled out into their own module (Listing 13-9).

Listing 13-9. The ObservationRange module

```
module ObservationRange =

    type Range =
        private
            | SingleOpposition of ArcLengthDays:int
            | MultiOpposition of FirstYear:int * LastYear:int

    let fromLine (oppositions : int option) (line : string) =
        match oppositions with
        | None ->
            None
        | Some o when o = 1 ->
            line
            |> Column.tryAsInt 128 131
            |> Option.map SingleOpposition
        | Some _ ->
            let firstYear = line |> Column.tryAsInt 128 131
            let lastYear = line |> Column.tryAsInt 133 136
```

```
match firstYear, lastYear with
| Some(fy), Some(ly) ->
    MultiOpposition(FirstYear=fy, LastYear=ly) |> Some
| _ ->
    None
```

This is a great pattern for F# code: define a domain type in a module of its own, and place one or more functions to create instances of that type (or otherwise work with it) in the same module. As we've discussed before in this book, the one issue this does give you is that of choosing names for the module and the type. Here I've settled on ObservationRange and Range – which is admittedly a little repetitive but is not unreasonable. I made both the case constructors for Range private, as we provide a means of creating instances within the module: the fromLine function. You might have to remove the private keyword if it caused problems with serialization or with use from other languages.

Incidentally I also experimented with calling the DU __ (double underscore) on the basis that you don't really use the DU name, only the case names. This works, but I can only imagine the wrath that would fall on my head from the F# community if I suggested it seriously.

A few other things I've changed in the observation range functions:

- I changed the layout of the DU so that each case is indented to the right of the keyword type. This isn't *required* by F#'s indentation rules, but the coding guidelines firmly recommend it.

- I named each of the fields of the DU (ArcLengthDays, FirstYear, and LastYear). This greatly improves *motivational transparency*. You might also notice that I used these labels when constructing the MultiOpposition instance near the end of Listing 13-9.

- I renamed the rangeFromLine function as fromLine. The module name now gives sufficient context. The function will be invoked thus:

- line |> ObservationRange.fromLine.

- I bound firstYear and lastYear values explicitly, rather than doing it on-the-fly in the match expression. Again, this reduces the cognitive load on the reader. Heavily nested calls, each level of which does some separate calculation, are the absolute bane of code readability. And they make step-debugging much harder.

- I tidied up some of the slightly idiosyncratic indentation.

The Importance of Alignment

The indentation changes merit a little more commentary. In one of the changes in Listing 13-9, this…

```
line |> columnAsInt 128 131
|> Option.map SingleOpposition
```

…has become this:

```
line
|> Column.tryAsInt 128 131
|> Option.map SingleOpposition
```

It's particularly heinous to mix new-line styles when writing pipelines. It makes the reader wonder whether there is some unnoticed reason why successive lines are different. To avoid this, the simple rule is this: single piping operations can go into a single line; multiple piping operations like this example should each go on a separate line. In this case the forward-pipe operators go at the beginning of each line.

The second indentation change in Listing 13-9 was this:

```
match (line |> columnAsInt 128 131),
      (line |> columnAsInt 133 136) with
| Some(firstObservedYear), Some(lastObservedYear) ->
    MultiOpposition(firstObservedYear,
       lastObservedYear) |> Some
| _ -> None
```

...to this:

```
let firstYear = line |> Column.tryAsInt 128 131
let lastYear = line |> Column.tryAsInt 133 136
match firstYear, lastYear with
| Some(fy), Some(ly) ->
    MultiOpposition(FirstYear=fy, LastYear=ly) |> Some
| _ ->
    None
```

Apart from the separate binding of `firstYear` and `lastYear`, the point here is that if *one* branch of a match expression (the bit after the `->`) is on the same line as the `->`, the *other* branches should also be on the same line. Conversely, as in this example, if *any* branch won't nicely fit on the same line, *all* the branches should begin on an indented new line.

Why am I banging on about indentation so much? It's to do with the way the human eye and brain process information. What we are aiming for is code laid out in a very *rectilinear* (lined-up) style, where items that perform a similar role (e.g., different branches of the same match expression, or different steps of the same pipeline) are all lined up with each other. Then the reader can run their eye down the code and quickly pick out all the lines of equivalent significance. This engages the visual pattern processing part of the brain, which works somewhat separately (and faster) than the part of the brain concerned with interpreting the language of the code itself. I've illustrated this in Figure 13-1, showing with boxes the kinds of categories the reader might be looking for. Finding them is so much easier when the boxes are left aligned!

```
let rangeFromLine (oppositions : int option) (line : string) =
    match oppositions with
    | None -> None
    | Some o when o = 1 ->
        line |> columnAsInt 128 131
             |> Option.map SingleOpposition
    | Some o ->
        match (line |> columnAsInt 128 131),
              (line |> columnAsInt 133 136) with
        | Some(firstObservedYear), Some(lastObservedYear) ->
            MultiOpposition(firstObservedYear,
                lastObservedYear) |> Some
        | _ -> None


let fromLine (oppositions : int option) (line : string) =
    match oppositions with
    | None ->
        None
    | Some o when o = 1 ->
        line
        |> Column.tryAsInt 128 131
        |> Option.map SingleOpposition
    | Some _ ->
        let firstYear = line |> Column.tryAsInt 128 131
        let lastYear = line |> Column.tryAsInt 133 136
        match firstYear, lastYear with
        | Some(fy), Some(ly) ->
            MultiOpposition(FirstYear=fy, LastYear=ly) |> Some
        | _ ->
            None
```

Figure 13-1. *Code is more readable when thoughtfully aligned*

The Minor Planet Type

Now we tackle the core "domain object": the type that represents an individual minor planet. Here's the initial state of the code (Listing 13-10).

Listing 13-10. Initial state of the minor planet type

```
type MinorPlanet = {
    Designation : string; AbsMag : float option
    SlopeParam : float option; Epoch : string
    MeanAnom : float option; Perihelion : float option
    Node : float option; Inclination : float option
    OrbEcc : float option; MeanDaily : float option
    SemiMajor : float option; Uncertainty : char option
    Reference : string; Observations : int option
    Oppositions : int option; Range : ObservationRange option
    RmsResidual : double option; PerturbersCoarse : string
    PerturbersPrecise : string; ComputerName : string
    Flags : char[]; ReadableDesignation : string
    LastOpposition : string }
```

It's horrible! In an effort to make the code more compact, two record fields have been put on each line. Some fields are divided by a semicolon, and others are not. Some of the field names, such as AbsMag are abbreviated, while others, such as PerturbersPrecise, are written out fully. There are no triple-slash comments on the fields, so the consumer won't get tool tips explaining the significance of each field, its units, etc. Let's move the type into its own module and tidy it up (Listing 13-11).

Listing 13-11. A tidier version of the minor planet type

```
module MinorPlanet =

    type Body = {
        /// Number or provisional designation (packed format)
        Designation : string
        /// Absolute magnitude
        H : float option
        /// Slope parameter
        G : float option
        /// Epoch in packed form
        Epoch : string
        /// Mean anomaly at the epoch (degrees)
        M : float option
```

367

```
/// Argument of perihelion, J2000.0 (degrees)
Perihelion : float option
/// Longitude of the ascending node, J2000.0 (degrees)
Node : float option
/// Inclination to the ecliptic, J2000.0 (degrees)
Inclination : float option
/// Orbital eccentricity
e : float option
/// Mean daily motion (degrees per day)
n : float option
/// Semimajor axis (AU)
a : float option
/// Uncertainty parameter
Uncertainty : char option
/// Reference
Reference : string
/// Number of observations
Observations : int option
/// Number of oppositions
Oppositions : int option
/// Year of first and last observation,
/// or arc length in days.
Range : ObservationRange.Range option
/// RMS residual (arcseconds)
RmsResidual : double option
/// Coarse indicator of perturbers
PerturbersCoarse : string
/// Precise indicator of perturbers
PerturbersPrecise : string
/// Computer name
ComputerName : string
/// Flags
```

```
Flags : char[]
/// Readable designation
ReadableDesignation : string
/// Date of last observation included in orbit solution (YYYYMMDD)
LastOpposition : string }
```

By the way, the code in Listing 13-11 is a lot more readable in an editor than on the printed page, simply because of the colors the editor adds.

I've put the type in its own module, MinorPlanet, and called the type itself Body. Each field has its own line and its own triple-slash comment. More controversially, I've used *shorter* names for some of the fields, such as H for absolute magnitude. I did this because this is the officially accepted domain term for the item. When astronomers see a value *H* in the context of a Solar System body, they know it means absolute magnitude. I've even reflected the fact that some accepted domain terms are lowercase, for example, *e* for orbital eccentricity. I think this is reasonable in a domain such as this, where there is an accepted terminology having some terms conventionally expressed in lowercase.

How far you take use of domain terminology is an interesting question. In math-related code, I have occasionally found myself using Greek letters and symbols as names, as in Listing 13-12.

Listing 13-12. Using Greek characters in code

```
let eccentricity ε h μ =
    1. + ((2. * ε * h * h) / (μ * μ))
    |> sqrt
```

This has the advantage that your code can look a lot like the accepted formula for a particular mathematical calculation. But it does mean a lot of copy and pasting or use of ALT-*xxx* keyboard codes, so it is probably not to be encouraged!

Getting back to the minor planet record type, we also need to place the related functions into our MinorPlanet module. Listing 13-13 shows the tidied-up function to create a MinorPlanet.Body instance from a string.

Listing 13-13. Creating a MinorPlanet.Body instance

```
let fromMpcOrbLine (line : string) =

    let oppositions = line |> Column.asString 124 126 |> Convert.tryInt
    let range = line |> ObservationRange.fromLine oppositions
```

```
{ Designation =              line |> Column.asString        1    7
  H =                        line |> Column.tryAsDouble      9   13
  G =                        line |> Column.tryAsDouble     15   19
  Epoch =                    line |> Column.asString        21   25
  M =                        line |> Column.tryAsDouble     27   35
  Perihelion =               line |> Column.tryAsDouble     38   46
  Node =                     line |> Column.tryAsDouble     49   57
  Inclination =              line |> Column.tryAsDouble     60   68
  e =                        line |> Column.tryAsDouble     71   79
  n =                        line |> Column.tryAsDouble     81   91
  a =                        line |> Column.tryAsDouble     93  103
  Uncertainty =              line |> Column.tryAsChar      106  106
  Reference =                line |> Column.asString       108  116
  Observations =             line |> Column.tryAsInt       118  122
  Oppositions =              oppositions
  Range =                    range
  RmsResidual =              line |> Column.tryAsDouble    138  141
  PerturbersCoarse =         line |> Column.asString       143  145
  PerturbersPrecise =        line |> Column.asString       147  149
  ComputerName =             line |> Column.asString       151  160
  Flags =                    line |> Column.asCharArray    162  165
  ReadableDesignation = line |> Column.asString            167  194
  LastOpposition =           line |> Column.asString       195  202 }
```

I've taken another potentially controversial step here: I've aligned the start-and-end index positions as if they were numbers in a table. There are advantages and disadvantages to this. The obvious *disadvantage* is that it's fiddly to do. And if you rename anything, you have to adjust the alignment. The *advantage*, and for me it's an overwhelming one, is again that you can run your eye down the code and spot patterns and anomalies.

If you are going to follow this approach, it's well worth being familiar with your editor's block selection features. In Visual Studio, you can ALT+drag to select a rectangular block, which makes it much easier to adjust alignment. In Visual Studio Code, it's SHIFT+ALT+drag. In any case, I would only do this kind of super-alignment in special cases such as Listing 13-13, where there are a lot of necessarily repetitive lines of code.

Listing 13-14 shows the original code for creating minor planet record instances from a sequence of strings.

Listing 13-14. Original code for creating minor planet instances

```
let createFromData (data : seq<string>) =
    data
    |> Seq.skipWhile (fun line ->
                                line.StartsWith("----------")
                                |> not) |> Seq.skip 1
    |> Seq.filter (fun line ->
                        line.Length > 0)
    |> Seq.map (fun line -> create line)
```

By now you probably recognize what needs doing here. We should move the header-skipping code to its own function, and we should get rid of the crazy indenting. A good principle to adopt is to indent things the minimum amount that is required by the compiler. Listing 13-15 shows the improved version (which should also go into in the MinorPlanet module).

Listing 13-15. Improved code for creating minor planet instances

```
let private skipHeader (data : seq<string>) =
    data
    |> Seq.skipWhile (fun line ->
        line.StartsWith("----------") |> not)
    |> Seq.skip 1

let fromMpcOrbData (data : seq<string>) =
    data
    |> skipHeader
    |> Seq.filter (fun line -> line.Length > 0)
    |> Seq.map fromMpcOrbLine
```

I've also renamed the createFromData function to fromMpcOrbData as this is a little more specific. The abbreviation MpcOrb is reasonable here because that is what the input file is called.

Finally, here's how the demonstration code needs to change to reflect the improvements we've made (Listing 13-16).

Listing 13-16. Calling the revised code

```
open System.IO

let demo() =

    // Brightest 10 minor planets (absolute magnitude)
    @"C:\Data\MinorPlanets\MPCORB.DAT"
    |> File.ReadLines
    |> MinorPlanet.fromMpcOrbData
    |> Seq.filter (fun mp ->
        mp.H |> Option.isSome)
    |> Seq.sortBy (fun mp ->
        mp.H.Value)
    |> Seq.truncate 10
    |> Seq.iter (fun mp ->
        printfn "Name: %s Abs. magnitude: %0.2f"
            mp.ReadableDesignation (mp.H |> Option.defaultValue nan))
> demo();;
Name: (136199) Eris Abs. magnitude: -1.10
Name: (134340) Pluto Abs. magnitude: -0.76
Name: (136472) Makemake Abs. magnitude: -0.20
Name: (136108) Haumea Abs. magnitude: 0.20
Name: (90377) Sedna Abs. magnitude: 1.50
Name: (225088) 2007 OR10 Abs. magnitude: 1.80
Name: (90482) Orcus Abs. magnitude: 2.20
Name: (50000) Quaoar Abs. magnitude: 2.40
Name: 2013 FY27 Abs. magnitude: 3.00
Name: (4) Vesta Abs. magnitude: 3.20
```

Recommendations

Use thoughtful naming and layout to maximize the readability of your code. In particular:

- Choose names for types and functions that reflect exactly what they represent or do – but don't be verbose. Remember that the name of the module in which items live can provide additional context, allowing you to keep the item names relatively short.

- When you are forced to bind a value that you don't later use, for example, in a match expression, use underscore to explicitly ignore it.

- Use the try... idiom when a function returns an option type.

- Don't force the reader to think about too much at a time. For example, a line with heavy nesting and multiple calculations might benefit from being broken up into separate, explicit steps.

- Isolate non-domain-specific items from domain-specific items, typically by placing them in separate modules. Different "domain objects" should also go into their own modules, along with closely associated functions. More generally, keep modules short by ruthlessly classifying items into small groupings. Sometimes this process can be helped by nesting modules.

- Where there is already established domain terminology, align the naming in your domain-specific code with that terminology.

- When using Discriminated Unions, seriously consider giving explicit names to any case payload fields, especially when there are several fields that could be confused.

- When a pipeline uses more than one forward-pipe operator, place each operation on a separate line. Never ever mix the single-line with the new-line style.

- Within a match expression, be consistent on whether the code following -> is on the same or a new line.

- When declaring and constructing records, place fields on separate lines unless the record definition is very small. Never mix single-line and new-line styles in the same record declaration or construction.

- For domain classes, record types and API functions; use triple-slash comments to document members, fields, and public functions. Only rarely can you cram sufficient information into the name.

- Above all, name items and align your code to maximize the eye's ability to spot patterns - and exceptions to those patterns. If you only take away one principle from this chapter, make it this one!

Summary

It's rare to be able to organize code perfectly on the first pass. It's absolutely fine to hack something together just to see if it works, and to help you understand the domain you are working on. This is in keeping with the exploratory spirit of F# coding. But what happens next is also important. Tirelessly polish your code using the principles from this chapter. What you are aiming for is code that, in the words of computer scientist Tony Hoare has "obviously no deficiencies":

> There are two ways of constructing a software design: One way is to make it so simple that there are obviously no deficiencies, and the other way is to make it so complicated that there are no obvious deficiencies. The first method is far more difficult.

As Hoare points out, achieving "obviously no deficiencies" isn't easy. But the cost of bugs escalates exponentially as they become embedded in a larger system and in the associated processes. So, designing code that has "obviously no deficiencies" is – even in the medium term – much cheaper. Remember what we said in Chapter 1 about complexity explosions!

In the next chapter we'll draw together the various threads from this book, and remind ourselves of the key practices required to produce truly stylish F# code.

Exercise

EXERCISE 13-1 – MAKING CODE READABLE

The following working code searches for files below a certain path, and returns those files whose names match a regular expression, and which have the `ReadOnly` attribute set.

```
open System.IO
open System.Text.RegularExpressions

let find pattern dir =
    let re = Regex(pattern)
    Directory.EnumerateFiles
                (dir, "*.*", SearchOption.AllDirectories)
    |> Seq.filter (fun path -> re.IsMatch(Path.GetFileName(path)))
    |> Seq.map (fun path ->
        FileInfo(path))
    |> Seq.filter (fun fi ->
                fi.Attributes.HasFlag(FileAttributes.ReadOnly))
    |> Seq.map (fun fi -> fi.Name)
```

How would you reorganize this code to make it easier to read, maintain, and extend?

Hint: You might want to add a couple of modules, which may each have only one function.

Exercise Solution

EXERCISE 13-1 – MAKING CODE READABLE

Here's my attempt to improve this code. How does yours compare?

```
open System.IO
open System.Text.RegularExpressions

module FileSearch =

    module private FileName =
```

```
        let isMatch pattern =
            let re = Regex(pattern)
            fun path ->
                let fileName = Path.GetFileName(path)
                re.IsMatch(fileName)

    module private FileAttributes =

        let hasFlag flag filePath =
            FileInfo(filePath)
                .Attributes
                .HasFlag(flag)

    /// Search below path for files whose file names match the specified
    /// regular expression, and which have the 'read only' attribute set.
    let findReadOnly pattern dir =
        Directory.EnumerateFiles(dir, "*.*", SearchOption.AllDirectories)
        |> Seq.filter (FileName.isMatch pattern)
        |> Seq.filter (FileAttributes.hasFlag FileAttributes.ReadOnly)
```

CHAPTER 14

Summary

We are what we repeatedly do. Excellence, then, is not an act, but a habit.

—Will Durant, Historian and Philosopher (paraphrasing Aristotle)

F# and the Sense of Style

Well, you reached the end - congratulations! I very much hope you picked up some useful habits from these pages. They're distilled from several years' very happy experience of using F# in a wide variety of industries. While you may not agree with everything I say, I hope I've helped you become a more reflective practitioner in the art of programming in F#.

Before I let you go, let me reiterate the key points from each of the preceding chapters. If any of these still feel unfamiliar, it might be worth turning back to the chapters in question.

Designing Functions with Types

In Chapter 2, "Designing Functions with Types," I talked about how to design and write that fundamental unit of work in F#: the function. My approach is to start by defining the required signature. Then I write a body that matches the signature. Likely as not, doing this causes me to rethink what the function should really do, and hence what its signature should be. I repeatedly refine the signature and body, trying to eliminate as many errors as possible at the signature (type) level – but also making sure any remaining potential errors are handled explicitly in the function body.

I also pointed out the usefulness of Single Case Discriminated Unions for modeling some business types. It's often useful to place such a union into a module, together with functions to create and work with instances of the union.

377

© Kit Eason 2018
K. Eason, *Stylish F#*, https://doi.org/10.1007/978-1-4842-4000-7_14

In passing, I also mentioned how you can sometimes simplify code by defining your own operators. It's a technique to use sparingly.

Missing Data

In Chapter 3, "Missing Data," I showed you ways to stop using null values for representing missing data. Either you can use Discriminated Unions to model cases where data items are present or absent. Or you can use option types, in situations where the possibilities are simply "value present" or "value not present." and where it's obvious from context why these cases would occur.

I talked about the `Option` module, in particular the `Option.bind`, `Option.map,` and `Option.defaultValue` functions, which you can use to make your option type handling pipeline friendly. There are also functions such as `Option.ofObj` and `Option.ofNull,` which can help you transition data between the nullable and the F# world.

Don't forget that the advent of "nullable reference types" in C# – that is, the potential for reference types to be non-nullable by default – may change the landscape here. You'll need to keep up with the latest language design thinking for both C# and F# to get the best from this change.

Finally, I mentioned that you should avoid exposing F#-specific types, such as DU's and option types, in API's that might be consumed by C# or other .NET languages.

Collection Functions

In Chapter 4, "Working Effectively with Collection Functions," I showed how vital the fluent use of collection functions is to effective F# programming. I encouraged you to get familiar with the many functions in the `Array`, `List`, and `Seq` modules, such as `map`, `iter`, and `filter`. I pointed out the importance of choosing and interpreting functions, particularly collection functions, by looking at their type signatures. Remember there are handy visual tables in this chapter to help you with this (Tables 4-1 through 4-11).

Be aware of the significance of partial functions and learn to handle their failure cases gracefully. Often this can be done by using a `try...` variant of a function, which returns an option type, or by writing such a variant yourself.

I pointed out the dangers of loops that use mutable values as counters and flags. There is almost always an easier way of achieving the same thing using a collection function. Learn to write neat, elegant pipelines of collection functions – but don't let them get too long, or maintainers may find them difficult to interpret and debug.

Immutability and Mutation

In Chapter 5, "Immutability and Mutation," I discussed how, though baffling at first, immutability-by-default is the key to the practical benefits of functional programming. Once you understand how to program in immutable style, try to get in the habit of coding in that style first, only falling back on mutation for performance reasons, or because what you're trying to do isn't possible to express clearly in immutable terms. I realize, though, that it may take a while before this approach seems natural to you. Remember that using the collection functions is often the way to move away from loop-based, mutable programming to mutable style.

Pattern Matching

In Chapter 6, "Pattern Matching," I showed how there's more to pattern matching than match expressions. I urged you to practice recognizing and using pattern matching wherever it can occur. Use Table 6-2 as a guide both to what syntax features are available and how freely to use them. Understand active patterns and use them where appropriate, but not at the expense of obfuscating your code. Remember that you can pattern match on types, which is indispensable when dealing with class hierarchies; and on the literal null, which may sometimes be useful when dealing with nullable values.

Record Types

In Chapter 7, "Record Types," I discussed how to use record types as the first choice for representing small collections of named items. Be familiar with the design considerations that drive the choice of records over classes: records are to be preferred when there are no "moving parts," and the external and internal representations of data can be the same.

When you need to "modify" a record type instance, reach for the `with` keyword rather than making the record instance or its fields mutable.

I discussed the difference between structural (content) equality, as implemented by default in record types; and reference equality, as implemented by default in classes.

You can add instance or static methods to records, but do so sparingly. Alternatives include placing the record type and closely related functions in a module; or – when behaviors need to be complex and closely coupled to the type – using a class instead.

Finally, I think it's worth understanding the implications of applying the `[<Struct>]` attribute to a record type.

Classes

In Chapter 8, "Classes," I discussed F#'s approach to .NET classes, which allow you represent combinations of private and public values and behaviors. I suggest you reach for classes rather than record types when you truly need asymmetric representation of data, or you need moving parts. Typically, having moving parts involves there being an internal mutable state, together with methods that indirectly let the caller change that state. Here F# classes are the most natural fit. Also consider using F# classes when you need to participate in a C#-style class hierarchy.

Conversely, be aware of the costs of using classes. I showed how using them can lead to accidental complexity, which often starts because of a need to implement equality and/or comparison between class instances.

Remember that object expressions can sometimes let you provide inheritance-like behavior with minimal code.

Programming with Functions

In Chapter 9, "Programming with Functions," I introduced the twin concepts of *currying* and *partial application*. Currying is the separation of function parameters into individual items, and partial application is providing just some of those parameters when using the function. Prefer curried style unless there is a special reason to tuple a function's parameters together. Define curried parameters in an order that best allows the caller to partially apply when necessary. Use partial application if it makes your code clearer or eliminates repetition.

I showed how functions are first-class values, meaning you can create them, bind them to other values, pass or receive them as parameters, and return them as the result of other functions – all with little more effort than it takes to do the same for, say, an integer.

I explained how you can compose functions using the >> operator, if the two functions return and take the same types. Consider using this feature if it genuinely simplifies or clarifies your code. Be wise to the costs of function composition in terms of readability and the ability to step through code and inspect intermediate values.

Asynchronous and Parallel Programming

In Chapter 10, "Asynchronous and Parallel Programming," I illustrated asynchronous programming using the analogy of ordering pizza at a restaurant – one which gives you a pager to tell you when your meal is ready. To make your code asynchronous, identify places where your code is "ordering pizza," typically requesting a disk or network operation. Use let!, use! or (from F#) 4.5 match! bindings in an async {} block to perform such operations, freeing up the thread to do other work until the result is available. Return the (promise of a) result of an async {} block using the return keyword.

I pointed out the difference between the F# "cold task" model for asynchronous calls, and C#'s "hot task" model – where the task is running as soon as it is defined. Be prepared to translate between the two worlds, for example, by using Async.StartAsTask to create a running, C#-style task. Use Async.RunSynchronously very sparingly to actually get the result of an asynchronous computation, remembering that doing so is equivalent to waiting at the restaurant counter for your pizza pager to go off. In an extended example, I took you through the process of implementing "async all the way down," at each layer of a stack of functions.

Where it makes sense to run several asynchronous computations in parallel, consider doing so with Async.Parallel, or Async.ParallelWithThrottle from the FSharpx.Async Nuget package.

For computations that don't need to be asynchronous, but which can usefully be run in parallel, simply use Array.Parallel.map or one of the other functions in the Array.Parallel module.

Railway Oriented Programming

In Chapter 11, "Railway Oriented Programming," I took you through the ROP style. This is an approach centered around the use of the `Result` type, which allows you to represent the results of computations that might pass or fail. I recast the ROP metaphor in terms of machine tools in a widget factory. Each machine tool is placed into an "adapter housing" so that we can put together a production line of units, each of which can bypass failures and process successes from the previous step. In ROP, the basic functions generally take a "naked" type as input and return a result wrapped in a `Result` type. We use an adapter function (`Result.bind`) to convert each such function so that it both *takes* a `Result` type and returns a `Result` type. Functions thus adapted can be composed using `>>`. ROP also uses `Result.map` to adapt functions that can never fail, so that they can also slot into the pipeline.

We can use a Discriminated Union to enumerate all the error possibilities, with some cases having payloads to convey further information about the error. Doing this means that errors that have occurred anywhere in the pipeline can be handled in a centralized way using `Result.mapError`.

I suggested that you use ROP judiciously. But even if you choose not to adopt it in your code, you should be sure to understand how it works, as doing so can yield insights that are applicable in your F# programming generally.

Performance

In Chapter 12, "Performance," I encouraged you to code with *mechanical sympathy*, being aware of the performance characteristics of the data structures and algorithms that you employ. For example, don't use indexed access into F# lists, and don't create large numbers of objects unnecessary, particularly if they will persist beyond Generation 0 of the garbage collection cycle.

Use collection functions combined with the appropriate collection types to write performant code. For example, `Array.map` and `Array.filter` might in some circumstances be a better choice than `List.map` and `List.filter`. If you don't want intermediate collections in a pipeline to be realized, consider using functions from the `Seq` module. Remember that comprehensions (code in `seq {}`, `[||]` or `[]`, combined with the `yield` keyword) can be a great way to combine somewhat imperative code with functional concepts, all in a performant way.

Where performance is critical, create repeatable benchmarks. I gave an example of doing this using BenchmarkDotNet. First write correct code, typically supported by unit tests. Then refine performance progressively, all while keeping an eye both on the benchmark results and the unit test results.

I suggested that you shouldn't optimize prematurely, nor micro-optimize unnecessarily, especially if doing so compromises the clarity or reliability of your code, or risks not getting the benefits of future compiler or platform improvements.

Layout and Naming

In Chapter 13, "Layout and Naming," I encouraged you to treat layout and naming as key drivers of the quality of your code. I suggested that you choose concise names that reflect exactly what an item does or represents. Placing items in carefully named modules can help with this. It's often useful to classify functions carefully, for example, separating generic from domain-specific functions, and placing each domain object and its closely related functions in its own module.

I gave a few tips on layout. These boil down to organizing your code to help the eye pick out patterns (and exceptions to those patterns) using consistent line breaks and indentation. You can also help the reader by using triple-slash comments to document public functions, types, etc., as these comments will appear as tool tips in most editors.

I also pointed you to the official F# Style Guide, which contains a wealth of more detailed recommendations on topics such as naming, spacing, and indentation.

Onwards!

You're now equipped to write stylish, performant, maintainable code. But if you ever find yourself in doubt, try applying the principles we established in Chapter 1.

- *Semantic focus.* When looking at a small piece of code, can the reader understand what is going on without needing a great deal of context from elsewhere in the codebase – or worse still, from outside it?

- *Revisability.* Can the maintainer make changes to the code and be confident that there won't be unexpected knock-on effects elsewhere?

- *Motivational Transparency.* Can the reader tell what the author of the code *intended* to achieve, and why each piece of code is as it is?

- *Mechanical Sympathy.* Does the code make best use of the facilities available in the platform and the language, for instance, by using the right data structure and accessing it in an efficient way?

Stick to these principles, learn what language features help you adhere to them, and you'll have an enjoyable and productive time with F#. Have fun!

Index

A

Abstract class
    abstract members, 211
    default member implementation, 211

Active pattern, 137, 149
    & operator, 143
    complete, 142
    default match, 141
    efficiency, 144
    multi case, 139
    parameterized, 141
    partial, 140
    single case, 137

ALGOL W, 29

Alignment, 364, 374

AllowNullLiteral attribute, 216

append, 65, 71

ArgumentException, 80

Array
    clamps [|||], 124, 320
    indexed access, 315
    vs. list, 317
    module, 63
    resize, 107
    vs. sequence, 318, 327
    slicing, 67

Array clamps ([|...|]), 320

Array2D module, 87

Array3D module, 87

Array4D module, 87

Array module, 61, 63
    average, 84
    contains, 343
    filter, 63
    find, 343
    head, 80
    init, 63
    iter, 64
    length, 320
    map, 346
    Parallel.map, 66, 340, 342, 346
    sort, 63
    sortInPlaceWith, 66
    tryAverage, 84
    tryFind, 343
    zip, 81

Asterisk (* int), 235

Asymmetric representation, 183

Asynchronous programming, 251, 259
    batching, 267
    cancellation token, 275
    imperative operation, 261
    lock expression, 266
    recommendations for design, 276
    testing downloads, 267
    throttling, 271

async computation expression, 260

CPSIA information can be obtained
at www.ICGtesting.com
Printed in the USA
FSHW011627081218
54335FS

9 781484 239995